Great Recipes

from

Great Gardeners

The Pennsylvania Horticultural Society Cookbook

Cooking and gardening are art forms: creative, original and occasionally
prepared with borrowings — a cup of sugar, a touch of thyme or a recipe. Here's a harvest
of invited recipes and hints, some original and some borrowed.

Published by: The Pennsylvania Horticultural Society

Library of Congress Number: 93-072675
ISBN: 0-9637494-0-4

First Printing _____ September 1993

Favorite Recipes® Press
Nashville, Tennessee 37230

Second Printing _____ February 1994
Third Printing _____ September 1997

Chapel Company
Moorestown, New Jersey 08057

Foreword

Gardeners are so often good cooks that it seems only natural for the Pennsylvania Horticultural Society to publish a cookbook. And, like many things around the Society, the book became reality because volunteers took the lead in mixing the ingredients, stirring the pot and ladling the stew.

Sally Graham and Sandy Manthorpe led the way in this gardening/cooking/publishing adventure, and my grateful thanks go to them and to the hundreds of volunteers and staff members who served on a host of committees. They've produced not only a wonderful selection of recipes, but also a beautiful introduction to the Pennsylvania Horticultural Society with text and photos.

Founded in 1827 with just 53 members, today the Society's membership includes thousands of gardeners. Their appetites for the programs and activities described here, along with the recipes, are ravenous. Together these members create a powerful force in the Delaware Valley, making it possible for the Society to engage in many activities, including producing the world's largest indoor Flower Show and running Philadelphia Green, the nation's largest and most comprehensive community greening program.

Behind all of these programs are hundreds of individuals who love to grow and garden, to show and to share. Their sharing makes the Society a special place for me, whether it's receiving seeds from a prize-winning pepper at the Harvest Show, visiting their gardens, reading about their plants in *Green Scene*, or the glory of winning an award with other club members at the Flower Show. Gardeners are generous people, and we invite you to enjoy this collection of their bounty. And thanks to you, too, for your sharing by purchasing a copy of this book. The revenues we raise through this project will be invested in Philadelphia Green.

Jane G. Pepper

Jane G. Pepper
President
Pennsylvania Horticultural Society

We dedicate this book to all who volunteer for the Pennsylvania Horticultural Society.
With their talents and enthusiasm, the Pennsylvania Horticultural Society
will continue to bloom and flourish.

Acknowledgements

Sally Graham and Sandy Manthorpe
Co-Chair, Cookbook Committee

Recipe Committee

Jill Evans (Chair), Tina Colehower, Blanche Epps, Wallace Evans, Roxie Gevjan,
Carol Kueppers, Flossie Narducci, Joanna McQuail Reed.

Editorial and Design Committee

Towney Cunningham (Chair), Amanda Manthorpe (Artwork Chair),
Ginny Tietjens and Sue Seltzer (Tips Co-Chair), Jean Byrne, Louis Cunningham, Elsa Efran,
Ross Feehrer, Anne Hayes, Joyce Langelier, Ed Lindemann, Betty Barr Mackey,
Gay Mason, Jane Ruffin, Lisa Stephano, Hope Wood.

Marketing and Finance Committee

Marie Todor (Chair), Linda Butler, Toni Cavanagh, Anne Donnell, Elsa Efran,
Millie Ewell, Sally Humphreys, Arlene Jarett, Mary Labold, Barbara Lockwood, Helen Lyman,
Martha Morris, Terry Mushovic, Paul Quintavalla, Margo Ross, Daryl Rynkiewicz,
Richard Scholl, Lisa Stephano, John Swan, Anne Symes, Alice Szarek, Sharon Turner,
Rosemarie Vassalluzzo, Carolyn Waite, Sandy Ward.

Design and Photography

Photographers: Ira Beckoff, Walter Chandoha, Betsy Gullan, Adam Laipson, Jane Ruffin.
Cover arrangement designed by Thom Piecara, A.I.F.D.; photographed by Ira Beckoff.
Menu border designed by Sandy Manthorpe; photographed by Jane Ruffin.
Border flowers donated by Philadelphia Flower Show exhibitors.
"Book title by John Swan"
Line art designed by Anne Fox Hayes. Icon designed by Joyce Langelier.

"To garden, to cook with care, joy and intelligence: to eat with pleasure and serenity. To break bread, to savour a steaming soup or delicate salad—nourishes and nurtures so much more than just the body."   J.B.

Contents

The Philadelphia Flower Show

The Pennsylvania Horticultural Society's Philadelphia Flower Show is the largest and most prestigious indoor flower show in the world. For 10 days every March, dedicated horticulturists transform 10 acres of bare concrete into fragrant, kaleidoscopic gardens surrounded by towering trees, cascading waterfalls, natural woodlands, city terraces and exotic flowers from around the world.

Flower Show competitors have come from almost every continent, representing the finest commercial and amateur talents in the international world of horticulture. Spectacular orchid displays, masses of perfectly forced roses and tall pastel delphiniums share space with tomato vines dripping with ripe fruit (in March!), thousands of pots bursting with bright spring bulbs, and popular African violets.

The goal of the Flower Show, aided by generous corporate support, the hardworking Pennsylvania Horticultural Society staff and 3,000 energetic volunteers, is to spread horticultural knowledge and enthusiasm and to raise money for the Pennsylvania Horticultural Society's acclaimed community program, Philadelphia Green.

This greening program gives low income neighborhood groups year 'round technical, educational and material assistance that covers everything from street trees to community gardens to window boxes. Flower Show revenues also support the Society's work to restore and revitalize Philadelphia's open spaces and gateway roads with landscaping and horticultural maintenance.

Fountains and waterfalls, bricks and stonework, statues and trellises enhance the Philadelphia Flower Show's landscaped exhibits. –Photography by Adam Laipson

Philadelphia Flower Show Celebration Dinner

Pesto-Cheese Pie *(page 22)*   Exotic Wild Mushroom Soup *(page 47)*
or   Boula Gratiné *(page 38)*

Blackened Veal with Salmon *(page 92)*   or   Pork Roast with Fennel *(page 89)*
or   Filet Mignon in Cognac Cream *(page 80)*

Michigan Baked Noodles *(page 149)*   or   Lemon Rice *(page 150)*

Beets in Orange Sauce *(page 130)*

Super Spinach Salad *(page 69)*

Grapefruit Alaska *(page 207)*   or   Crustless Cranberry Pie *(page 235)*   or
Candied Apple Pie *(page 232)*

Silver and ivy arrangement (page 11)

Baked Artichoke Hearts

1   13-ounce can whole artichoke hearts
3 ounces cream cheese or Boursin cheese
1/2 cup melted garlic butter
3/4 cup grated Parmesan cheese
3/4 cup bread crumbs   1/4 cup toasted pine nuts

Open artichoke heart centers gently. Stuff with cream cheese. Dip into butter, then mixture of Parmesan cheese and crumbs. Press pine nuts into cheese. Place on foil-lined baking sheet. Bake at 350 degrees for 30 minutes. May flavor cream cheese with any favorite herbs. Yield: 8 servings.

Approx Per Serving: Cal 251; Prot 6 g; Carbo 11 g; Fiber <1 g; T Fat 20 g; 72% Calories from Fat; Chol 49 mg; Sod 457 mg.

Baked Brie with Strawberries

1   1 to 1 1/2-pound round loaf whole grain bread
1 1/2 to 2-pound wheel of Brie cheese
1 pint fresh strawberries

Slice off top 1/2 inch of bread loaf; scoop out center leaving 1-inch shell. Place cheese in center; wrap in foil. Bake at 350 degrees for 30 minutes or until heated through. Arrange strawberries around top and outside loaf. Cut into wedges and serve. Yield: 20 servings.

Approx Per Serving: Cal 245; Prot 12 g; Carbo 18 g; Fiber 3 g; T Fat 14 g; 51% Calories from Fat; Chol 45 mg; Sod 429 mg.

Broccoli and Cauliflower

1 tablespoon sugar
1 tablespoon dillweed
1 tablespoon MSG
1 teaspoon salt
1 teaspoon coarsely ground pepper
1 tablespoon garlic salt
1 cup cider vinegar
3/4 cup oil
1 bunch broccoli, cut into bite-sized pieces
1 head cauliflower, cut into bite-sized pieces

Combine sugar, dillweed, MSG, salt, pepper, garlic salt, vinegar and oil in large bowl; mix well. Add broccoli and cauliflower, tossing to coat. Chill overnight, stirring occasionally. Drain to serve. Yield: 15 servings.

Approx Per Serving: Cal 116; Prot 1 g; Carbo 5 g; Fiber 1 g; T Fat 11 g; 81% Calories from Fat; Chol 0 mg; Sod 1420 mg.

Select a large silver container for the center of the table. Purchase a large hanging pot of ivy, remove wire hangers and place in silver bowl...Presto! On either side of the centerpiece, place one or more silver candlesticks of various sizes and shapes. Purchase a large mirror at a second-hand store or garage sale. Have it cut to make two runners down the center of the table. Place the silver on this mirror runner...elegant!

Dilled Carrot Fritters

2 pounds carrots, grated
1 tablespoon grated ginger
1 cup minced scallion
1 teaspoon white pepper
1½ teaspoons salt
1 cup sifted flour
2 eggs, beaten
Corn oil for deep frying
1 cup heavy cream
1 cup sour cream
1 tablespoon minced dill

Combine carrots, ginger, scallion, white pepper, salt, flour and eggs in large bowl; mix well. Shape by tablespoonfuls into balls; place on tray. Freeze for 1 hour. Heat oil to 350 degrees in saucepan. Deep-fry fritters until golden brown; drain. Serve with dill crème fraîche. To make dill crème fraîche, whisk heavy cream and sour cream in bowl; pour into covered container. Let stand in warm place for 12 hours or until thickened. Stir in dill. Chill, covered, for 36 hours. Yield: 50 servings.

Approx Per Serving: Cal 47; Prot 1 g; Carbo 4 g; Fiber 1 g; T Fat 3 g; 57% Calories from Fat; Chol 17 mg; Sod 77 mg. Nutritional analysis does not include oil for deep frying.

Cheese and Mushroom en Croûte

1   8-count can crescent rolls
1 to 2 teaspoons dried minced onion
1   4-ounce can sliced mushrooms, drained
1   12-ounce round Gouda cheese

Unroll crescent rolls. Place 1 rectangle on baking sheet, sealing perforations. Sprinkle half the onion and mushrooms over dough; place cheese in center. Sprinkle with remaining onion and mushrooms. Fold up edges of dough to enclose cheese; seal edges. Place remaining portion of dough over top, folding edges down and sealing. Bake at 375 degrees for 20 to 25 minutes or until golden brown. Yield: 10 servings.

Approx Per Serving: Cal 204; Prot 10 g; Carbo 10 g; Fiber <1 g; T Fat 14 g; 60% Calories from Fat; Chol 38 mg; Sod 510 mg.

To substitute dried herbs for fresh, use ⅓ teaspoon powdered or ½ teaspoon crushed dried herbs for each tablespoon chopped fresh herbs.

Cheese Puffs

3 ounces cream cheese
4 ounces sharp Cheddar cheese, cubed
1/2 cup butter
2 egg whites, stiffly beaten
1 1-pound loaf unsliced white bread, crusts trimmed,
cut into 1-inch cubes

Melt cream cheese, Cheddar cheese and butter in top of double boiler; remove from heat. Fold in egg whites. Dip bread cubes in mixture to coat. Place on baking sheet; cover with plastic wrap. Chill or freeze overnight. Bake at 375 degrees for 10 to 12 minutes or until browned. Freezes well. Yield: 60 servings.

Approx Per Serving: Cal 39; Prot 1 g; Carbo 2 g; Fiber <1 g;
T Fat 3 g; 65% Calories from Fat; Chol 8 mg; Sod 54 mg.

Make a beautiful appetizer tray of *Flower-Glazed Cheeses*. Soften 1 envelope plain gelatin in 2 cups cold water or white wine and heat to dissolve. Decorate cheeses with edible flowers and herbs such as nasturtiums, marigolds, violets, roses, pansies, basil, chives, lavender or rosemary. Brush with gelatin mixture and chill until set.

Cream Cheese-Pesto Ring

16 ounces cream cheese, softened
16 ounces unsalted butter, softened
1/2 cup pine nuts
2 cloves of garlic
4 cups fresh basil
6 sprigs of parsley
1/2 cup olive oil
1/2 cup freshly grated Parmesan or Romano cheese

Beat cream cheese and butter in mixer bowl until light and fluffy. Line bottom and sides of 10-inch ring mold with cheese mixture, approximately 1/2 inch thick; reserve remaining cheese mixture. Process pine nuts, garlic, basil and parsley in food processor until smooth. Add oil gradually, processing until smooth paste forms. Add Parmesan cheese. Process just until mixed. Pour over cheese layer to within 1 inch of top of mold. Cover with reserved cheese mixture to enclose pesto sauce. Chill until firm. Unmold onto serving plate; garnish with greens and edible flowers. Yield: 25 servings.

Approx Per Serving: Cal 264; Prot 3 g; Carbo 3 g; Fiber 1 g;
T Fat 28 g; 90% Calories from Fat; Chol 61 mg; Sod 90 mg.

Spanakopita

1 onion, chopped
2 tablespoons butter
3/4 tablespoon flour
1/2 cup milk
3 eggs, beaten
8 ounces feta cheese, crumbled
8 ounces dry curd cottage cheese
1   10-ounce package frozen chopped spinach,
thawed, drained
Salt and pepper to taste
12 sheets phyllo dough, thawed
1/4 cup melted butter

Sauté onions in 2 tablespoons butter in saucepan. Stir in flour. Cook until bubbly, stirring frequently. Add milk. Cook until thickened, stirring constantly. Combine eggs, feta cheese, cottage cheese, spinach, salt and pepper in bowl; mix well. Stir in white sauce. Layer 6 sheets of phyllo dough in 9x13-inch baking dish, brushing each sheet with melted butter and keeping remaining dough covered with a moist towel. Spread with spinach mixture. Top with remaining phyllo, brushing each sheet with remaining butter. Bake at 350 degrees for 1 hour.
Yield: 12 servings.

Approx Per Serving: Cal 217; Prot 11 g; Carbo 18 g; Fiber 2 g;
T Fat 12 g; 47% Calories from Fat; Chol 88 mg; Sod 379 mg.

Cheesy Green Chili Tart

2 all ready pie pastries
1 cup shredded Cheddar cheese
1   4-ounce can chopped green chilies, drained
1 cup shredded Monterey Jack cheese
1/4 teaspoon chili powder
Garlic powder to taste
1 cup salsa

Let pie pastries stand at room temperature for 15 minutes. Place 1 pastry circle on greased baking sheet. Layer with Cheddar cheese, green chilies and Monterey Jack cheese. Place remaining pie pastry over layers, sealing edge with fork. Prick surface with fork; sprinkle with chili powder and garlic powder. Bake at 450 degrees for 10 to 15 minutes or until golden brown. Let stand for 5 minutes. Cut into wedges; serve with salsa.
Yield: 16 servings.

Approx Per Serving: Cal 174; Prot 5 g; Carbo 11 g; Fiber <1 g;
T Fat 12 g; 62% Calories from Fat; Chol 14 mg; Sod 358 mg.

Make a quick *Chili Spread* by mixing 8 ounces cream cheese, one 15-ounce can chili without beans and 2 cups shredded Cheddar cheese in quiche pan. Bake at 350 degrees for 20 minutes and serve warm with corn chips.

Dentist Buffalo Wings

3 pounds chicken wings, tips trimmed
3 cloves of garlic, crushed
2 teaspoons salt
2 teaspoons pepper
1¹/₂ tablespoons Worcestershire sauce
1 teaspoon dry mustard
¹/₄ cup tarragon vinegar
¹/₃ cup oil

Rinse chicken wings; pat dry. Place in shallow dish. Combine garlic, salt, pepper, Worcestershire sauce, mustard and vinegar in blender. Add oil gradually, processing until mixture is slightly thickened. Pour over chicken wings. Marinate in refrigerator for 3 hours to overnight; drain. Place on baking sheet. Bake at 475 degrees for 30 minutes. Yield: 25 servings.

Approx Per Serving: Cal 146; Prot 11 g; Carbo <1 g; Fiber <1 g; T Fat 11 g; 69% Calories from Fat; Chol 35 mg; Sod 213 mg.

How many hors d'oeuvres to prepare? If preceding dinner, plan on 4 pieces per person. If just a cocktail party, plan on 10 pieces per person. If a reception with no dinner to follow, prepare 10 to 15 pieces for each guest.

Chicken Nouri Roulade

8 ounces chicken, boned, skinned
2 sheets dried seaweed paper
2 tablespoons flour
1 tablespoon wasabi
2 scallions
¹/₂ ounce pickled ginger
2 egg yolks, beaten
1 cup sifted flour
¹/₂ cup water
Corn oil for deep frying

Rinse chicken; pat dry. Pound chicken until very thin. Lay out seaweed sheets, overlapping half way lengthwise. Flour chicken; place on seaweed. Top with wasabi, scallions and pickled ginger. Roll up to enclose filling, sealing edges with water. Beat egg yolks, flour and water in small bowl until smooth. Dip chicken roll into batter. Deep-fry in 350-degree oil in saucepan for 12 minutes or until golden brown. Remove with slotted spoon; drain on wire rack for 10 minutes. Slice into 10 portions. Yield: 10 servings.

Approx Per Serving: Cal 82; Prot 5 g; Carbo 10 g; Fiber <1 g; T Fat 2 g; 24% Calories from Fat; Chol 53 mg; Sod 12 mg. Nutritional information does not include wasabi, pickled ginger and oil for deep frying.

Cheesy Chicken Roll-Ups

4 ounces cooked chicken breast filets
1 small onion, finely chopped
1 tablespoon finely chopped parsley
2 tablespoons grated Parmesan cheese
2 tablespoons (or more) mayonnaise
1/2 teaspoon Dijon mustard
1/4 teaspoon salt
1/8 teaspoon white pepper
1/2 teaspoon lemon juice
12 slices bacon, cut into halves

Mash chicken, onion, parsley, Parmesan cheese, mayonnaise, mustard, salt, pepper and lemon juice together in bowl, adding additional mayonnaise if needed for desired consistency. Spread mixture on bacon halves; roll up. Place seam side down on broiler rack. Broil until bacon is browned. Yield: 24 servings.

Approx Per Serving: Cal 38; Prot 3 g; Carbo <1 g; Fiber <1 g; T Fat 3 g; 67% Calories from Fat; Chol 8 mg; Sod 94 mg.

Add a small amount of crushed marjoram, dill, basil, thyme and garlic powder to a block of cream cheese; mix well. This makes an easy *Herbed Spread* for crackers or Melba toast.

Crab Grass

1/2 onion, finely chopped
1/2 cup melted butter
1   10-ounce package frozen chopped spinach, cooked, drained
7 to 8 ounces crab meat
3/4 cup grated Parmesan cheese

Sauté onion in butter in skillet. Stir in spinach, crab meat and Parmesan cheese, mixing well. Spoon into chafing dish; serve with Melba rounds. Yield: 10 servings.

Approx Per Serving: Cal 143; Prot 8 g; Carbo 2 g; Fiber 1 g; T Fat 12 g; 71% Calories from Fat; Chol 52 mg; Sod 278 mg.

Crostini

3 loaves sourdough French bread
1 bunch scallions, chopped
1/4 cup olive oil
8 ounces goat cheese, thinly sliced

Slice bread lengthwise; cut into 4-inch slices. Process scallions and olive oil in food processor until puréed. Spread over bread slices. Top with thin slices of cheese. Place on baking pan. Broil until cheese melts; serve immediately. Yield: 36 servings.

Approx Per Serving: Cal 126; Prot 5 g; Carbo 19 g; Fiber <1 g; T Fat 4 g; 26% Calories from Fat; Chol 5 mg; Sod 263 mg.

Crab Puffs

10 slices whole wheat bread
12 ounces crab meat, cooked, flaked
8 ounces Swiss cheese, shredded
1/3 cup mayonnaise
2 tablespoons sherry
1 tablespoon lemon juice
Salt and cayenne pepper to taste
1/2 teaspoon dillweed
1/4 cup grated Parmesan cheese
Paprika to taste

Cut 4 rounds from each bread slice with small cookie cutter. Place on baking sheet. Toast at 350 degrees for 3 to 4 minutes or until light brown; cool. Combine crab meat, Swiss cheese, mayonnaise, sherry, lemon juice, salt, cayenne pepper and dillweed in bowl; mix well. Spread on toasted bread rounds. Sprinkle with Parmesan cheese and paprika. Bake for 15 to 20 minutes longer or until lightly browned. May be frozen and baked later at 350 degrees for 25 minutes. Yield: 40 servings.

Approx Per Serving: Cal 64; Prot 4 g; Carbo 3 g; Fiber 1 g; T Fat 4 g; 51% Calories from Fat; Chol 15 mg; Sod 103 mg.

Ramirez Hot Crab Spread

16 ounces cream cheese, softened
2 tablespoons milk
1 pound fresh lump backfin crab meat, cooked
1/4 cup Worcestershire sauce
1/2 cup chopped green bell pepper
1/2 cup chopped scallions, including part of green tops
1/2 teaspoon salt
Pepper to taste
1/4 cup slivered almonds

Beat cream cheese with milk in bowl until smooth. Add crab meat, Worcestershire sauce, green pepper, scallions, salt and pepper; mix well. Spoon into small baking dish; top with almonds. Bake at 350 degrees for 15 minutes or until bubbly and heated through. Serve with crackers or toasted bread rounds. Yield: 20 servings.

Approx Per Serving: Cal 112; Prot 6 g; Carbo 2 g; Fiber <1 g; T Fat 9 g; 73% Calories from Fat; Chol 43 mg; Sod 201 mg.

 Add a few rose geranium leaves, a whole clove and 1 slice of lemon to tea for a relaxing drink.

Clam Puffs

1 10-ounce can minced clams
1/4 cup butter
3/4 cup flour
2 eggs
1 teaspoon salt
1/8 teaspoon white pepper
1/4 teaspoon crushed dillseed
1/4 teaspoon thyme
1/4 teaspoon paprika
1/2 teaspoon chopped chives

Drain clams and set aside, reserving 1/2 cup clam juice. Heat butter and reserved clam juice in saucepan until mixture boils; reduce heat. Add flour, stirring constantly until mixture leaves side of pan and forms ball. Beat in eggs 1 at a time. Stir in clams, salt, pepper, dillseed, thyme, paprika and chives. Drop by 1/2 teaspoonfuls into greased baking pan. Bake at 400 degrees for 20 minutes or until golden brown. May freeze and reheat at 350 degrees for 10 to 15 minutes. Yield: 36 servings.

Approx Per Serving: Cal 37; Prot 3 g; Carbo 2 g; Fiber <1 g; T Fat 2 g; 44% Calories from Fat; Chol 21 mg; Sod 90 mg.

Clams Casino

2 6-ounce cans minced clams, drained
Juice of 1/2 lemon
1 medium onion, finely chopped
1/2 green bell pepper, finely chopped
2 to 3 cloves of garlic, minced
1/2 cup butter
1 teaspoon oregano
1 teaspoon parsley flakes
1 teaspoon hot sauce
1/2 cup Italian bread crumbs
6 slices American cheese
1/2 cup grated Parmesan cheese

Simmer clams in lemon juice in saucepan for 10 minutes. Sauté onion, green pepper and garlic in butter in skillet until tender. Stir in oregano, parsley, hot sauce and clam mixture. Add bread crumbs gradually until of desired consistency. Spoon into quiche pan. Cover with sliced cheese; sprinkle with Parmesan cheese. Bake at 350 degrees for 15 to 20 minutes or until bubbly. Serve with nacho or corn chips. Yield: 20 servings.

Approx Per Serving: Cal 121; Prot 8 g; Carbo 4 g; Fiber <1 g; T Fat 8 g; 62% Calories from Fat; Chol 34 mg; Sod 236 mg.

Festive Florentine Crescents

1 10-ounce package frozen chopped spinach,
thawed, drained
1½ cups shredded sharp Cheddar cheese
2 tablespoons bread crumbs
3 slices bacon, crisp-fried, crumbled
2 8-count cans crescent rolls

Combine spinach, cheese, bread crumbs and bacon in saucepan. Cook over low heat until cheese is melted, stirring occasionally. Unroll crescent roll dough; separate into 16 triangles. Cut triangles into halves. Spread each with rounded teaspoonful of spinach mixture. Roll up from wide end. Place on greased baking sheet. Bake at 375 degrees for 11 to 13 minutes or until golden brown. Yield: 32 servings.

Approx Per Serving: Cal 79; Prot 3 g; Carbo 6 g; Fiber <1 g;
T Fat 5 g; 55% Calories from Fat; Chol 6 mg; Sod 168 mg.

Make *Green Pepper Dip* by mixing 8 ounces cream cheese, 1 chopped green bell pepper, ¼ chopped onion, 1 tablespoon sour cream, 1 teaspoon Worcestershire sauce and salt to taste. Serve chilled with crackers.

Marinated Pretzels

1 envelope ranch dressing mix   1 cup oil
1¼ teaspoons each dillweed, oregano and onion powder
2 teaspoons garlic powder
1 13-ounce package small pretzels

Combine first 6 ingredients in large bowl; mix well. Add pretzels, tossing to coat. Let stand until liquid is absorbed, stirring every 20 minutes. Store in airtight container in refrigerator. Yield: 6 servings.

Approx Per Serving: Cal 537; Prot 6 g; Carbo 52 g; Fiber 3 g;
T Fat 39 g; 60% Calories from Fat; Chol 0 mg; Sod 1307 mg.

Spiced Ham Spread

4 cups minced baked ham
2 tablespoons Dijon mustard   ¼ cup mayonnaise
1 teaspoon cinnamon   1 clove of garlic, crushed
2 tablespoons unsalted butter, softened
Crushed water-pack green peppercorns to taste

Combine ham, mustard, mayonnaise, cinnamon, garlic and butter in bowl; mix well. Add peppercorns gradually to desired taste. Pack mixture into oiled 4-cup mold. Chill until firm. Serve with crackers or party bread or use as stuffing for fresh vegetables. Yield: 32 servings.

Approx Per Serving: Cal 48; Prot 4 g; Carbo <1 g; Fiber <1 g;
T Fat 3 g; 61% Calories from Fat; Chol 13 mg; Sod 267 mg.

Meatless Meatballs

1 cup ground pecans   1 cup cracker crumbs
1 cup shredded sharp Cheddar cheese   4 eggs, beaten
Salt and pepper to taste   1 teaspoon sage
1   10-ounce can cream of mushroom soup
1 soup can water

Mix first 7 ingredients in bowl. Shape into 24 small balls. Brown in nonstick skillet. Place in baking dish. Add mixture of soup and water. Bake at 350 degrees for 1 hour. May freeze and heat at 200 degrees. Yield: 24 servings.

Approx Per Serving: Cal 125; Prot 3 g; Carbo 5 g; Fiber 1 g; T Fat 10 g; 73% Calories from Fat; Chol 42 mg; Sod 182 mg.

Melitzano Salata

2 medium eggplant   2 cloves of garlic, crushed
1/4 cup finely chopped parsley   1/2 teaspoon salt
1/4 teaspoon freshly ground pepper
2 teaspoons fresh lemon juice   1/3 cup mayonnaise

Prick eggplants several times with fork. Place 1 eggplant between 2 layers of paper towels. Microwave on High for 12 minutes; cool. Repeat with second eggplant. Cut into halves lengthwise; scoop out centers. Mash with remaining ingredients in bowl. Yield: 24 servings.

Approx Per Serving: Cal 30; Prot <1 g; Carbo 2 g; Fiber 1 g; T Fat 2 g; 70% Calories from Fat; Chol 2 mg; Sod 63 mg.

Aztec Stuffed Mushrooms

42 large mushrooms   1 pound ground venison
1 cup wheat tortilla bread crumbs
1/2 cup minced coriander   Salt and pepper to taste
2 tablespoons corn oil

Remove stems from mushrooms and chop finely; reserve caps. Combine chopped stems and remaining ingredients in bowl; mix well. Stuff mixture into reserved mushroom caps. Place on baking sheet. Bake at 350 degrees for 25 to 30 minutes or until heated through. Yield: 42 servings.

Approx Per Serving: Cal 29; Prot 3 g; Carbo 2 g; Fiber <1 g; T Fat 1 g; 32% Calories from Fat; Chol 5 mg; Sod 15 mg.

Mushroom Paté

8 ounces mushrooms   1 medium onion, cut into quarters
3 tablespoons melted butter   1 tablespoon lemon juice
1 teaspoon Worcestershire sauce
1/2 teaspoon each salt, pepper and garlic powder
2 tablespoons mayonnaise

Mince mushrooms and onion in food processor. Sauté in butter in skillet until tender. Stir in next 5 ingredients. Simmer over medium heat for 15 minutes or until liquid evaporates; cool. Stir in mayonnaise; chill. Yield: 24 servings.

Approx Per Serving: Cal 26; Prot <1 g; Carbo 1 g; Fiber <1 g; T Fat 2 g; 80% Calories from Fat; Chol 5 mg; Sod 66 mg.

Stuffed Mushrooms

12 large mushrooms
1 small onion, finely chopped
4 tablespoons butter
1 cup soft fine bread crumbs
1/2 cup unsalted pecans, chopped
2 tablespoons cream
1 tablespoon sherry
Salt and pepper to taste

Remove stems from mushrooms and chop finely; reserve caps. Sauté chopped stems and onion in 1 tablespoon butter in skillet for 2 minutes. Stir in bread crumbs, pecans, cream and sherry. Season with salt and pepper; set aside. Brush mushroom caps with melted butter; place cup side down on rack in broiler pan. Broil for 2 minutes. Invert; fill with stuffing mixture. Brush with remaining butter. Broil for 3 minutes longer. Yield: 12 servings.

Approx Per Serving: Cal 95; Prot 1 g; Carbo 4 g; Fiber 1 g; T Fat 8 g; 77% Calories from Fat; Chol 14 mg; Sod 54 mg.

For an easy centerpiece spray black a large can that has 2 rubber bands around it. Fill with floral foam and flowers. Place about 25 spears of asparagus around black can, secured by the 2 rubber bands.

Molded Liver Paté

1 envelope unflavored gelatin
1/4 cup cold water
1   10-ounce can madrilene consommé
1 teaspoon dillweed
1 teaspoon lemon juice
Seasoned salt to taste
3 ounces cream cheese, softened
4 ounces mild liverwurst

Soften gelatin in cold water. Heat consommé in saucepan. Stir in gelatin, dillweed, lemon juice and seasoned salt. Pour a small amount of mixture into shallow 6 to 8-inch mold; chill until firm. Process cream cheese and liverwurst in blender. Add remaining consommé mixture. Process until very smooth. Pour over gelatin in mold. Chill until firm. Unmold onto serving plate; serve with wafers. Yield: 16 servings.

Approx Per Serving: Cal 48; Prot 3 g; Carbo 1 g; Fiber <1 g; T Fat 4 g; 74% Calories from Fat; Chol 17 mg; Sod 130 mg.

Oyster Pie

1½ to 2 pints oysters
2 tablespoons butter
2 tablespoons flour
1 cup half and half
3 egg yolks, beaten
3 tablespoons sherry
1½ teaspoons lemon juice
Salt and pepper to taste
1 recipe 2-crust deep-dish pie pastry
¼ cup fine bread crumbs

Heat oysters in their juice in saucepan over medium heat until edges begin to curl. Remove from heat and set aside. Melt butter in small saucepan; blend in flour. Cook until golden brown. Add half and half, stirring until mixture is smooth and thickened; remove from heat. Drain a small amount of juice from oysters and mix with egg yolks in small bowl. Drain remaining juice from oysters, reserving ¼ cup. Combine egg mixture, oysters, ¼ cup reserved juice, sherry, lemon juice, salt and pepper with cream sauce; mix well. Line deep-dish pie plate with 1 pie pastry. Pour in oyster mixture; sprinkle with bread crumbs. Top with remaining pie pastry. Bake at 350 degrees for 15 to 20 minutes or until golden brown. Yield: 8 servings.

Approx Per Serving: Cal 431; Prot 13 g; Carbo 28 g; Fiber 5 g; T Fat 80 g; 82% Calories from Fat; Chol 365 mg; Sod 478 mg.

Pesto-Cheese Pie

¼ cup herb-seasoned bread crumbs
2 tablespoons grated Parmesan cheese
16 ounces cream cheese, softened
1 cup ricotta cheese
½ cup grated Parmesan cheese
Salt and cayenne pepper to taste
3 eggs
½ cup prepared pesto sauce
¼ cup pine nuts

Spray side and bottom of 8-inch springform pan with nonstick cooking spray. Combine bread crumbs and Parmesan cheese in small bowl; mix well. Pat into prepared pan. Beat cream cheese, ricotta cheese, ½ cup Parmesan cheese, salt and cayenne pepper at medium speed in mixer bowl. Add eggs 1 at a time, beating well after each addition. Spoon half the mixture into small bowl and set aside. Add pesto sauce to remaining mixture, beating well. Pour pesto mixture into prepared pan; pour plain cheese mixture over top. Sprinkle with pine nuts. Bake at 325 degrees for 1 hour or until lightly browned. Cool completely. Cover with plastic wrap and chill overnight. Serve at room temperature. Yield: 8 servings.

Approx Per Serving: Cal 440; Prot 16 g; Carbo 9 g; Fiber 1 g; T Fat 39 g; 78% Calories from Fat; Chol 166 mg; Sod 460 mg.

Sweet Pepper Appetizer

2 cups finely chopped onions
1/4 cup olive oil
1 1/2 cups each finely chopped red, green and yellow
bell peppers
3/4 cup finely chopped celery
2 cloves of garlic, minced
1/2 teaspoon dried oregano
2 bay leaves
20 stuffed green olives, sliced
1   2-ounce bottle of capers
Juice of 1 lemon
1   14-ounce can peeled whole tomatoes
1/8 teaspoon nutmeg
Salt and pepper to taste
1/2 cup brandy

Sauté onions in olive oil in large skillet until tender. Add bell peppers, celery, garlic, oregano, bay leaves, olives, capers with juice, lemon juice, undrained tomatoes and nutmeg. Cook for 20 minutes, stirring frequently. Season with salt and pepper. Remove from heat; stir in brandy. Remove bay leaves. Serve at room temperature with sliced French bread, party rye bread or crackers.
Yield: 20 servings.

Approx Per Serving: Cal 59; Prot 1 g; Carbo 6 g; Fiber 1 g;
T Fat 4 g; 55% Calories from Fat; Chol 0 mg; Sod 131 mg.
Nutritional information does not include capers.

Sweet Onion Pizza

3 large Vidalia onions, sliced
2 tablespoons olive oil
1 clove of garlic, minced
1   8-ounce can pizza dough
1/2 teaspoon dried basil
1 cup crumbled Gorgonzola cheese

Sauté onions in olive oil in large skillet until browned. Add garlic; remove from heat. Spread pizza dough on 10x15-inch baking sheet. Top with onion mixture. Sprinkle with basil and cheese. Bake at 400 degrees for 8 minutes or until lightly browned and cheese bubbles. Cut into small pieces. Serve hot or cold. May substitute 1 1/2 cups Swiss cheese for Gorgonzola cheese or Maui onions for Vidalia onions. Yield: 20 servings.

Approx Per Serving: Cal 97; Prot 3 g; Carbo 9 g; Fiber <1 g;
T Fat 6 g; 53% Calories from Fat; Chol 8 mg; Sod 41 mg.

To help avoid tears when chopping onions, peel under cold running water; close your mouth and breathe through your nose; hold a bread crust or celery stalk in your mouth or chop near an open flame.

Rosemary Pizza

2¹/₂ cups flour
¹/₂ teaspoon salt
1 envelope rapid-rise yeast
1 cup warm water
1 tablespoon sugar
3 cloves of garlic, thinly sliced
3 tablespoons rosemary
¹/₄ cup (about) olive oil
Salt and freshly ground pepper to taste

Combine flour, salt, yeast, warm water and sugar in large bowl; mix well. Knead on floured surface for 15 minutes; shape into ball. Place in greased bowl, turning to grease surface. Let rise, covered, in a warm place for 1 to 1¹/₂ hours or until doubled in bulk. Punch dough down; let rise until doubled in bulk. Punch dough down. Roll out on floured surface to a ¹/₂-inch thick 6-inch circle. Brush pizza pan with small amount of olive oil. Place dough on pan. Make indentations over surface of dough; insert garlic slice and some rosemary in each indentation. Sprinkle with olive oil; smooth over surface with fingertips. Sprinkle with additional salt and pepper to taste. Bake at 400 degrees for 15 minutes or until golden brown. Remove garlic before serving. Yield: 6 servings.

Approx Per Serving: Cal 285; Prot 6 g; Carbo 43 g; Fiber 2 g; T Fat 10 g; 31% Calories from Fat; Chol 0 mg; Sod 180 mg.

Fresh Vegetable Pizza

2 8-count cans crescent rolls
16 ounces cream cheese, softened
1 cup mayonnaise
1 envelope ranch dressing mix
¹/₂ cup chopped broccoli
¹/₂ cup chopped cauliflower
¹/₂ cup chopped red bell pepper
¹/₂ cup chopped green bell pepper
¹/₂ cup shredded carrot
¹/₂ cup sliced green or black olives
¹/₂ cup shredded Cheddar cheese

Spread crescent roll dough in 10x15-inch baking dish, sealing perforations. Bake at 375 degrees for 11 to 13 minutes or until golden brown. Mix cream cheese, mayonnaise and ranch dressing mix in bowl until blended. Spread over prepared crust. Top with broccoli, cauliflower, bell peppers, carrot, olives and cheese. Cut into serving portions. Yield: 15 servings.

Approx Per Serving: Cal 351; Prot 5 g; Carbo 15 g; Fiber 1 g; T Fat 31 g; 77% Calories from Fat; Chol 46 mg; Sod 617 mg.

For a more mellow flavor, add herbs earlier in the cooking process. If a strong flavor is required, sprinkle them in just prior to serving.

Mini Quiches

1   10-count can refrigerator biscuits
1   7-ounce can cocktail shrimp, drained
3 eggs
1/2 cup light cream
1/4 teaspoon Worcestershire sauce
1/2 teaspoon dry mustard
2 drops Tabasco sauce
1 tablespoon brandy
Salt to taste
1 1/3 ounces Gruyère cheese, sliced

Separate biscuits; split into halves crosswise. Press into greased miniature muffin cups. Place 2 to 3 shrimp in each cup. Combine eggs, cream, Worcestershire sauce, mustard, Tabasco sauce, brandy and salt in bowl; mix well. Pour into prepared muffin cups. Top each with slice of Gruyère cheese. Bake at 350 degrees for 15 to 20 minutes or until lightly browned. Yield: 20 servings.

Approx Per Serving: Cal 83; Prot 5 g; Carbo 6 g; Fiber <1 g; T Fat 5 g; 50% Calories from Fat; Chol 58 mg; Sod 161 mg.

To make *Tuna Paté*, combine 8 ounces cream cheese, 2 tablespoons chili sauce, 2 tablespoons parsley, 2 teaspoons minced onion, 1/2 teaspoon hot pepper sauce and 12 ounces canned tuna. Pack into 4-cup mold and chill overnight.

Zucchini Quiche

4 eggs, beaten   1/2 cup biscuit mix
2 tablespoons oil
3 to 4 cups grated zucchini
1 cup shredded Cheddar cheese
Pepper, onion salt and parsley to taste

Mix eggs, biscuit mix and oil in bowl. Stir in zucchini, cheese, pepper, onion salt and parsley. Pour into 9-inch pie plate. Bake at 350 degrees for 30 minutes or until knife inserted near center comes out clean. Yield: 6 servings.

Approx Per Serving: Cal 239; Prot 12 g; Carbo 13 g; Fiber 2 g; T Fat 16 g; 60% Calories from Fat; Chol 162 mg; Sod 299 mg.

Easy Sausage Appetizer

1 1/2 to 2 pounds sweet Italian sausage
1 1/2 to 2 pounds hot Italian sausage
3   9-ounce jars pepper salad

Place sausage in large roasting pan. Bake at 325 degrees for 1 hour or until cooked through. Slice crosswise into 1/2-inch slices. Place in large glass bowl. Add pepper salad; mix well. Chill, covered, until serving time. Warm in microwave. Serve with wooden picks. Yield: 20 servings.

Approx Per Serving: Cal 137; Prot 9 g; Carbo 1 g; Fiber 0 g; T Fat 11 g; 73% Calories from Fat; Chol 33 mg; Sod 393 mg.
Nutritional information does not include pepper salad.

Sausage Stars

1 pound sausage
1¹/2 cups shredded Cheddar cheese
1¹/2 cups shredded Monterey Jack cheese
1 cup prepared ranch salad dressing
1 2-ounce can sliced black olives, drained
¹/2 cup chopped red bell pepper
1 16-ounce package won ton wrappers, cut into fourths
1 tablespoon oil

Brown sausage in skillet, stirring until crumbly; drain and blot with paper towels to remove excess grease. Combine with Cheddar cheese, Monterey Jack cheese, salad dressing, olives and bell pepper in bowl; mix well. Grease miniature muffin cups. Place won ton wrapper in each cup. Brush with oil. Bake at 350 degrees for 5 minutes or until golden brown. Remove from muffin cups; place on baking sheet. Fill with sausage mixture. Bake for 5 minutes or until bubbly. Yield: 60 servings.

Approx Per Serving: Cal 75; Prot 3 g; Carbo 5 g; Fiber <1 g;
T Fat 5 g; 59% Calories from Fat; Chol 10 mg; Sod 150 mg.

Dress up poached fish or Salmon Mousse with cucumber slices. Thinly slice unpeeled cucumbers and arrange in overlapping rows to resemble scales.

Salmon Mousse

1 envelope unflavored gelatin
¹/2 cup cold water
2 tablespoons lemon juice
1 small onion, sliced
¹/2 cup mayonnaise
2 tablespoons prepared horseradish
1 teaspoon dillweed
¹/2 teaspoon salt
¹/4 teaspoon paprika
1 15-ounce can salmon, drained, flaked
1 cup whipping cream
2 teaspoons oil
2 medium cucumbers, thinly sliced

Soften gelatin in water in saucepan for 1 minute. Heat over medium heat until gelatin is dissolved, stirring constantly. Process gelatin mixture, lemon juice and onion in food processor for 10 seconds. Add mayonnaise, horseradish, dillweed, salt, paprika, salmon and cream. Process at medium speed until smooth. Pour salmon mixture into 4-cup mold brushed with oil. Chill, covered, for 2 hours to overnight or until firm. Unmold onto plate; arrange cucumbers around mousse. (See hint to left.)
Yield: 32 servings.

Approx Per Serving: Cal 76; Prot 3 g; Carbo 1 g; Fiber <1 g;
T Fat 7 g; 77% Calories from Fat; Chol 19 mg; Sod 131 mg.

Salmon Rouladen

10 ounces center-cut smoked salmon, sliced lengthwise
7 ounces whitefish salad
1/2 tablespoon parsley flakes

Place 10x24-inch sheet of plastic wrap on smooth surface. Place salmon on wrap in single layer, 3 inches from edge, overlapping slices 1/4 inch. Cover with second sheet of plastic wrap. Flatten with rolling pin; remove top sheet of plastic wrap. Spread whitefish salad evenly over salmon, leaving 1/4-inch edge. Sprinkle with parsley. Roll up salmon starting from long side; cover with plastic wrap. Freeze until firm. Slice diagonally into 1/4-inch slices; arrange on serving plate. Serve with Cajun Remoulade (page 151). Chill until serving time. Yield: 16 servings.

Approx Per Serving: Cal 21; Prot 3 g; Carbo <1 g; Fiber <1 g; T Fat 1 g; 35% Calories from Fat; Chol 4 mg; Sod 139 mg. Nutritional information does not include whitefish salad.

To make a party *Shrimp Mold*, mix 8 ounces cream cheese, 3/4 cup mayonnaise, 1/2 cup chopped celery, 1/4 cup chopped onion, 1/2 teaspoon salt and 2 cups chopped cooked shrimp. Soften 1 envelope gelatin in 1/2 can tomato soup in saucepan and heat to dissolve gelatin. Add shrimp mixture and chill in mold until set.

Shrimp Toast

8 slices dry white bread, crusts trimmed
2 teaspoons pale dry sherry
2 teaspoons cornstarch
1 egg white, beaten
1/2 teaspoon salt
1/2 teaspoon finely chopped gingerroot
8 ounces shrimp, shelled, deveined, finely chopped
1/4 cup finely chopped water chestnuts
1 scallion, finely chopped
2 teaspoons sesame seed
4 cups peanut oil for deep frying

Cut each bread slice into 4 squares or triangles. Arrange on tray; set aside. Combine sherry and cornstarch in small bowl. Stir in beaten egg white, salt and ginger. Add shrimp, water chestnuts and scallion, stirring until paste forms. Spread 1/2 tablespoon of mixture over each bread square. Sprinkle with sesame seed, pressing in lightly. Heat oil in wok or deep-fryer to 375 degrees. Fry bread squares in batches shrimp side down for 2 minutes; turn. Fry for 1 minute longer or until golden brown and crisp; drain. Yield: 32 servings.

Approx Per Serving: Cal 22; Prot 2 g; Carbo 3 g; Fiber <1 g; T Fat <1 g; 15% Calories from Fat; Chol 11 mg; Sod 73 mg. Nutritional information does not include peanut oil for deep frying.

Crab Cocktail Mold

1   3-ounce package lemon gelatin   1 cup hot water
³/4 cup chili sauce   2 tablespoons vinegar
Worcestershire and Tabasco sauce to taste
2 tablespoons prepared horseradish
2 cups crab meat, flaked

Dissolve gelatin in hot water in bowl. Stir in remaining ingredients. Spoon into oiled fish-shaped mold. Chill until firm. May use shrimp. Yield: 16 servings.

Approx Per Serving: Cal 52; Prot 4 g; Carbo 8 g; Fiber <1 g; T Fat <1 g; 6% Calories from Fat; Chol 17 mg; Sod 240 mg.

Cheesesteak Stromboli

1 loaf frozen bread dough, thawed
16 ounces thinly sliced steaks   2 onions, thinly sliced
8 ounces fresh mushrooms, sliced
2 tablespoons oil   8 ounces mozzarella cheese, sliced

Pat out bread dough to form large rectangle. Fry steaks, onions and mushrooms in oil in skillet until cooked through; drain. Add cheese, stirring until melted. Spread in center of dough. Fold up sides, tucking ends under and sealing seam. Place on baking sheet. Let rise for 1 hour. Bake at 350 degrees for 20 minutes. Yield: 10 servings.

Approx Per Serving: Cal 277; Prot 17 g; Carbo 28 g; Fiber 1 g; T Fat 12 g; 37% Calories from Fat; Chol 43 mg; Sod 375 mg.

Vegetable and Chip Dip

1 cup mayonnaise
¹/2 cup sour cream
1 tablespoon lemon juice
1 teaspoon Worcestershire sauce
1 teaspoon salt
¹/4 teaspoon each paprika and garlic powder
1 teaspoon each thyme, celery seed, parsley
and curry powder
1 tablespoon each onion flakes and chives
1 tablespoon capers

Combine mayonnaise, sour cream, lemon juice, Worcestershire sauce, salt, seasonings and capers in bowl; mix well. Chill, covered, for 4 hours. Serve with vegetables or chips. Yield: 12 servings.

Approx Per Serving: Cal 153; Prot 1 g; Carbo 1 g; Fiber <1 g; T Fat 17 g; 96% Calories from Fat; Chol 15 mg; Sod 291 mg.
Nutritional information does not include capers.

To make *Walnut Cream Cheese Spread*, combine 8 ounces cream cheese, 1 bunch chopped scallions, 1 chopped green bell pepper, 5 ounces walnuts and 1 tablespoon sugar. Serve with bagels or pumpernickel.

Sun-Dried Tomatoes and Cheese

1   8-ounce jar oil-pack sun-dried tomatoes
2 cloves of garlic   2/3 cups pitted Calamata olives
1 loaf French bread, sliced   12 ounces feta cheese

Process tomatoes with oil and garlic in food processor until smooth. Stir in olives. Spoon into serving bowl; surround with French bread slices and cheese. Yield: 4 servings.

Approx Per Serving: Cal 576; Prot 21 g; Carbo 64 g; Fiber 4 g; T Fat 28 g; 42% Calories from Fat; Chol 61 mg; Sod 1332 mg.

Marinated Vegetables

2   10-ounce packages frozen artichokes
2 pounds fresh mushrooms, sliced
2 pounds cherry tomatoes
1/2 head cauliflowerets   1 cup cider vinegar
1/2 cup oil   1 clove of garlic, cut into halves
1 1/2 tablespoons salt
1/2 teaspoon each thyme, chervil, oregano and black peppercorns

Cook artichokes using package directions; drain and cool. Combine with remaining ingredients in large bowl; mix well. Chill, covered, overnight. Serve with wooden picks. Yield: 12 servings.

Approx Per Serving: Cal 142; Prot 4 g; Carbo 13 g; Fiber 7 g; T Fat 10 g; 56% Calories from Fat; Chol 0 mg; Sod 836 mg.

Marinated Brussels Sprouts

1 envelope lemon-dill sauce mix
1/4 cup margarine
1/2 cup milk
1 pound fresh Brussels sprouts
1/8 teaspoon baking soda
6 to 8 small red or yellow bell peppers, cut into julienne strips

Prepare lemon-dill sauce mix with 1/4 cup margarine and 1/2 cup milk using package directions; set aside. Steam Brussels sprouts with baking soda in a small amount of water in saucepan until tender; drain. Pour lemon-dill sauce over Brussels sprouts in bowl, tossing gently to coat. Top with pepper strips; garnish with fresh dill. Serve with wooden picks. May substitute two 10-ounce packages frozen Brussels sprouts for fresh sprouts. Yield: 10 servings.

Approx Per Serving: Cal 102; Prot 3 g; Carbo 10 g; Fiber 3 g; T Fat 7 g; 54% Calories from Fat; Chol 2 mg; Sod 255 mg.

To rehydrate dried ingredients such as chilies and sun-dried tomatoes in the microwave, place in self-sealing plastic bag with 1 cup of hot water. Seal the bag and set in a dish. Cook on High until softened—about 6 to 8 minutes.

The World's Best Bloody Mary

1 quart rich thick tomato juice   1 quart V-8 juice
16 ounces concentrated lemon juice
24 ounces vodka   1 tablespoon Worcestershire sauce
1¹/₂ teaspoons Tabasco sauce
1 tablespoon freshly ground pepper
1 tablespoon celery salt

Combine all ingredients in pitcher; mix well. Serve over ice in large glasses. Garnish with sprigs of celery and squeeze of lime. Yield: 12 servings.

Approx Per Serving: Cal 170; Prot 1 g; Carbo 11 g; Fiber 1 g; T Fat <1 g; 1% Calories from Fat; Chol 0 mg; Sod 981 mg.

Spencer's Cocktail

³/₄ ounce apricot brandy   1¹/₂ ounces dry gin
1 dash of bitters   ¹/₄ teaspoon orange juice

Combine all ingredients in pitcher. Shake with cracked ice; strain into 3-ounce cocktail glass. Garnish with cherry and a twist of orange peel. Yield: 1 serving.

Approx Per Serving: Cal 149; Prot <1 g; Carbo 8 g; Fiber <1 g; T Fat <1 g; 0% Calories from Fat; Chol 0 mg; Sod 1 mg.

These 2 recipes above are Philadelphia Flower Show Bartenders' Drinks.

Apple-Grape Punch

2 cups apple juice
2 cups water
1 apple, cored, thinly sliced
1 tablespoon lemon juice
1 cup seedless grapes
6 cups apple juice
4 cups grape juice
1   6-ounce can frozen lemonade concentrate, thawed
4 cups carbonated lemon-lime drink, chilled

Combine 2 cups apple juice and water in bowl. Sprinkle apple slices with lemon juice. Arrange with grapes in 5-cup ring mold. Pour ³/₄ cup apple juice mixture in mold; freeze. Add remaining juice mixture; freeze. Combine 6 cups apple juice, grape juice and lemonade concentrate in bowl; mix well and chill. Pour into punch bowl. Stir in lemon-lime drink. Unmold ice ring and float on top. Yield: 28 servings.

Approx Per Serving: Cal 88; Prot <1 g; Carbo 22 g; Fiber <1 g; T Fat <1 g; 2% Calories from Fat; Chol 0 mg; Sod 7 mg.

Place dried goldenrod and mint leaves into a tea ball and steep in hot water for 15 minutes. This makes a very relaxing tea.

French Hot Chocolate Mix

2¹/₂ ounces unsweetened chocolate
¹/₂ cup cold water   ³/₄ cup sugar
Salt to taste   ¹/₂ teaspoon vanilla extract
¹/₂ cup heavy cream, whipped

Melt chocolate with water in saucepan over medium-high heat, stirring constantly with whisk until smooth. Add sugar and salt. Cook for 3 minutes. Let stand until cool. Stir in vanilla. Fold in whipped cream. Store in refrigerator until serving time. Combine 1 tablespoon chocolate mixture with enough hot milk to fill 1 cup for each serving. Yield: 24 servings.

Approx Per Serving: Cal 57; Prot <1 g; Carbo 7 g; Fiber <1 g; T Fat 3 g; 50% Calories from Fat; Chol 7 mg; Sod 2 mg.

Bridge Club Punch

1   4-ounce can frozen orange juice concentrate, thawed
¹/₄ cup lemon juice
1   46-ounce can unsweetened pineapple juice
1   28-ounce bottle of raspberry soda, chilled

Mix orange juice concentrate with lemon juice and pineapple juice in bowl; chill. Pour into punch bowl; stir in raspberry soda just before serving. Yield: 8 servings.

Approx Per Serving: Cal 161; Prot 1 g; Carbo 40 g; Fiber 1 g; T Fat <1 g; 1% Calories from Fat; Chol 0 mg; Sod 15 mg.

Cranberry Cassis Punch

1 cup black currant syrup
3 cups cranberry juice cocktail
¹/₂ cup fresh orange juice   ¹/₂ cup fresh lemon juice
3 cups ginger ale   1 cup vodka

Combine first 4 ingredients in bowl; chill overnight. Stir in ginger ale and vodka before serving. Pour over ice in punch bowl; garnish with mint leaves. Yield: 8 servings.

Approx Per Serving: Cal 282; Prot <1 g; Carbo 56 g; Fiber <1 g; T Fat <1 g; <1% Calories from Fat; Chol 0 mg; Sod 27 mg.

Fish House Punch

1   1-pound package light brown sugar
4 cups lemon juice   2 quarts Jamaican rum
1 quart brandy   4 ounces peach brandy
2 quarts water   Ice ring

Mix brown sugar and lemon juice in bowl. Combine rum, brandy and peach brandy in large bowl; chill. Pour lemon juice and rum mixtures into punch bowl. Add water; mix well. Float ice ring on top. This is the original 18th century recipe. It is delicious tasting and therefore dangerous! Serve with a non-alcoholic alternative. Yield: 12 servings.

Approx Per Serving: Cal 705; Prot <1 g; Carbo 75 g; Fiber <1 g; T Fat <1 g; 0% Calories from Fat; Chol 0 mg; Sod 21 mg.

Yummy Irish Creme

1³/4 cups whiskey
1   14-ounce can sweetened condensed milk
1 cup heavy cream
4 eggs
2 tablespoons chocolate syrup
2 teaspoons instant coffee
1 teaspoon vanilla extract
¹/2 teaspoon almond extract

Process all ingredients in blender until mixed; chill. Garnish servings with edible flowers. Yield: 8 servings.

Approx Per Serving: Cal 423; Prot 8 g; Carbo 31 g; Fiber <1 g; T Fat 18 g; 39% Calories from Fat; Chol 164 mg; Sod 113 mg.

Pink Lemonade

1   6-ounce can frozen lemonade concentrate, thawed
1   6-ounce can grenadine
6 cans water

Combine lemonade concentrate, grenadine and water in bowl; mix well. Pour over ice in punch bowl. This is a nice substitute for a Bacardi cocktail. Yield: 8 servings.

Approx Per Serving: Cal 118; Prot <1 g; Carbo 19 g; Fiber <1 g; T Fat <1 g; 1% Calories from Fat; Chol 0 mg; Sod 2 mg.

Sangria

1 orange, sliced   1 lemon, sliced
1 lime, sliced   ¹/2 cup brandy
1   750-milliliter bottle of red or white wine
1   750-milliliter bottle of sparkling cider

Marinate orange, lemon and lime in brandy in large bowl for 1 to 2 hours. Stir in wine and cider; chill. Pour in pitcher to serve; do not add ice to pitcher. Yield: 8 servings.

Approx Per Serving: Cal 154; Prot 1 g; Carbo 21 g; Fiber 1 g; T Fat <1 g; 1% Calories from Fat; Chol 0 mg; Sod 8 mg.

Garden Sangria

2 small oranges, sliced
1 small apple, cored, sliced
1 lemon, cut into ¹/2-inch slices
1   750-milliliter bottle of red wine
¹/3 cup sugar   ¹/4 cup brandy
3 cups club soda

Cut orange slices into quarters. Combine with apple, lemon, wine, sugar, brandy and soda in bowl; mix well. Pour into pitcher to serve. Use inexpensive wine and substitute any fruits available from the garden, such as strawberries or peaches. Yield: 10 servings.

Approx Per Serving: Cal 108; Prot <1 g; Carbo 15 g; Fiber 1 g; T Fat <1 g; 1% Calories from Fat; Chol 0 mg; Sod 19 mg.

Aunt Essie's Iced Tea

3 quarts water   12 decaffeinated tea bags
1 cup sugar   1/2 cup fresh orange juice
1/2 cup fresh lemon juice   5 to 6 sprigs of fresh mint

Bring water to a boil in saucepan; add tea bags. Steep for 10 minutes; discard tea bags. Combine sugar, orange juice and lemon juice in large glass bowl. Stir in tea; add mint. Let stand for 30 minutes; discard mint. Chill until serving time. Yield: 12 servings.

Approx Per Serving: Cal 73; Prot <1 g; Carbo 19 g; Fiber <1 g; T Fat <1 g; 1% Calories from Fat; Chol 0 mg; Sod 7 mg.

Cape May Hospitality Tea

3 quarts water   4 tea bags
1 cup sugar
3 cups orange juice
1 tablespoon (heaping) whole cloves

Bring water to a boil in large saucepan; add tea bags. Steep for 4 minutes; discard tea bags. Stir in sugar, orange juice and cloves; let stand for 5 minutes. Strain into pitcher, discarding cloves. Serve hot or cold. Yield: 12 servings.

Approx Per Serving: Cal 94; Prot <1 g; Carbo 24 g; Fiber <1 g; T Fat <1 g; 1% Calories from Fat; Chol 0 mg; Sod 8 mg.

Strawberry Festival Tea

1 quart fresh strawberries, hulled, sliced into halves
1 1/3 cups sugar   1 gallon tea
2 6-ounce cans frozen lemonade concentrate, thawed

Sprinkle strawberries with sugar in bowl. Mix tea and lemonade concentrate in large pitcher; add sweetened strawberries; stir. Serve over ice. This recipe is a favorite of Antoinette Kuzmanich Hatfield, wife of Senator Mark Hatfield. Yield: 20 servings.

Approx Per Serving: Cal 93; Prot <1 g; Carbo 24 g; Fiber 1 g; T Fat <1 g; 1% Calories from Fat; Chol 0 mg; Sod 7 mg.

Whiskey Sours

1 6-ounce can frozen lemonade concentrate, thawed
1 6-ounce can frozen orange juice concentrate, thawed
1/4 cup confectioners' sugar
4 jiggers (6 ounces) Southern Comfort
2 cups crushed ice

Combine lemonade concentrate, orange juice concentrate, sugar, Southern Comfort and ice in pitcher. Stir until ice is almost melted. May add additional ice cubes. Serve with orange slice and cherry. Yield: 6 servings.

Approx Per Serving: Cal 180; Prot 1 g; Carbo 29 g; Fiber <1 g; T Fat <1 g; 1% Calories from Fat; Chol 0 mg; Sod 2 mg.

The Philadelphia Flower Show

Behind the Scenes

The Pennsylvania Horticultural Society's Philadelphia Flower Show shines as brightly for novices as it does for experts. While beginning gardeners absorb plant names and landscaping ideas, experienced growers share the newest cultivars and pick up the latest trends and techniques from professionals.

The Show attracts a wide array of media attention. Early morning network shows broadcast from dazzling springtime gardens; prominent newspapers and national magazines carry the horticultural experts' wisdom and experience to readers around the world.

A few statistics help explain the Flower Show's success:

- Approximately 300,000 people attend the Philadelphia Flower Show every year.

- Fifty tractor trailer loads of mulch provide the basics before the first flower arrives.

- Each night during the Show, 60 major landscape and floral exhibitors replace faded flowers and tired perennials. At 6:00 a.m. on most mornings, members of 70 garden clubs and hundreds of exhibitors converge with hundreds of competitive entries, so visitors see fresh new designs, new flowers and plants throughout the week.

- More than 200 certified judges from across the United States pay their own expenses to judge 500 competitive classes in the amateur horticultural and artistic arrangements sections of the show. Besides pride in being asked to judge the best Flower Show in the country, the judges' only compensation is a special lunch cooked and served by volunteers; one of the Judges' Luncheon menus appears in this section.

Philadelphia Flower Show exhibitors successfully force trees, shrubs and thousands of bright flowers to bloom in cold, early March. – Photography by Walter Chandoha

Philadelphia Flower Show Judges' Luncheon

White Wine Spritzers

Festive Florentine Crescents *(page 19)*   or   Fresh Vegetable Pizza *(page 24)*

Chicken-Cranberry Mold *(page 59)* and Cheese Tetrazzini *(page 189)*
(garnished with parsley or watercress and sliced peaches or orange sections)

Pineapple-Buttermilk Sherbet *(page 216)*   and   Cookies
Lemon Bars *(page 229)*   Caramel-Oatmeal Bars *(page 229)*
Pecan Wafers *(page 230)*   Swedish Christmas Cookies *(page 231)*

Coffee and Tea

Line a large rustic basket with plastic. Place wet floral foam block in basket. Fill basket with green apples and artichokes. Wind ivy over handle then insert roses into floral foam.

Summer Borscht

1 16-ounce can beets with juice
1 16-ounce can pickled beets with juice
1 cup tomato purée   2 teaspoons salt
1 teaspoon seasoned salt
1 small onion, chopped
3 tablespoons lemon juice
2 cups sour cream

Drain beets, reserving juices. Add enough water to beet juices to measure 6 cups. Purée all ingredients except sour cream in batches in blender until smooth. Chill in refrigerator. Serve with bowl of sour cream. May store in refrigerator for several days. This is a meatless, cabbage-less, greasesless, no-cook soup created by Charlotte Archer and Ed Lindemann (The Philadelphia Flower Show Designer) in 1976 for the Bicentennial Preview Dinner, Philadelphia Flower Show. For the Fourth of July, serve borscht in glass bowls on bright blue place mats; garnish with a spoonful of sour cream on top of each serving. Yield: 6 to 8 servings.

Variations: Serve with **Horseradish Cream** made by mixing equal parts of sour cream, horseradish and mayonnaise instead of sour cream. Sprinkle with chopped fresh dill. Add a small amount of sugar and/or some red wine vinegar to your taste. Garnish with chopped cucumber.

Approx Per Serving: Cal 196; Prot 3 g; Carbo 20 g; Fiber 3 g; T Fat 12 g; 54% Calories from Fat; Chol 26 mg; Sod 1032 mg.

Chilled Black Bean Soup

1 10-ounce can black bean soup
1 10-ounce can consommé
1 cup sour cream
1 tablespoon curry powder
4 lemon slices

Combine undiluted soups, sour cream and curry powder in blender container. Process until smooth. Chill until serving time. Top with lemon slices. Yield: 4 servings.

Approx Per Serving: Cal 212; Prot 9 g; Carbo 16 g; Fiber 2 g; T Fat 13 g; 55% Calories from Fat; Chol 26 mg; Sod 1088 mg.

Borage Soup

6 cups chicken broth   2 onions, chopped
2 cups packed chopped borage   1 teaspoon salt
1 teaspoon pepper   2 cups half and half

Combine chicken broth and onions in large saucepan. Simmer for 20 minutes; add borage. Cook for 5 minutes longer. Purée in blender; season with salt and pepper. Warm half and half in saucepan. Stir into puréed mixture; serve hot. Substitute buttermilk for half and half to serve cold. Yield: 8 servings.

Approx Per Serving: Cal 126; Prot 7 g; Carbo 7 g; Fiber 1 g; T Fat 8 g; 58% Calories from Fat; Chol 23 mg; Sod 891 mg.

Soups

Boula Gratiné

2 10-ounce cans clear green turtle soup
2 10-ounce cans green pea soup
1 tablespoon flour
1/4 cup sherry
2 cups heavy cream, whipped
3/4 cup grated Parmesan cheese

Cook soups in top of double boiler over boiling water until heated through. Stir in flour. Cook until thickened, stirring constantly. Stir in sherry. Ladle into 6 ovenproof bowls; arrange on baking sheet. Top with whipped cream; sprinkle with Parmesan cheese. Broil for 2 to 3 minutes or until cheese is melted and lightly browned.
Yield: 6 servings.

Approx Per Serving: Cal 454; Prot 12 g; Carbo 23 g; Fiber 1 g; T Fat 35 g; 69% Calories from Fat; Chol 117 mg; Sod 930 mg. Nutritional information does not include turtle soup.

A few fresh or dried marigold petals can spruce up a chicken soup recipe and make a tasty garnish for beef stews.

Cream of Brussels Sprouts Soup

4 cups coarsely chopped Brussels sprouts
5 cups chicken broth
5 tablespoons butter
1/4 cup flour
3 cups light cream
Salt and pepper to taste

Cook Brussels sprouts in 3 cups chicken broth in large saucepan over medium heat until tender. Purée in blender. Melt butter in saucepan. Add flour, stirring until blended. Stir in cream. Simmer for 2 minutes. Add puréed mixture, remaining 2 cups broth, salt and pepper. Simmer for 4 minutes longer. Garnish with chopped parsley.
Yield: 10 servings.

Approx Per Serving: Cal 307; Prot 6 g; Carbo 8 g; Fiber 2 g; T Fat 29 g; 82% Calories from Fat; Chol 96 mg; Sod 470 mg.

When your parsley begins to get tired, chop it in the food processor and freeze in small plastic bags. Put into soups, sauces or stews.

Carrot Soup

2 teaspoons oil
1 pound carrots, thinly sliced
1 large onion, chopped
2/3 cup chopped celery
1 1/2 cups chopped peeled potatoes
1 clove of garlic, minced
1/2 teaspoon sugar
5 whole cloves
White pepper to taste
4 cups chicken broth
Dillweed to taste

Heat oil in large saucepan. Add carrots, onion, celery, potatoes, garlic and sugar. Cook, covered, over low heat for 10 minutes, stirring occasionally. Add cloves, pepper and chicken broth. Bring to a boil; reduce heat. Cook, partially covered, for 20 minutes or until vegetables are tender; remove and discard cloves. Process a small amount at a time in blender until puréed. Sprinkle servings with dillweed. This is the best carrot soup yet and contains no butter or cream. Yield: 6 servings.

Approx Per Serving: Cal 114; Prot 5 g; Carbo 18 g; Fiber 4 g; T Fat 3 g; 21% Calories from Fat; Chol 1 mg; Sod 558 mg.

Herbed Cauliflower Soup

Flowerets of 1 large head cauliflower
6 cups chicken broth
6 cloves of garlic, chopped
1 large onion, sliced
4 ounces feta cheese, crumbled
1 teaspoon dried oregano
2 tablespoons chopped fresh basil
1 teaspoon salt
1/2 teaspoon freshly ground white pepper
1/4 cup grated Romano cheese
2 scallions, chopped

Cook cauliflower in chicken broth in large saucepan over low heat for 15 to 20 minutes. Add garlic and onion. Simmer until tender, stirring occasionally. Drain, reserving stock. Purée vegetables in food processor. Add 1/2 cup reserved stock, feta cheese, oregano, basil, salt and white pepper. Process until smooth. Return to saucepan with reserved stock. Simmer until heated through, stirring frequently. Sprinkle individual servings with Romano cheese and scallions. Yield: 6 servings.

Approx Per Serving: Cal 135; Prot 12 g; Carbo 8 g; Fiber 2 g; T Fat 7 g; 44% Calories from Fat; Chol 22 mg; Sod 1399 mg.

Chestnut Soup

1 pound carrots, peeled, sliced
2 onions, sliced
1 clove of garlic, crushed
2 ounces butter
Juice of 2 oranges
Grated rind of 1 orange
1/8 teaspoon curry powder
4 cups chicken stock
12 to 14 canned chestnuts
1/4 cup crushed tomatoes
Salt and pepper to taste
1 teaspoon brown sugar

Cook carrots, onions and garlic in butter in large covered saucepan over low heat for 10 minutes, Add orange juice, orange rind, curry powder, chicken stock, chestnuts, tomatoes, salt and pepper; mix well. Bring to a boil; reduce heat. Simmer until vegetables are tender. Process a small amount at a time in blender until puréed. Return to saucepan; add brown sugar. Cook until heated through. Yield: 8 servings.

Approx Per Serving: Cal 129; Prot 4 g; Carbo 14 g; Fiber 3 g; T Fat 7 g; 45% Calories from Fat; Chol 16 mg; Sod 470 mg.

Boil fresh chestnuts for 25 minutes. Peel with knife while still warm. Put in plastic freezer bags and freeze.

Barbecued Chicken Soup

6 cups low-sodium chicken stock
1 barbecued chicken breast, boned, shredded
1/2 8-ounce package spiral pasta
2 tomatoes, seeded, chopped
1 small green bell pepper, seeded, chopped
1/2 cup dry sherry
3 to 5 shallots, thinly sliced
1/3 teaspoon curry powder
Salt and freshly ground pepper to taste

Combine chicken stock, chicken, pasta, tomatoes, green pepper, sherry, shallots, curry powder, salt and pepper in large saucepan. Simmer over low heat for 1 hour, stirring occasionally. Serve with oregano-flavored dumplings. Yield: 5 servings.

Chicken Barbecuing Marinade: Mix extra-virgin olive oil with either dry sherry, hot pepper sherry, lemon juice, wine or cider vinegar. Add crushed garlic, chopped onion, shallots or scallions and herbs, such as thyme, oregano or marjoram. Stir in white Worcestershire sauce or soy sauce. Loosen skin on chicken to allow marinade to penetrate meat. Marinate chicken in plastic bag for at least 3 hours and grill until tender.

Approx Per Serving: Cal 315; Prot 16 g; Carbo 52 g; Fiber 3 g; T Fat 2 g; 7% Calories from Fat; Chol 10 mg; Sod 179 mg.
Nutritional information does not include marinade for chicken.

Soupe au Citron Froide

1 14-ounce can chicken broth
2 egg yolks, beaten   2 tablespoons lemon juice
Salt and cayenne pepper to taste

Heat broth in saucepan until warmed but not hot. Stir a small amount into egg yolks; add egg yolk mixture to broth. Cook over very low heat until slightly thickened, stirring constantly. Remove from heat; cool. Chill until serving time. Stir in lemon juice, salt and cayenne pepper. Serve in blue glass bowls. Garnish with lemon slices and chopped parsley. Yield: 2 servings.

Approx Per Serving: Cal 98; Prot 8 g; Carbo 2 g; Fiber <1 g; T Fat 6 g; 55% Calories from Fat; Chol 214 mg; Sod 640 mg.

Clam Chowder

1 small onion, chopped   ½ red bell pepper, chopped
2 stalks celery, chopped   3 tablespoons butter
2 10-ounce cans clams   1 8-ounce bottle of clam juice
2 8-ounce cans tomato sauce   6 ounces chicken broth
1 bay leaf   Salt and pepper to taste

Sauté vegetables in butter in saucepan. Add remaining ingredients. Simmer for 30 minutes. Discard bay leaf. Yield: 6 servings.

Approx Per Serving: Cal 139; Prot 10 g; Carbo 11 g; Fiber 2 g; T Fat 13 g; 59% Calories from Fat; Chol 75 mg; Sod 729 mg.

Cream of Experience Soup

1 carrot, sliced
1 medium potato, peeled, cubed
1 medium onion, chopped
1 cup water
1 low-salt beef or chicken bouillon cube
1 cup cooked green beans
1 sprig of parsley, chopped
1 large clove of garlic, minced
1 cup tomato juice
1 tablespoon margarine
1 teaspoon Worcestershire sauce
¼ teaspoon basil
⅛ teaspoon pepper
1 tablespoon sherry
2 small round kielbasa sausages, sliced*

Cook carrot, potato and onion in water with bouillon cube in saucepan until tender. Add green beans. Purée in food processor until smooth; return to saucepan. Add parsley, garlic, tomato juice, margarine, Worcestershire sauce, basil, pepper, sherry and sausages. Bring to a boil; reduce heat. Garnish servings with sour cream. May substitute any leftover vegetables for green beans. *May omit kielbasa. Yield: 5 servings.

Approx Per Serving: Cal 286; Prot 10 g; Carbo 16 g; Fiber 2 g; T Fat 20 g; 64% Calories from Fat; Chol 42 mg; Sod 912 mg.

Armenian Cucumber Soup

1 cup yogurt   2 cups cold water
1/4 teaspoon garlic powder   Salt to taste
1 medium cucumber, peeled, thinly sliced
2 tablespoons finely chopped fresh mint

Whisk yogurt in bowl. Add water, garlic powder and salt; whisk vigorously. Fold in cucumber; chill. Sprinkle servings with mint. Yield: 4 servings.

Approx Per Serving: Cal 44; Prot 2 g; Carbo 5 g; Fiber 1 g; T Fat 2 g; 38% Calories from Fat; Chol 7 mg; Sod 28 mg.

Cold Eggplant Soup

1 pound eggplant, cubed
1 green bell pepper, coarsely chopped
2 cloves of garlic, crushed   6 tablespoons olive oil
1/2 cup water   1 teaspoon freshly chopped mint
3 cups plain yogurt   Salt and pepper to taste
1/2 cup milk   2 tablespoons chopped chives

Simmer eggplant, green pepper, garlic, olive oil and water in saucepan for 15 minutes. Purée in food processor; return to saucepan. Add mint, yogurt, salt, pepper and milk; mix well. Chill for 4 to 5 hours. Ladle into soup bowls; sprinkle with chives. Yield: 8 servings.

Approx Per Serving: Cal 169; Prot 4 g; Carbo 9 g; Fiber 2 g; T Fat 14 g; 70% Calories from Fat; Chol 13 mg; Sod 48 mg.

Escarole Soup

3 to 4 pounds escarole
2 pounds lean ground beef
9 eggs
1 1/2 cups grated Parmesan or Romano cheese
Grated rind of 1 1/2 lemons
Salt, pepper and garlic to taste
5 quarts chicken stock

Clean escarole under cold water. Cook in boiling water in large saucepan for 40 minutes; drain and cool. Cut into bite-sized pieces; set aside. Combine ground beef, 2 eggs, 1/2 cup cheese, grated rind of 1/2 lemon, salt, pepper and garlic in bowl; mix well. Shape into small balls. Drop into large kettle of boiling water. Simmer over medium-high heat for 35 to 40 minutes; drain. Bring chicken stock to a boil in large kettle. Beat 7 eggs, remaining lemon rind and 1 cup cheese in bowl. Pour into boiling stock, stirring constantly. Cook for 10 minutes. Add escarole and meatballs. Simmer for 1 hour, stirring frequently. Serve hot. Garnish with additional grated cheese and croutons. Yield: 20 servings.

Approx Per Serving: Cal 210; Prot 20 g; Carbo 5 g; Fiber 1 g; T Fat 12 g; 53% Calories from Fat; Chol 131 mg; Sod 966 mg.

 For best results, rotate your vegetable crops in the garden.

Crab Meat Bisque

1/3 cup finely chopped green bell pepper
1/3 cup finely chopped onion
1 whole scallion, chopped
1/4 cup chopped parsley
1 1/2 cups sliced fresh mushrooms
6 tablespoons butter
2 tablespoons flour
1 cup milk
1 teaspoon salt
1/8 teaspoon white pepper
Tabasco sauce to taste
1 1/2 cups half and half
1 pound lump crab meat
1/4 cup dry sherry

Sauté green pepper, onion, scallion, parsley and mushrooms in 4 tablespoons butter in skillet for 5 minutes or until tender. Melt remaining 2 tablespoons butter in saucepan. Blend in flour. Add milk gradually. Cook until thickened and smooth, stirring constantly. Add salt, pepper, Tabasco sauce, sautéed vegetables and half and half. Bring to a boil; reduce heat. Add crab meat. Simmer for 5 minutes, stirring constantly. Stir in sherry before serving. May substitute cooked shrimp for crab meat.
Yield: 6 servings.

Approx Per Serving: Cal 314; Prot 19 g; Carbo 9 g; Fiber 1 g; T Fat 21 g; 63% Calories from Fat; Chol 134 mg; Sod 707 mg.

Baked Fish Chowder

2 pounds flounder filets, cut into bite-sized pieces
4 new potatoes, peeled, sliced
Celery leaves to taste
1 bay leaf
2 teaspoons salt
4 whole cloves
1 clove of garlic, minced
1 large Spanish onion, chopped
1/2 cup butter
1 teaspoon dillseed
1/4 teaspoon white pepper
1 cup dry white wine
3 cups boiling water

Combine flounder, potatoes, celery leaves, bay leaf, salt, cloves, garlic, onion, butter, dillseed, pepper, wine and water in bowl; mix well. Spoon into 3-quart baking dish. Bake, covered, at 375 degrees for 1 hour. Discard bay leaf and cloves before serving. May substitute any white fish for flounder. This chowder recipe comes from Maine where you would expect lobster, but this chowder tastes better than lobster. Yield: 8 servings.

Approx Per Serving: Cal 254; Prot 23 g; Carbo 6 g; Fiber 1 g; T Fat 13 g; 46% Calories from Fat; Chol 93 mg; Sod 728 mg.

Fish Soup with Brandy

1 tablespoon minced garlic
1 cup thinly sliced leeks
1 teaspoon saffron threads
1/2 teaspoon dried thyme
3 tablespoons olive oil
11/2 pounds flounder filets
1 cup dry white wine
1 cup bottled clam juice
3 cups water
2 tomatoes, peeled, seeded, chopped
1 teaspoon fennel seed, crushed
1 bay leaf
Salt, freshly ground pepper and Tabasco sauce to taste
3 tablespoons brandy

Cook garlic, leeks, saffron and thyme in olive oil in large saucepan over medium heat until leeks are wilted. Add flounder. Simmer for several minutes or until fish begins to flake. Add wine, clam juice, water, tomatoes, fennel seed, bay leaf, salt, pepper and Tabasco sauce; mix well. Bring to a boil; reduce heat. Simmer for 20 minutes, stirring occasionally. Discard bay leaf; add brandy. Ladle into soup bowls; garnish with chopped parsley. May substitute halibut, bass or haddock for flounder.
Yield: 4 servings.

Approx Per Serving: Cal 348; Prot 34 g; Carbo 12 g; Fiber 2 g
T Fat 12 g; 32% Calories from Fat; Chol 93 mg; Sod 285 mg.

Icy Cold Spanish Gazpacho

1 cup finely chopped peeled tomatoes
1/2 cup finely chopped green bell pepper
1/2 cup finely chopped celery
1/2 onion, minced
2 teaspoons chopped parsley
1 teaspoon minced chives
1 small clove of garlic, minced
1 teaspoon salt
1/4 teaspoon pepper
2 tablespoons tarragon vinegar
2 tablespoons olive oil
1/2 teaspoon Worcestershire sauce
2 cups tomato juice

Combine tomatoes, green pepper, celery, onion, parsley, chives, garlic, salt and pepper with vinegar, oil, Worcestershire sauce and tomato juice in glass bowl; mix well. Chill, covered, for 4 hours. Serve in chilled cups, garnished with seasoned croutons and additional minced vegetables. Yield: 2 servings.

Approx Per Serving: Cal 208; Prot 4 g; Carbo 21 g; Fiber 5 g; T Fat 14 g; 56% Calories from Fat; Chol 0 mg; Sod 1996 mg.

Mung beans are an olive green variety that may be used in purées, soups or stews; they are ideal for sprouting.

Hearthside Soup

2 medium leeks (white part only), thinly sliced
1 clove of garlic, minced
1¹/₂ tablespoons butter
2 14-ounce cans chicken broth
1 14-ounce can chopped tomatoes
2 carrots, thinly sliced
1 zucchini, cut into ¹/₂-inch cubes
1 cup sliced mushrooms
1 8-ounce can red kidney beans, drained, rinsed
¹/₂ cup frozen peas
Salt and pepper to taste
1 tablespoon Dijon mustard

Sauté leeks and garlic in butter in 3-quart saucepan. Add broth, tomatoes and carrots. Simmer for 5 minutes; add zucchini, mushrooms, beans and peas. Simmer for 5 minutes. Stir in salt, pepper and mustard. Serve hot, garnished with grated Parmesan cheese. Yield: 6 servings.

Approx Per Serving: Cal 134; Prot 8 g; Carbo 18 g; Fiber 6 g; T Fat 5 g; 29% Calories from Fat; Chol 8 mg; Sod 777 mg.

By refrigerating soup or stew overnight you can easily remove any excess fat that has solidified on the top. This will bring an extra dimension of healthiness to your food.

Holiday House Chowder

1 pound sausage
1 cup water
2 15-ounce cans red kidney beans, drained
1 29-ounce can whole tomatoes
2 onions, chopped
2 bay leaves
2 cloves of garlic, finely chopped
2 teaspoons salt
¹/₂ teaspoon thyme
¹/₈ teaspoon each caraway seed and black pepper
Crushed red pepper to taste
2 cups chopped unpeeled potatoes
1 green bell pepper, chopped

Brown sausage in skillet, stirring until crumbly; drain. Combine with water, beans, tomatoes, onions, bay leaves, garlic, salt, thyme, caraway seed, black pepper and red pepper in large saucepan; mix well. Simmer for 1 hour. Add potatoes and green pepper. Simmer for 20 minutes longer or until potatoes are tender. Remove bay leaves before serving. Yield: 4 servings.

Approx Per Serving: Cal 554; Prot 27 g; Carbo 74 g; Fiber 22 g; T Fat 18 g; 29% Calories from Fat; Chol 43 mg; Sod 2838 mg.

Italian Wedding Soup

3 quarts water
1 large whole chicken breast
1 whole onion
3 carrots, chopped
2 stalks celery
Salt and pepper to taste
12 ounces ground beef
1 egg
2 cloves of garlic, minced
1/2 cup bread crumbs
2   10-ounce packages frozen chopped spinach,
cooked, drained
1 cup white rice, cooked

Combine water, chicken breast, onion, carrots, celery, salt and pepper in 5-quart saucepan. Bring to a boil; reduce heat to medium. Simmer for 45 minutes. Remove chicken breast; cool. Shred meat, discarding bone, and add to soup. Combine ground beef, egg, garlic and bread crumbs in bowl; mix well. Shape into small balls. Drop into soup mixture. Cook for 45 minutes longer. Remove onion; discard. Stir in cooked spinach and rice. Simmer until heated through. This is a traditional Calabrian soup. Yield: 16 servings.

Approx Per Serving: Cal 140; Prot 10 g; Carbo 16 g; Fiber 2 g; T Fat 4 g; 26% Calories from Fat; Chol 36 mg; Sod 88 mg.

Cheesy Leek and Potato Soup

White part of 1 leek, cut into 1/2-inch slices
1 clove of garlic, minced
1 tablespoon butter
2 new potatoes, peeled, cubed
2 1/2 cups chicken broth
2 ounces Stilton cheese
1/2 cup milk
1/4 teaspoon dried thyme
Salt and freshly ground white pepper to taste
Hot pepper sauce to taste
1 tablespoon minced scallion

Sauté leek and garlic in butter in large saucepan until tender. Add potatoes and broth. Simmer, covered, for 20 minutes or until potatoes are tender. Remove potatoes and leek with slotted spoon. Process in blender with 1/2 cup cooking liquid and cheese; return to saucepan. Add milk, thyme, salt, pepper and hot pepper sauce. Simmer over low heat until heated through. Stir in scallion; serve hot. Yield: 2 servings.

Approx Per Serving: Cal 297; Prot 16 g; Carbo 17 g; Fiber 1 g; T Fat 19 g; 56% Calories from Fat; Chol 51 mg; Sod 1564 mg.

For a clearer and more flavorful soup, bring soup slowly to a boil while carefully skimming off any foam or residue that rises to the top.

Exotic Wild Mushroom Soup

1 cup heavy cream
1 cup sour cream
1/2 cup brandy
2 teaspoons minced garlic
2 pounds onions, sliced
1 cup butter
1 1/2 cups sliced oyster mushrooms
1 1/2 cups sliced shiitake mushrooms
4 1/2 quarts vegetable broth
1 cup white wine
1 cup sherry
1/4 cup flour
2 bay leaves

Make crème fraîche 2 days ahead. Beat heavy cream and sour cream in bowl until blended. Flambé brandy in saucepan. Stir into cream mixture. Let stand, covered, in warm place for 12 hours or until thickened to make brandied crème fraîche. Stir well. Chill for 36 hours. Sauté garlic and onions in half the butter in skillet for 10 minutes. Add mushrooms. Cook for 5 minutes longer. Combine vegetable broth, wine and sherry in large saucepan. Bring to a boil. Melt remaining butter in small saucepan. Blend in flour. Stir into broth; add mushroom mixture and bay leaves. Simmer for 35 minutes, stirring occasionally. Remove bay leaves before serving. Ladle into soup bowls; top with brandied crème fraîche. Yield: 16 servings.

Approx Per Serving: Cal 303; Prot 8 g; Carbo 11 g; Fiber 1 g; T Fat 22 g; 65% Calories from Fat; Chol 59 mg; Sod 987 mg.

Cream of Mushroom Soup

1 pound fresh mushrooms
3 tablespoons butter
1 tablespoon lemon juice
Salt and pepper to taste
2 tablespoons minced shallots
3 tablespoons minced onions
2 tablespoons flour
6 cups chicken broth
1 bay leaf
2 sprigs of parsley
Cayenne pepper to taste
3/4 cup heavy cream

Remove stems from mushrooms; chop finely and set aside. Slice caps. Sauté caps with 2 tablespoons butter and lemon juice in large saucepan for 3 minutes. Season with salt and pepper; remove mushrooms to warmed plate. Sauté shallots and onions in remaining 1 tablespoon butter in saucepan until tender. Add chopped mushroom stems. Cook for 2 minutes. Stir in flour. Cook over low heat for 2 minutes, stirring constantly. Stir in chicken broth. Add bay leaf, parsley and cayenne pepper. Cook over low heat for 15 minutes, stirring occasionally. Strain liquid; return to saucepan. Add sliced mushroom caps and cream. Cook over low heat until heated through. Yield: 6 servings.

Approx Per Serving: Cal 225; Prot 8 g; Carbo 8 g; Fiber 2 g; T Fat 19 g; 72% Calories from Fat; Chol 57 mg; Sod 839 mg.

Mushroom Consommé

1 pound fresh mushrooms, sliced
1 tablespoon beef stock
2 tablespoons Burgundy

Simmer mushrooms in beef stock and water to cover in saucepan for 30 minutes. Strain, pressing mushrooms to release essence. Adjust seasoning. Add Burgundy just before serving. Yield: 4 servings.

Approx Per Serving: Cal 33; Prot 2 g; Carbo 5 g; Fiber 2 g; T Fat <1 g; 12% Calories from Fat; Chol <1 mg; Sod 17 mg.

Nothing Soup

4 egg whites   ¼ teaspoon salt   4 egg yolks
4 cups milk   ⅓ cup sugar
½ teaspoon vanilla extract

Beat egg whites with salt in mixer bowl until stiff peaks form. Combine egg yolks, milk, sugar and vanilla in 5-quart saucepan; mix well. Cook over low heat until mixture begins to simmer, stirring occasionally. Drop scoops of egg white mixture onto milk mixture. Simmer, covered, for 5 minutes. Ladle milk broth into bowls; float egg whites on top. Garnish with cinnamon. Serve hot or cold. Yield: 4 servings.

Approx Per Serving: Cal 293; Prot 14 g; Carbo 28 g; Fiber 0 g; T Fat 14 g; 42% Calories from Fat; Chol 246 mg; Sod 294 mg.

Italian Parsley Soup

1 large onion, thinly sliced
White portion of 1 large leek, chopped
2 large carrots, thinly sliced
2 tablespoons butter
1 large potato, thinly sliced
4 cups chicken stock
1 cup packed flat-leaf Italian parsley
1 to 2 tablespoons fresh chervil or rosemary

Sauté onion, leek and carrots in butter in skillet until onion is tender. Add potato. Cook for 5 minutes longer. Heat chicken stock in large saucepan; add vegetables. Simmer, covered, for 30 minutes or until carrots are tender; cool slightly. Purée in blender with parsley and chervil; return to saucepan. Simmer until heated through. Garnish with fresh parsley sprigs. Yield: 6 servings.

Approx Per Serving: Cal 108; Prot 5 g; Carbo 12 g; Fiber 2 g; T Fat 5 g; 40% Calories from Fat; Chol 11 mg; Sod 566 mg.

Make *Easy Chicken and Corn Chowder* by mixing 1 can potato soup, 1 can cream-style corn, 1 can chunk chicken, 1 envelope chicken broth mix and 2 cups milk in saucepan and heating to serving temperature.

Parsley Purée

2 carrots, chopped
2 potatoes, chopped
2 onions, chopped
1 tablespoon butter
1 bunch parsley, stems removed
1   14-ounce can chicken broth
Salt and freshly ground pepper to taste
1/8 teaspoon curry powder
1/4 teaspoon Worcestershire sauce
2 cups milk

Combine carrots, potatoes, onions and butter with a small amount of water in saucepan. Simmer, covered, until vegetables are tender. Process in blender until puréed. Add parsley, chicken broth, salt, pepper, curry powder and Worcestershire sauce to blender. Process until smooth. Pour milk into top of double boiler; stir in vegetable mixture. Cook over boiling water until heated through. Serve with chowder crackers or croutons; garnish with chopped chives. In spring substitute tender dandelion greens for parsley. Yield: 4 servings.

Approx Per Serving: Cal 222; Prot 9 g; Carbo 30 g; Fiber 4 g; T Fat 8 g; 31% Calories from Fat; Chol 25 mg; Sod 417 mg.

Chick-Pea Soup

2 to 3 cloves of garlic, cut into halves
1/4 cup olive oil
1 to 2 sprigs of rosemary
1/2   8-ounce can tomato sauce
2   15-ounce cans chick-peas
1 to 2 cups chicken broth
Salt to taste
1 cup broken spinach noodles

Sauté garlic in oil in skillet until browned; discard garlic. Add rosemary. Brown for 1 to 2 minutes. Add tomato sauce. Cook for 5 to 10 minutes or until reduced to desired consistency. Press undrained chick-peas through sieve, discarding skins. Add to skillet. Add enough chicken broth to make of desired consistency. Cook for 15 to 20 minutes, stirring occasionally. Add salt and noodles. Cook until noodles are tender. Yield: 2 servings.

Approx Per Serving: Cal 270; Prot 96 g; Carbo 304 g; Fiber 85 g; T Fat 57 g; 24% Calories from Fat; Chol 1 mg; Sod 1103 mg.

To remove liquid fat from the top of soup, stew or gravy, drape a paper towel across the surface. When towel is soaked, lift off. Repeat as necessary.

Cream of Curried Pea Soup

1 cup shelled fresh peas
1 medium onion, sliced
1 medium carrot, sliced
1 large stalk celery, sliced
1 medium potato, peeled, sliced
1 clove of garlic
1 teaspoon salt
1½ teaspoons curry powder
2 cups chicken stock
1 cup half and half

Combine peas, onion, carrot, celery, potato, garlic, salt, curry powder and 1 cup chicken stock in saucepan. Bring to a boil; reduce heat. Simmer, covered, for 15 minutes or until vegetables are tender. Process in food processor until smooth. Add remaining stock and half and half gradually, processing constantly. Chill in refrigerator until serving time. Serve in chilled soup bowls; garnish with chopped chives. Yield: 4 servings.

Approx Per Serving: Cal 181; Prot 8 g; Carbo 21 g; Fiber 4 g; T Fat 8 g; 39% Calories from Fat; Chol 23 mg; Sod 965 mg.

Red Pepper Soup

2 pounds red bell peppers, sliced
¼ cup butter
4 cups beef broth
2 egg yolks, beaten
1 cup whipping cream

Sauté red peppers in butter in saucepan for 3 to 5 minutes. Add broth. Simmer until peppers are tender. Remove with slotted spoon to food processor. Process until puréed; return to broth. Beat egg yolks with ¼ cup cream and small amount of hot broth. Add egg mixture to broth, whisking vigorously. Stir in remaining cream. Cook over low heat until heated through. Yield: 8 servings.

Approx Per Serving: Cal 205; Prot 4 g; Carbo 7 g; Fiber 2 g; T Fat 19 g; 80% Calories from Fat; Chol 110 mg; Sod 456 mg.

Make *Cold Blueberry Soup* by simmering 1 pint blueberries in 2 cups water with 1 sliced lemon, ½ cup sugar and 1 cinnamon stick in saucepan for 15 minutes. Remove cinnamon stick. Cool slightly before puréeing in a blender to desired consistency; chill. Serve with sour cream.

Frankhouser's Potato Soup

1/4 cup butter
1/4 cup flour
1   12-ounce can evaporated milk
1 quart water
6 potatoes, cubed
1 teaspoon salt
2 chicken bouillon cubes
1/4 teaspoon pepper
1/4 cup chopped parsley
1 tablespoon dried minced onion
2 hard-boiled eggs, sliced

Melt butter in microwave-safe bowl. Blend in flour and evaporated milk. Microwave on High until mixture becomes thick paste, stirring every 3 minutes; set aside. Combine water, potatoes, salt, bouillon cubes, pepper, parsley and onion in large saucepan. Bring to a boil. Cook until potatoes are tender. Add paste mixture. Cook until soup thickens slightly, stirring constantly. Serve topped with sliced eggs. Yield: 6 servings.

Approx Per Serving: Cal 311; Prot 9 g; Carbo 38 g; Fiber 2 g; T Fat 14 g; 41% Calories from Fat; Chol 109 mg; Sod 894 mg.

Spicy Potato-Cheese Soup

2 1/2 cups cubed peeled potatoes
1 cup chopped onion
1/2 cup thinly sliced celery
2 1/2 cups water
2 1/2 teaspoons salt
1/4 cup butter
1/4 cup flour
1/2 teaspoon hot pepper
1/4 teaspoon each freshly ground black pepper
and dry mustard
1 1/2 teaspoons steak sauce
2 cups milk
8 ounces sharp Cheddar cheese, shredded
1 tablespoon chopped fresh parsley
1   14-ounce can stewed tomatoes, chopped
2 teaspoons fresh dill

Combine potatoes, onion, celery, water and 1 teaspoon salt in medium saucepan. Bring to a boil. Simmer, covered, for 15 minutes. Melt butter in large saucepan; blend in flour. Add remaining 1 1/2 teaspoons salt, hot pepper, black pepper, dry mustard, steak sauce and milk. Simmer until smooth and thickened, stirring constantly. Add vegetable mixture, cheese, parsley and tomatoes. Simmer until heated through. Sprinkle with fresh dill. Yield: 6 servings.

Approx Per Serving: Cal 370; Prot 15 g; Carbo 27 g; Fiber 2 g; T Fat 23 g; 55% Calories from Fat; Chol 72 mg; Sod 1447 mg.

Curried Pumpkin Soup

1/2 large onion
1 clove of garlic
1 teaspoon fresh ginger
1 tablespoon peanut oil
1/4 medium pumpkin
1 14-ounce can chicken broth
Red pepper to taste
1 teaspoon curry powder
1/4 cup whipping cream
1/2 cup frozen baby peas
2 tablespoons chopped fresh coriander

Chop onion, garlic and ginger in food processor. Sauté in oil in 3-quart saucepan for 5 minutes or until onion is tender. Scoop out pumpkin with melon baller. Add pumpkin balls and chicken broth to saucepan. Bring to a boil; reduce heat. Simmer for 15 to 20 minutes or until pumpkin is tender. Stir in red pepper, curry, cream and peas. Cook over low heat until heated through, stirring frequently. Sprinkle with coriander. Yield: 6 servings.

Approx Per Serving: Cal 92; Prot 3 g; Carbo 6 g; Fiber 2 g; T Fat 6 g; 61% Calories from Fat; Chol 14 mg; Sod 229 mg.

Dutch Pumpkin Soup

1 pumpkin or Hubbard squash
2 large carrots, thinly sliced
1 cup chopped onion   2 tablespoons butter
5 cups chicken broth
1 teaspoon each cumin, paprika and dried ginger
1   28-ounce can pumpkin purée
3/4 cup light cream   Salt and pepper to taste
3 tablespoons thinly sliced scallions
2/3 cup cherry tomatoes, thinly sliced, drained
1/2 cup sunflower seed, roasted, salted

Hollow out pumpkin or Hubbard squash to use as a tureen. Cut small slice from bottom to stabilize if necessary. Sauté carrots and onion in butter in saucepan until carrots are slightly brown and glazed. Add 1 cup chicken broth and seasonings. Simmer for 20 minutes. Cool. Purée in blender. Combine carrot purée, pumpkin purée and remaining 4 cups broth in 2-quart saucepan; whisk to blend. Add cream; season with salt and pepper. Stir in scallions. Heat to serving temperature. Pour soup into hollowed pumpkin or squash. Top with tomato slices. Serve with sunflower seed. Yield: 10 servings.

Approx Per Serving: Cal 205; Prot 7 g; Carbo 19 g; Fiber 5 g; T Fat 13 g; 53% Calories from Fat; Chol 27 mg; Sod 466 mg.

Ukrainian Sauerkraut Soup

8 ounces dried green split peas
10 cups water
3 slices bacon, chopped
2 large onions, finely chopped
3 cloves of garlic, chopped
2 pounds sauerkraut
2 bay leaves
1/2 teaspoon caraway seed
1 tablespoon tomato paste
3 to 4 pounds country-style spare ribs

Combine split peas with 2 cups water in saucepan. Bring to a boil; reduce heat. Simmer over low heat for 45 to 60 minutes or until tender. Fry bacon in large saucepan until crisp. Add onions and garlic. Sauté until onions are tender. Add sauerkraut, remaining 8 cups water, bay leaves, caraway seed, tomato paste and spare ribs. Bring to a boil; reduce heat. Cook over low heat for 2 to 3 hours. Add peas and liquid. Remove spare ribs; cool. Cut meat into bite-sized pieces, discarding bones. Return to saucepan. Heat to serving temperature. Remove bay leaves before serving. May also add 1 to 2 pounds sliced kielbasa sausage and 2 cups freshly shredded cabbage. The longer this soup cooks the more flavorful it becomes. Make it in the morning or the day before and reheat. Yield: 10 servings.

Approx Per Serving: Cal 392; Prot 28 g; Carbo 21 g; Fiber 6 g; T Fat 22 g; 51% Calories from Fat; Chol 85 mg; Sod 700 mg.

Tamale Soup

8 ounces ground beef
2 medium onions, chopped
4 cloves of garlic, minced
3 tablespoons oil
2 cups shredded cooked roast beef
3 cups tomato sauce
4 cups water
2 4-ounce cans sliced black olives, drained
2 4-ounce cans chopped green chilies
1 16-ounce can whole kernel corn, drained
2 jalapeño peppers, finely chopped
2 tablespoons cumin
3 tablespoons chili powder
2 cups chopped tomatoes
2 cups shredded Monterey Jack cheese

Brown ground beef with onions and garlic in oil in large soup kettle, stirring until ground beef is crumbly; drain. Add roast beef, tomato sauce, water, olives, green chilies, corn, jalapeño peppers, cumin, chili powder and tomatoes. Simmer for 20 minutes, stirring occasionally. Sprinkle servings with cheese. May substitute ground turkey for ground beef. Yield: 14 servings.

Approx Per Serving: Cal 243; Prot 15 g; Carbo 15 g; Fiber 3 g; T Fat 16 g; 55% Calories from Fat; Chol 41 mg; Sod 737 mg.

Tomato Soup Forever

1/2 cup unsalted butter
2 tablespoons olive oil
1 large onion, thinly sliced
2 sprigs of fresh thyme or 1/2 teaspoon dried thyme
4 basil leaves, chopped, or 1/2 teaspoon dried basil
Salt and pepper to taste
2 1/2 pounds tomatoes, chopped
3 tablespoons unsalted tomato paste
3 3/4 cups low-salt chicken broth
1/4 cup flour
1 teaspoon sugar
1 cup whipping cream
1/4 cup unsalted butter

Heat 1/2 cup butter and olive oil in large saucepan. Add onion, thyme, basil, salt and pepper. Cook until onion is tender. Stir in tomatoes and tomato paste. Simmer for 10 minutes. Blend 5 tablespoons chicken broth with flour in small bowl. Stir into tomato mixture. Add remaining mixture through fine sieve; return to saucepan. Add sugar and cream. Simmer over low heat for 5 minutes, stirring occasionally. Add 1/4 cup butter, stirring until melted. Serve topped with garlic croutons. May substitute canned tomatoes when fresh is unavailable. Yield: 8 servings

Approx Per Serving: Cal 351; Prot 4 g; Carbo 14 g; Fiber 3 g;
T Fat 32 g; 80% Calories from Fat; Chol 87 mg; Sod 57 mg.

Turkey Meatball-Escarole Soup

1 pound ground turkey
1 cup fresh bread crumbs
1 tablespoon grated onion
1/2 teaspoon celery seed
1/2 teaspoon dried sage
2 tablespoons olive oil
1/3 cup uncooked orzo
3 1/2 cups chicken broth
1 small head escarole, coarsely sliced

Combine turkey, bread crumbs, onion, celery seed and sage in bowl; mix well. Shape into 3/4-inch meatballs. Brown in oil in skillet; drain and set aside. Cook orzo using package instructions; set aside. Bring chicken broth to a boil in large saucepan. Add escarole. Cool until wilted. Add meatballs and orzo. Simmer for 10 minutes. The original Sicilian version of this, called Wedding Soup, uses cannellini beans and ground lamb. Yield: 6 servings.

Approx Per Serving: Cal 227; Prot 19 g; Carbo 8 g; Fiber 1 g;
T Fat 13 g; 52% Calories from Fat; Chol 48 mg; Sod 562 mg.

Make "soup bags" by mixing together 2 teaspoons each of thyme, parsley and marjoram, 1 teaspoon savory, 4 teaspoons celery leaves and 1/2 teaspoon of sage leaves. Divide into 6 portions and enclose each portion in a piece of cheesecloth. Next time you make soup or stew, add a "soup bag" while it is cooking.

Roasted Vegetable Soup

12 large plum tomatoes, cut into halves
6 green bell peppers, cut into quarters
1 large onion, coarsely chopped
2 fennel bulbs, coarsely chopped
2 garlic bulbs
1 tablespoon olive oil
2 eggplant, cut into halves lengthwise
Sherry vinegar, salt and pepper to taste
4 cups (or less) tomato juice
Polenta Croutons and Pesto (next column)

Place tomatoes, bell pepper, onion and fennel on baking sheet. Roast at 400 degrees until lightly charred. Rub garlic bulbs with olive oil; wrap in foil. Roast until tender; cool. Squeeze garlic cloves from skin. Place eggplant cut side down on baking sheet. Roast until tender. Scrape pulp from skin. Combine all vegetables in bowl. Purée in several batches in food processor. Combine in saucepan. Season with sherry vinegar, salt and pepper. Heat to serving temperature over medium heat, adding tomato juice until of desired consistency. Ladle into soup bowls; top with Polenta Croutons and Pesto. May substitute chicken stock for tomato juice. Yield: 8 servings.

Approx Per Serving: Cal 114; Prot 4 g; Carbo 23 g; Fiber 8 g; T Fat 3 g; 17% Calories from Fat; Chol 0 mg; Sod 461 mg. Nutritional information does not include Polenta Croutons and Pesto and fennel bulbs.

Polenta Croutons and Pesto

2 cups chopped mixed savory herbs such as
parsley, rosemary, sage, thyme, oregano
or winter savory
3/4 cup olive oil
2 cloves of garlic, chopped
1/2 cup pine nuts
3/4 cup grated Parmesan cheese
5 cups water
1 tablespoon aniseed, toasted
1 tablespoon olive oil
1/2 teaspoon each salt and pepper
2 cups cornmeal

Combine savory herbs with 3/4 cup olive oil, garlic, pine nuts and cheese in food processor container; process until smooth. Bring water, aniseed, 1 tablespoon olive oil, salt and pepper to a boil in saucepan; reduce heat. Whisk in cornmeal gradually. Cook for 2 to 3 minutes, stirring constantly with wooden spoon; remove from heat. Let stand for 20 minutes, stirring every 5 to 10 minutes. Spread evenly in shallow baking sheet; cool to room temperature. Cut into 3/4x4-inch strips; cut into croutons. Bake at 400 degrees until crisp and golden brown. May fry croutons if preferred. Serve Pesto and Polenta Croutons with Roasted Vegetable Soup. Yield: 8 servings.

Approx Per Serving: Cal 411; Prot 7 g; Carbo 31 g; Fiber 4 g; T Fat 30 g; 64% Calories from Fat; Chol 6 mg; Sod 287 mg.

Black Bean Salad

1 small white onion   4 whole cloves
1 pound dried black turtle beans
2 bay leaves   2 cloves of garlic, minced
Juice and grated zest of 1 lime
1/2 cup sherry wine vinegar
1/4 cup fresh orange juice
1 tablespoon chili powder
1 tablespoon cumin powder, toasted
2 teaspoons salt   Cayenne pepper to taste
1/2 cup peanut oil
1 red onion, finely chopped
1 each red and green bell pepper, finely chopped
1 carrot, finely chopped
1/4 cup chopped fresh coriander

Stud white onion with cloves. Combine with beans, bay leaves and water to cover by 4 inches in saucepan. Bring to a boil over high heat; reduce heat. Simmer just until beans are tender, adding additional water if necessary for desired consistency. Drain and cool beans, discarding onion and bay leaves. Combine garlic, lime juice and zest, vinegar, orange juice, chili powder, cumin, salt and cayenne pepper in small bowl; mix well. Whisk in peanut oil. Combine beans with red onion, bell peppers, carrot and coriander in salad bowl. Add dressing; mix well. May store in refrigerator for up to 2 days. Serve with small rounds of fresh chevre cheese sprinkled with pepper and baked at 400 degrees until soft. Yield: 12 servings.

Approx Per Serving: Cal 227; Prot 9 g; Carbo 29 g; Fiber 2 g; T Fat 10 g; 37% Calories from Fat; Chol 0 mg; Sod 369 mg.

Five-Bean Salad

2/3 cup sugar   2/3 cup vinegar
1/3 cup oil   3 tablespoons mustard
Salt to taste   1 onion, thinly sliced
1 16-ounce can cut green beans, drained
1 16-ounce can cut wax beans, drained
1 16-ounce can chick-peas, drained
1 16-ounce can pink kidney beans, drained
1 16-ounce can red kidney beans, drained

Combine sugar, vinegar, oil, mustard and salt in saucepan; mix well. Bring to a boil, stirring until sugar is dissolved. Pour over onion and beans in large bowl; mix well. Chill overnight. Yield: 12 servings.

Approx Per Serving: Cal 226; Prot 7 g; Carbo 36 g; Fiber 7 g; T Fat 7 g; 27% Calories from Fat; Chol 0 mg; Sod 615 mg.

Snap Bean Salad

1 pound whole green snap beans, ends trimmed
1/2 cup French dressing   1 pimento, sliced

Cook beans in a small amount of water in saucepan until tender-crisp; drain. Refresh in ice water. Marinate in dressing in refrigerator for several hours. Stack in serving dish; crisscross with pimento slices. Yield: 4 servings.

Approx Per Serving: Cal 204; Prot 2 g; Carbo 11 g; Fiber 3 g; T Fat 18 g; 75% Calories from Fat; Chol 0 mg; Sod 373 mg.

Cold Broccoli Salad

1 bunch broccoli, chopped
8 ounces Cheddar cheese, shredded
1/2 onion, finely chopped
1 cup mayonnaise-type salad dressing
1/2 cup sugar   2 teaspoons apple cider vinegar
8 ounces bacon, crisp-fried, crumbled

Combine broccoli, cheese and onion in salad bowl. Mix salad dressing, sugar and vinegar in small bowl. Pour over broccoli mixture; add bacon. Toss to coat. Chill, covered, for 2 hours. Yield: 8 servings.

Approx Per Serving: Cal 341; Prot 11 g; Carbo 23 g; Fiber 2 g; T Fat 24 g; 61% Calories from Fat; Chol 45 mg; Sod 533 mg.

Celery and Olive Salad

10 stalks celery, cut into bite-sized pieces
1   4-ounce jar Spanish olives, cut into halves
1 cup olive oil
Salt and pepper to taste

Combine celery and olives in bowl; mix well. Add olive oil, salt and pepper; mix well. Chill for 30 minutes. Yield: 10 servings.

Approx Per Serving: Cal 210; Prot <1 g; Carbo 2 g; Fiber 1 g; T Fat 23 g; 96% Calories from Fat; Chol 0 mg; Sod 307 mg.

Italian Cauliflower Salad

3/4 cup wine vinegar
1/2 cup light olive oil
2 tablespoons sugar
1/2 cup water
2 teaspoons Italian seasoning
1 teaspoon salt
1 head cauliflower, cut into bite-sized pieces
2 carrots, cut into 2-inch narrow strips
1 green bell pepper, cut into 1-inch squares
1 red bell pepper, cut into 1-inch squares
2 stalks celery, cut into 1-inch pieces
4 ounces green salad olives

Combine vinegar, oil, sugar, water, Italian seasoning and salt in skillet. Bring to a boil. Add cauliflower, carrots, bell peppers and celery. Bring to a boil; reduce heat. Simmer for 5 minutes, stirring frequently. Remove from heat; stir in olives. Chill, covered, overnight. Yield: 10 servings.

Approx Per Serving: Cal 141; Prot 1 g; Carbo 8 g; Fiber 2 g; T Fat 13 g; 75% Calories from Fat; Chol 0 mg; Sod 504 mg.

Olive oil can go rancid quickly in warm weather. Store it in a cool, dark spot but not in the refrigerator. Only buy in a size you will use in 2 months.

Chinese Chicken Salad

2 tablespoons Hoisin sauce   1/4 cup white wine
1/4 cup soy sauce   1 tablespoon garlic powder
1 teaspoon sesame oil
2 1/2 to 3 pounds boneless chicken breasts
4 cups vegetable oil for deep frying
1/2 16-ounce package egg roll wrappers
1 tablespoon cornstarch   3/4 cup white vinegar
1/4 cup sugar
2 teaspoons Tabasco sauce
1 teaspoon salt
1/2 teaspoon pepper
6 tablespoons soy sauce
2 tablespoons sesame oil
6 tablespoons vegetable oil
1 head iceberg lettuce, cut into bite-sized pieces
1 bunch scallions, cut into 1-inch strips
1 16-ounce can bean sprouts, rinsed, drained
3 tomatoes, cut into 1/2-inch cubes
3 tablespoons sesame seed, toasted

Combine Hoisin sauce, wine, 1/4 cup soy sauce, garlic powder and 1 teaspoon sesame oil in bowl; mix well. Rinse chicken and pat dry; pound thin. Pour marinade over chicken in shallow bowl. Marinate in refrigerator for 4 hours to overnight. Heat 4 cups vegetable oil in deep-fryer. Cut egg roll wrappers into 1-inch strips. Deep-fry in hot oil for 5 to 10 seconds or until puffed and golden; drain. Break into small pieces; set aside. Drain chicken, discarding marinade; place in baking dish. Bake at 375 degrees for 20 minutes. Cool; cut into 3/4-inch strips.

Dissolve cornstarch in a small amount of water; set aside. Combine vinegar, sugar, Tabasco sauce, salt, pepper, 6 tablespoons soy sauce, 2 tablespoons sesame oil and 6 tablespoons vegetable oil in saucepan. Bring to a boil. Stir in cornstarch mixture. Cook until thickened, stirring constantly; remove from heat to cool. Combine chicken strips, lettuce, scallions, bean sprouts and tomatoes in large bowl. Add dressing, tossing to coat. Stir in fried egg roll wrappers and sesame seed. May make ahead and assemble before serving. Yield: 12 servings.

Approx Per Serving: Cal 344; Prot 31 g; Carbo 22 g; Fiber 2 g; T Fat 14 g; 37% Calories from Fat; Chol 72 mg; Sod 1211 mg. Nutritional information does not include oil for deep frying.

Chicory Salad

1 bunch chicory, torn
1 1-ounce jar pine nuts, roasted
1 4-ounce package dried cherries, cut into thirds
2 tablespoons raspberry vinegar
1 teaspoon sugar
1/4 cup olive oil
1 shallot, sliced

Combine chicory, pine nuts and cherries in salad bowl. Mix vinegar, sugar, oil and shallot in small bowl. Pour over chicory mixture, tossing to coat. Yield: 6 servings.

Approx Per Serving: Cal 174; Prot 2 g; Carbo 16 g; Fiber 2 g; T Fat 13 g; 60% Calories from Fat; Chol 0 mg; Sod 18 mg.

Chicken-Cranberry Mold

2 envelopes unflavored gelatin
1 cup cranberry juice cocktail
5 tablespoons lemon juice
1   16-ounce can whole cranberry sauce
3/4 cup cold water
1 cup mayonnaise
3/4 teaspoon salt
2 tablespoons chopped parsley
1 1/2 cups chopped cooked chicken
1/2 cup chopped celery
1/4 cup coarsely chopped toasted almonds

Soften 1 envelope gelatin in cranberry juice in saucepan. Heat until gelatin dissolves, stirring to mix well. Stir in 2 tablespoons lemon juice and cranberry sauce. Pour into greased 6-cup ring mold; chill until partially set. Soften remaining envelope gelatin in cold water in saucepan. Heat until warmed through, stirring until gelatin is dissolved. Add mayonnaise, remaining 3 tablespoons lemon juice, salt, parsley, chicken, celery and almonds; mix well. Spoon over cranberry layer in mold. Chill until firm. Unmold onto serving plate. Yield: 8 servings.

Approx Per Serving: Cal 385; Prot 10 g; Carbo 29 g; Fiber 2 g; T Fat 26 g; 60% Calories from Fat; Chol 40 mg; Sod 405 mg.

Chicken Salad Deluxe

1 1/4 cups buttermilk salad dressing
1/2 cup mayonnaise
3 tablespoons half and half
1 3/4 teaspoons Beau Monde seasoning
1 teaspoon salt
1/2 teaspoon pepper
12 ounces slivered almonds
5 chicken breasts, cooked, chopped
10 ounces shell pasta, cooked, drained
2 1/2 cups green grapes, cut into halves
3 cups chopped celery
1/2 cup chopped onion
2   7-ounce cans water chestnuts, drained

Combine salad dressing, mayonnaise, half and half, Beau Monde seasoning, salt and pepper in small bowl; mix well. Chill, covered, overnight. Reserve 1 tablespoon almonds for garnish. Combine remaining almonds, chicken, pasta, grapes, celery, onion and water chestnuts in large bowl. Add dressing; mix gently. Serve with cantaloupe on lettuce-lined serving plates. Garnish with reserved almonds and parsley. Yield: 20 servings.

Approx Per Serving: Cal 338; Prot 12 g; Carbo 22 g; Fiber 4 g; T Fat 23 g; 59% Calories from Fat; Chol 26 mg; Sod 295 mg.

Yum-Yum Chinese Salad

1/2 cup sesame seed
3/4 cup sliced almonds
3 tablespoons butter
8 scallions, sliced
1 head lettuce, torn
2 cups chopped cooked chicken
2 3-ounce packages ramen noodles, broken
1 cup oil
1/4 cup sugar
1/3 cup red wine vinegar
2 teaspoons salt
1 teaspoon pepper

Brown sesame seed and almonds in butter in skillet; cool. Combine scallions, lettuce, chicken, noodles, sesame seed and almonds in salad bowl. Mix oil, sugar, vinegar, salt and pepper in small bowl. Pour over salad mixture, tossing to coat. May substitute ham, turkey, beef, shrimp or crab for chicken. Yield: 6 servings.

Approx Per Serving: Cal 751; Prot 23 g; Carbo 30 g; Fiber 4 g; T Fat 63 g; 73% Calories from Fat; Chol 57 mg; Sod 1229 mg.

Leaves from the lovage plant are a delicious addition to salads. The aroma and flavor of this herb are reminiscent of celery, only more pungent.

Couscous Salad

6 cups chicken stock
9 tablespoons olive oil
1/2 teaspoon ginger
1/4 teaspoon saffron
3 cups uncooked couscous
3/4 cup currants
3/4 cup chopped pitted dates
2 1/4 cups finely chopped celery
1 1/2 cups chopped carrots
1 cup minced scallions
1/2 cup minced parsley
2 1/4 tablespoons lemon juice
3/4 teaspoon salt
1/2 teaspoon cinnamon
3/4 cup toasted pine nuts

Combine chicken stock, 6 tablespoons olive oil, ginger and saffron in saucepan. Bring to a boil. Add couscous. Boil until liquid is absorbed; remove from heat. Fold in currants and dates. Let stand, covered, for 15 minutes. Stir in celery, carrots and scallions. Combine parsley, lemon juice, salt, cinnamon and remaining 3 tablespoons olive oil in small bowl; mix well. Pour over couscous, tossing well. Chill, covered, overnight. Sprinkle with pine nuts before serving. Yield: 16 servings.

Approx Per Serving: Cal 313; Prot 7 g; Carbo 45 g; Fiber 2 g; T Fat 12 g; 34% Calories from Fat; Chol <1 mg; Sod 424 mg.

Cranberry Relish Salad

2 oranges, seeded, cut into fourths
1 quart fresh cranberries
1¹/₂ cups sugar
2 envelopes unflavored gelatin
1¹/₂ cups cranberry juice cocktail

Grind oranges and cranberries in food grinder. Combine with sugar in bowl, mixing well. Soften gelatin in 1 cup cold cranberry juice in top of double boiler. Cook over boiling water, stirring until gelatin is dissolved; remove from heat. Stir in remaining ¹/₂ cup cranberry juice. Pour into cranberry mixture, stirring well. Pour into greased 3-cup mold. Chill until firm. Unmold onto serving plate. Yield: 12 servings.

Approx Per Serving: Cal 144; Prot 1 g; Carbo 36 g; Fiber 2 g; T Fat <1 g; 1% Calories from Fat; Chol 0 mg; Sod 3 mg.

When you've removed the tender leaves to preserve your herbs for winter, save the stems. Tie these stems into bundles about 2 inches thick and secure with pliable vines. When thrown on a fire these bundles impart a lovely fragrance to the house.

Cranberry Waldorf

3 cups fresh cranberries
2 cups miniature marshmallows
³/₄ cup sugar
2 large tart apples, chopped
¹/₂ cup seedless grapes, chopped
¹/₂ cup walnuts, chopped
1 cup heavy cream, whipped

Grind cranberries in food grinder. Combine with marshmallows and sugar in bowl. Let stand in refrigerator overnight. Stir in apples, grapes and walnuts. Fold in whipped cream. Yield: 8 servings.

Approx Per Serving: Cal 324; Prot 2 g; Carbo 47 g; Fiber 3 g; T Fat 16 g; 42% Calories from Fat; Chol 41 mg; Sod 26 mg.

Make **Pink Lady Salad** by bringing one 20-ounce can pineapple and one 6-ounce package strawberry gelatin to a boil in saucepan and cool. Mix in 8 ounces creamed cheese. Beat 1 well chilled can evaporated milk until fluffy and fold into salad. Chill until firm.

Cucumber and Pimento Salad

2 unpeeled cucumbers, sliced lengthwise
5 tablespoons lemon juice
2 tablespoons honey
3/4 teaspoon salt
1/2 teaspoon freshly ground white pepper
1/2 teaspoon onion powder
1/2 cup sour cream
1/4 cup mayonnaise
1   2-ounce jar chopped pimento, drained

Scoop out seed in cucumbers; slice thinly. Pat dry with paper towels. Whisk lemon juice, honey, salt, pepper and onion powder in medium bowl. Add cucumbers, tossing to coat. Chill for 2 hours to overnight, stirring occasionally. Combine sour cream, mayonnaise and pimento in bowl. Chill for 1 to 2 hours. Drain cucumbers, reserving 2 to 3 tablespoons marinade. Pat dry with paper towels. Whisk reserved marinade into sour cream mixture. Stir in cucumbers. Serve on lettuce-lined plates.
Yield: 6 servings.

Approx Per Serving: Cal 147; Prot 1 g; Carbo 11 g; Fiber 1 g; T Fat 12 g; 67% Calories from Fat; Chol 14 mg; Sod 331 mg.

 Use nasturtiums as a colorful garnish for salads.

Cucumbers with Dressing

2 eggs, beaten   3/4 cup sugar
1 teaspoon flour   1/2 cup cider vinegar
1/4 cup water
3 large cucumbers, peeled, seeded, sliced
1 large onion, chopped   Salt and pepper to taste

Beat eggs in bowl until frothy. Stir in mixture of sugar and flour. Add vinegar and water. Cook in top of double boiler over medium heat until thickened, stirring frequently. Pour over mixture of cucumbers and onion in salad bowl, tossing to coat. Season with salt and pepper. Chill until serving time. Yield: 6 servings.

Approx Per Serving: Cal 155; Prot 3 g; Carbo 32 g; Fiber 2 g; T Fat 2 g; 12% Calories from Fat; Chol 71 mg; Sod 27 mg.

Dandelion Salad

6 cups young unsprayed dandelion leaves
1/2 clove of garlic   3 tablespoons virgin olive oil
1 tablespoon flavored vinegar   Salt and pepper to taste

Wash and drain dandelion leaves. Rub clove half over wooden salad bowl. Mix oil, vinegar, salt and pepper in small bowl. Pour over dandelion leaves in prepared salad bowl, tossing to coat. Yield: 4 servings.

Approx Per Serving: Cal 128; Prot 2 g; Carbo 8 g; Fiber 1 g; T Fat 11 g; 70% Calories from Fat; Chol 0 mg; Sod 63 mg.

Egg Salad Ring Mold

2 tablespoons unflavored gelatin
1/2 cup cold water
1 cup boiling water
3/4 teaspoon salt
3 tablespoons lemon juice
3 tablespoons catsup
1/2 tablespoon horseradish
12 hard-boiled eggs, riced
2 cups mayonnaise

Soften gelatin in cold water. Add to boiling water in bowl, stirring until dissolved. Add salt, lemon juice, catsup and horseradish, mixing well. Fold in riced eggs and mayonnaise. Spoon into 10-inch ring mold rinsed in cold water. Chill for several hours to overnight. Unmold onto lettuce-lined serving plate. Garnish with tomato wedges and olives. Fill center with crab meat. This was the centerpiece at summer luncheons at the seashore 50 years ago when cholesterol and calories were not important.
Yield: 12 servings.

Approx Per Serving: Cal 352; Prot 8 g; Carbo 3 g; Fiber <1 g; T Fat 35 g; 88% Calories from Fat; Chol 235 mg; Sod 453 mg. Nutritional information does not include filling for center of ring.

Red Lettuce Spears

1/2 cup mayonnaise
2 tablespoons fresh tangerine juice
1 clove of garlic, pressed
1/4 teaspoon grated tangerine rind
1/8 teaspoon white pepper
1 head red leaf lettuce
12 ounces Italian green beans
1/2 teaspoon olive oil
1 to 2 tablespoons tangerine juice
1 small red or yellow bell pepper, sliced into 16 strips
2 medium tangerines, cut into wedges

Combine mayonnaise, 2 tablespoons tangerine juice, garlic, tangerine rind and pepper in small bowl; mix well. Chill, covered, for 30 minutes to 2 days. Cut lettuce vertically through core and leaves into eighths, trimming away most of core but keeping leaves attached. Rinse and drain; chill. Cook beans in 3 inches of boiling water for 2 to 3 minutes or until tender-crisp; drain. Rinse in cold water; drain and chill. Toss beans with olive oil in small bowl. Place lettuce and beans on 8 salad plates. Sprinkle with remaining tangerine juice. Spoon tangerine mayonnaise over beans. Top with bell pepper strips. Serve with tangerine wedges. May substitute oranges for tangerines.
Yield: 8 servings.

Approx Per Serving: Cal 134; Prot 2 g; Carbo 8 g; Fiber 2 g; T Fat 11 g; 73% Calories from Fat; Chol 8 mg; Sod 84 mg.

Salads

Lemon-Beet Mold

1 16-ounce can sliced beets, cut into shoestring strips
1/4 cup vinegar   1/4 cup sugar
1 3-ounce package lemon gelatin
1/2 cup cold water
1 tablespoon prepared horseradish

Drain beets, reserving liquid. Combine reserved liquid with enough water to measure 1 cup. Mix beet liquid, vinegar and sugar in saucepan. Bring to a boil. Add gelatin. Cook until gelatin dissolves, stirring frequently. Add cold water and horseradish, stirring well. Stir in beets. Pour into 4-cup mold. Chill until firm.
Yield: 8 servings.

Approx Per Serving: Cal 82; Prot 2 g; Carbo 20 g; Fiber 1 g; T Fat <1 g; 0% Calories from Fat; Chol 0 mg; Sod 185 mg.

Mill Dam Salad

3 heads lettuce, torn   1 bunch radishes, sliced
1 cup peas   1 cup black olives, sliced
1/2 red onion, sliced   1 cup Monterey Jack cheese cubes
6 hard-boiled eggs, cut into halves

Combine all ingredients in large salad bowl; toss lightly. Serve with olive oil dressing. Yield: 8 servings.

Approx Per Serving: Cal 160; Prot 10 g; Carbo 6 g; Fiber 3 g; T Fat 11 g; 61% Calories from Fat; Chol 173 mg; Sod 215 mg.

Mesclun Salad with Fresh Herbs

2 tablespoons lemon juice
1/4 cup extra-virgin olive oil
Salt and pepper to taste
4 to 5 cups mixed young salad greens
6 to 8 leaves each sorrel, basil and sage
12 to 15 long slender chive sprigs

Whisk lemon juice, oil, salt and pepper in salad bowl until creamy. Add salad greens, tossing to coat. Spoon onto individual salad plates. Tuck herb leaves into greens; top with crisscrossed chive sprigs. "Mesclun" is the French name for a salad of mixed young greens, such as arugula, red and green leaf lettuce or mache. Fresh herbs make this salad as good as any served in the south of France. Yield: 4 servings.

Approx Per Serving: Cal 134; Prot 1 g; Carbo 3 g; Fiber 1 g; T Fat 14 g; 88% Calories from Fat; Chol 0 mg; Sod 6 mg.

 A thyme-flavored vinaigrette dressing is lovely on assorted greens with artichoke hearts.

Salade Niçoise

4 pounds green beans, trimmed
10 ripe tomatoes, cut into eighths
5 heads romaine lettuce, torn
9 to 12 large new potatoes, cooked, cubed
12 hard-boiled eggs
6 pounds tuna, cooked
2 cups Niçoise olives
2 cups olive oil
1 cup vinegar
1 tablespoon Dijon mustard
Salt and pepper to taste

Blanch green beans for 3 to 5 minutes; drain and cool. Combine with tomatoes, lettuce, potatoes, eggs, tuna and olives in large serving bowl. Whisk oil, vinegar, mustard, salt and pepper in small bowl until creamy. Pour vinaigrette over salad, tossing to coat. Yield: 50 servings.

Approx Per Serving: Cal 220; Prot 16 g; Carbo 9 g; Fiber 2 g; T Fat 14 g; 55% Calories from Fat; Chol 73 mg; Sod 78 mg.

Mix 1 cup of fresh citrus peel with 1 cup of clover or orange blossom honey for a treat on waffles or French toast.

Orange and Fennel Salad

12 cups 1-inch romaine lettuce strips
4 navel oranges, peeled, thinly sliced
1 bulb fennel, thinly sliced
1/4 cup thinly sliced red onion
4 teaspoons fresh lemon juice
1/2 teaspoon salt
1/4 teaspoon freshly ground pepper
2 tablespoons extra-virgin olive oil

Combine lettuce, oranges, fennel and onion in salad bowl. Whisk lemon juice with salt and pepper in bowl. Add oil, whisking until creamy. Pour over salad, tossing to coat. May make salad ahead of time, adding dressing just before serving. Yield: 8 servings.

Approx Per Serving: Cal 78; Prot 2 g; Carbo 11 g; Fiber 3 g; T Fat 4 g; 39% Calories from Fat; Chol 0 mg; Sod 141 mg. Nutritional information does not include fennel.

Head lettuce should not be too hard or solid. A slight springiness indicates the presence of air pockets between the leaves, which means the lettuce is at the right stage of development. Store lettuce in a plastic bag with a dry paper towel. The lettuce will last much longer.

Honeyed Orange Salad

1/3 cup sugar
2 1/2 tablespoons lemon juice
2 1/2 tablespoons honey
2 tablespoons vinegar
1/2 teaspoon each dry mustard and paprika
1/8 teaspoon each salt and celery seed
1/2 cup oil
1 head Boston lettuce, torn
6 large oranges, peeled, sliced

Combine sugar, lemon juice, honey, vinegar, mustard, paprika, salt and celery seed in blender. Process until smooth, adding oil gradually. Chill, covered, until serving time. Arrange lettuce on salad plates; top with orange slices. Drizzle with dressing. Garnish with sliced kiwifruit. Yield: 6 servings.

Approx Per Serving: Cal 321; Prot 2 g; Carbo 41 g; Fiber 5 g; T Fat 19 g; 49% Calories from Fat; Chol 0 mg; Sod 47 mg.

 A handful of orange peels in a pot of boiling water fills your home with a wonderful citrus fragrance. Place old potpourri in water in an old teapot on stove or kerosene heater to freshen air.

Champagne Hearts of Palm

1/4 cup red raspberry vinegar
1 tablespoon prepared mustard
1/2 teaspoon salt
1/4 teaspoon pepper
1/2 cup peanut oil
1/4 cup Champagne or sparkling white wine
1 12-ounce can hearts of palm, drained,
cut into halves lengthwise
1 12-ounce can small black olives
1/2 cup chopped red onion
1 hard-boiled egg, sliced
2 teaspoons fresh dillweed

Whisk vinegar, mustard, salt and pepper in bowl. Add oil slowly, whisking constantly. Whisk in Champagne. Arrange hearts of palm, olives, onion and egg on salad plates. Drizzle with dressing; sprinkle with dillweed. Yield: 4 servings.

Approx Per Serving: Cal 445; Prot 4 g; Carbo 7 g; Fiber 4 g; T Fat 49 g; 91% Calories from Fat; Chol 53 mg; Sod 1407 mg.

When serving salads on a bed of lettuce, try a mix of different lettuces for interest.

English Pea Salad

1 cup sour cream
1 teaspoon seasoned salt
1/4 teaspoon lemon pepper
1/4 teaspoon garlic salt
1 20-ounce package frozen peas, thawed
1 6-ounce jar artichoke hearts, drained
4 ounces bacon, crisp-fried, crumbled
1 small white onion, chopped

Combine sour cream, seasoned salt, lemon pepper and garlic salt in bowl; mix well. Add peas, artichoke hearts, bacon and onion, tossing to coat. Chill, covered, overnight. Yield: 5 servings.

Approx Per Serving: Cal 246; Prot 10 g; Carbo 21 g; Fiber 6 g; T Fat 14 g; 50% Calories from Fat; Chol 26 mg; Sod 749 mg.

Make *Green Bean and Pea Salad* by mixing 1 can of French-style green beans, 1 can of tiny green peas, 4 chopped stalks of celery, 1 can of chopped pimento, 3/4 cup sugar, 1/2 cup vinegar and 1/4 cup oil. Marinate in refrigerator overnight.

Pear and Curly Endive Salad

1/4 cup sherry wine vinegar
4 teaspoons Dijon mustard   3/4 cup olive oil
1 teaspoon dried thyme, crumbled
Salt and freshly ground pepper to taste
1 head curly endive, torn
4 large ripe pears, cut into fourths

Combine vinegar and mustard in small bowl. Whisk in oil gradually. Stir in seasonings. Combine with endive and pears in large bowl, tossing to coat. Garnish with blueberries or raspberries. Yield: 6 servings.

Approx Per Serving: Cal 331; Prot 1 g; Carbo 22 g; Fiber 4 g; T Fat 28 g; 73% Calories from Fat; Chol 0 mg; Sod 96 mg.

New Potatoes in Vinaigrette

1/4 cup wine vinegar   Salt and pepper to taste
1/2 cup extra-virgin olive oil   1 clove of garlic, crushed
2 shallots, finely chopped   1 pound new red potatoes

Mix vinegar, salt and pepper in small bowl. Whisk in oil gradually. Stir in garlic and shallots. Boil potatoes until tender; do not overcook. Slice into halves or fourths. Pour vinaigrette over hot potatoes in large bowl, tossing gently. Chill, covered, overnight. Yield: 6 servings.

Approx Per Serving: Cal 262; Prot 2 g; Carbo 24 g; Fiber 2 g; T Fat 18 g; 60% Calories from Fat; Chol 0 mg; Sod 9 mg.

Merry Mermaid Salad

1/8 teaspoon Old Bay seasoning
2 tablespoons honey-Dijon ranch dressing
1/2 cup mayonnaise   1/4 cup sliced celery
2/3 cup cooked pasta
8 ounces cooked medium shrimp, peeled, split

Mix Old Bay seasoning, ranch dressing and mayonnaise in bowl. Stir in celery, pasta and shrimp. Chill overnight for best flavor. Use for stuffed tomatoes or on bed of lettuce garnished with cherry tomatoes and parsley sprigs. Yield: 3 servings.

Approx Per Serving: Cal 410; Prot 18 g; Carbo 9 g; Fiber 1 g; T Fat 34 g; 74% Calories from Fat; Chol 173 mg; Sod 430 mg.

Shrimp for the Gods

1 pound cooked shrimp   1 pound cottage cheese
1 cup sour cream   1/2 cup chutney
2 teaspoons (or more) curry powder
1/2 teaspoon garlic powder

Combine all ingredients in bowl; mix well. Chill until serving time. Serve on lettuce-lined plates; garnish with mandarin oranges and avocado slices. Yield: 6 servings.

Approx Per Serving: Cal 254; Prot 27 g; Carbo 8 g; Fiber <1 g; T Fat 12 g; 44% Calories from Fat; Chol 176 mg; Sod 611 mg.

Caraway Coleslaw

3/4 cup mayonnaise   1/2 cup sour cream
2 tablespoons cider vinegar   1 tablespoon brown sugar
2 teaspoons caraway seed   Salt and pepper to taste
4 cups shredded green cabbage
4 cups shredded red cabbage

Combine first 7 ingredients in small bowl; mix well. Combine green and red cabbage in 3-quart bowl. Add dressing, tossing to moisten. Chill for 6 hours or longer. Yield: 10 servings.

Approx Per Serving: Cal 161; Prot 1 g; Carbo 5 g; Fiber 1 g; T Fat 16 g; 84% Calories from Fat; Chol 15 mg; Sod 110 mg.

Celery-Walnut Slaw

4 cups thinly sliced celery
3 tablespoons chopped walnuts
1/2 cup shredded carrots   3 tablespoons raisins
2/3 cup plain yogurt   1 tablespoon vinegar
2 teaspoons salt   1/2 teaspoon white pepper

Combine celery, walnuts, carrots and raisins in large bowl. Mix yogurt, vinegar, salt and pepper in small bowl. Pour over celery mixture, tossing to coat. Chill before serving. Serve on lettuce-lined plates. Yield: 8 servings.

Approx Per Serving: Cal 54; Prot 2 g; Carbo 7 g; Fiber 2 g; T Fat 2 g; 38% Calories from Fat; Chol 2 mg; Sod 598 mg.

Avocado and Spinach Salad

1 cup oil   1/2 cup sugar   1/3 cup cider vinegar
1 tablespoon poppy seed   1 teaspoon salt
1 teaspoon dry mustard   1/4 teaspoon paprika
1 pound fresh spinach, torn   1 purple onion, sliced
1 ripe avocado, thinly sliced lengthwise
1 pint strawberries, hulled, sliced lengthwise

Whisk first 7 ingredients in small bowl until creamy. Arrange spinach, onion, avocado and strawberries on salad plates. Drizzle with dressing. Yield: 6 servings.

Approx Per Serving: Cal 492; Prot 4 g; Carbo 29 g; Fiber 8 g; T Fat 43 g; 75% Calories from Fat; Chol 0 mg; Sod 420 mg.

Super Spinach Salad

2 teaspoons grated onion   1 teaspoon salt
1/2 teaspoon pepper   2 teaspoons prepared mustard
2 tablespoons wine vinegar   1/2 cup oil
1/4 teaspoon lemon juice   1 pound fresh spinach, torn
Sections of 4 oranges and grapefruit

Mix first 5 ingredients in small bowl. Whisk in oil gradually until mixture is thickened. Add lemon juice. Arrange spinach on salad plates; top with orange and grapefruit sections. Drizzle with salad dressing. Yield: 8 servings.

Approx Per Serving: Cal 214; Prot 3 g; Carbo 22 g; Fiber 6 g; T Fat 14 g; 55% Calories from Fat; Chol 0 mg; Sod 328 mg.

Strawberry-Spinach Salad

1/4 cup sugar   Juice of 1 lemon
1 egg yolk, beaten   6 tablespoons oil
10 ounces fresh spinach, torn
1 pound fresh strawberries, hulled, sliced

Whisk sugar and lemon juice in small bowl until sugar is almost dissolved. Add egg yolk, whisking until sugar is completely dissolved. Add oil 1 tablespoon at a time, whisking after each addition until thickened. Place spinach in salad bowl; top with strawberries. Drizzle with dressing. Yield: 6 servings.

Approx Per Serving: Cal 198; Prot 2 g; Carbo 16 g; Fiber 4 g; T Fat 15 g; 65% Calories from Fat; Chol 36 mg; Sod 40 mg.

Sweet Potato Salad

3 pounds sweet potatoes, peeled, cubed
4 scallions, chopped
1/2 bunch parsley, coarsely chopped
1   2-inch piece of fresh ginger, grated
4 to 5 tablespoons olive oil   Juice of 1 lime

Cook sweet potatoes in boiling water until tender; drain and cool. Combine with remaining ingredients in large bowl, tossing to mix. Yield: 10 servings.

Approx Per Serving: Cal 208; Prot 2 g; Carbo 34 g; Fiber 5 g; T Fat 7 g; 31% Calories from Fat; Chol 0 mg; Sod 21 mg.

Salads

Warm Swordfish Salad

1 head radicchio
2 heads Bibb lettuce
4 slices French bread, toasted
1 clove of garlic
3 ounces prepared vinaigrette dressing
8 ounces swordfish, cut in julienne strips
1/4 cup each julienned carrot, celery and leek
2 tablespoons olive oil
Salt and pepper to taste
4 ounces unsweetened coconut milk
2 ounces bourbon

Remove outer leaves of radicchio, reserving inner leaves. Arrange on 1 side of salad plates. Remove outer leaves from Bibb lettuce, reserving inner leaves. Arrange on opposite side of salad plates. Rub toasted French bread with garlic clove; cut into small cubes. Place in center of salad plates. Slice reserved radicchio and Bibb lettuce leaves into julienne strips. Toss with vinaigrette dressing in bowl. Spoon over garlic croutons. Sauté swordfish, carrot, celery and leek in oil in skillet until fish flakes easily and vegetables are tender-crisp. Season with salt and pepper. Place equal portion of mixture on salad plates. Add coconut milk and bourbon to skillet. Cook until liquid is reduced by 3/4. Drizzle over salads. Yield: 4 servings.

Approx Per Serving: Cal 446; Prot 17 g; Carbo 24 g; Fiber 3 g;
T Fat 28 g; 60% Calories from Fat; Chol 23 mg; Sod 277 mg.

Tomato-Potato Caper

2 to 4 large lettuce leaves
1 medium potato, boiled, peeled, cubed
1 large tomato, chopped
2 scallions, chopped
1 tablespoon capers
1 teaspoon caper juice
1 tablespoon prepared mustard
2 tablespoons olive oil
Basil to taste
Salt and white pepper to taste

Line 2 salad plates with lettuce leaves. Combine potato, tomato, scallions and capers in medium bowl. Spoon equal portion onto salad plates. Whisk caper juice, mustard, oil, basil, salt and pepper in small bowl. Pour over salads. Yield: 2 servings.

Approx Per Serving: Cal 205; Prot 3 g; Carbo 18 g; Fiber 3 g;
T Fat 14 g; 60% Calories from Fat; Chol 0 mg; Sod 110 mg.
Nutritional information does not include capers and caper juice.

To speed the ripening of tomatoes, even green tomatoes, enclose them in a brown paper bag at room temperature.

Tomato and Mozzarella Salad

14 ounces mozzarella cheese, at room temperature
2   8-ounce tomatoes
1 large red onion, sliced
1/2 teaspoon each garlic powder and oregano
2 tablespoons minced fresh basil
Salt to taste
Freshly ground black pepper to taste
3 tablespoons extra-virgin olive oil

Slice mozzarella into six 1/2-inch rounds. Slice each tomato into three 1/2-inch thick rounds. Alternate overlapping slices of cheese, tomato and onion on large platter. Sprinkle with garlic powder, oregano, basil, salt and pepper. Drizzle with olive oil. Let stand for 30 minutes before serving. This blissfully simple summer appetizer takes on the colors of the Italian flag. It only takes minutes to put together and only uses a few ingredients that most have on hand. Yield: 4 servings.

Approx Per Serving: Cal 405; Prot 21 g; Carbo 10 g; Fiber 2 g; T Fat 31 g; 69% Calories from Fat; Chol 77 mg; Sod 380 mg.

Do not slice tomatoes directly into salads as their high water content will dilute the dressing, and the lettuce will wilt more quickly. Instead, serve separately or at the last minute arrange the tomatoes on the top of the salad.

Vegetable Aspic

2 envelopes unflavored gelatin
1   46-ounce can vegetable juice cocktail
1 bay leaf
1/4 cup fresh lemon juice
2 teaspoons grated onion
1/2 teaspoon Worcestershire sauce
1/2 cup mayonnaise
1 tablespoon raspberry vinegar

Soften gelatin in 1 cup vegetable juice cocktail. Heat remaining vegetable juice with bay leaf in saucepan until mixture begins to boil; remove bay leaf. Add gelatin mixture, stirring until dissolved. Stir in lemon juice, onion and Worcestershire sauce. Pour into 1-quart mold. Chill until firm. Unmold onto serving plate lined with salad greens. Serve with mixture of mayonnaise and raspberry vinegar. Garnish with avocado slices. Yield: 12 servings.

Approx Per Serving: Cal 92; Prot 2 g; Carbo 6 g; Fiber 1 g; T Fat 7 g; 69% Calories from Fat; Chol 5 mg; Sod 452 mg.

 The seeds of fresh papaya are edible. Use them as a garnish, in sauces or salad dressings.

Spring Violet Salad

8 cups mixed salad greens,
torn into bite-sized pieces
8 sprigs of fresh chervil, torn
8 lemon balm leaves, torn
10 violet leaves, torn
Chopped chives, bronze fennel and
watercress to taste
6 tablespoons olive oil
2 tablespoons rice wine vinegar
1 teaspoon honey
40 violet flowers

Toss salad greens, chervil, lemon balm, violet leaves and herbs in large salad bowl. Whisk oil, vinegar and honey in small bowl until creamy. Drizzle over salad. Top with violet flowers. Yield: 6 servings.

Approx Per Serving: Cal 137; Prot 1 g; Carbo 4 g; Fiber 1 g; T Fat 14 g; 86% Calories from Fat; Chol 0 mg; Sod 7 mg.

Lemon balm is easy to grow and adds a bright lemony-mint flavor to beverages, marinades, preserves, salads, lamb, and anything else that benefits from lemon and mint.

Watercress and Bacon Salad

3 bunches fresh watercress
2 eggs
1 teaspoon Dijon mustard
3 tablespoons lemon juice
2 tablespoons white vinegar
2 tablespoons sugar
Salt and lemon-pepper to taste
6 slices bacon, crisp-fried, crumbled

Trim and rinse watercress; drain in colander and chill. Whisk eggs, mustard, lemon juice, vinegar, sugar, salt and lemon-pepper in heavy enamel saucepan. Cook on high heat until thickened, stirring constantly. Place saucepan in cold water. Toss watercress and crumbled bacon in salad bowl. Pour warm dressing over salad and serve immediately. Yield: 6 servings.

Approx Per Serving: Cal 84; Prot 4 g; Carbo 6 g; Fiber <1 g; T Fat 5 g; 54% Calories from Fat; Chol 76 mg; Sod 150 mg.

Make *Crystallized Violets* by dipping the blossoms into a mixture of 1 egg white beaten with 1 tablespoon water. Sprinkle with sugar and dry for 12 hours. Store in airtight container.

Wild Rice-Smoked Turkey Salad

3¹/₂ cups cooked wild rice
1³/₄ pounds smoked turkey, cut into bite-sized pieces
2 avocados, cubed
1 tablespoon lemon juice
1 bunch cilantro leaves
³/₄ cup chopped red onion
¹/₄ cup red wine vinegar
¹/₂ cup olive oil
Salt and freshly ground pepper to taste

Combine rice and turkey in large bowl. Drizzle avocados with lemon juice. Add to rice mixture with cilantro, onion, vinegar, oil, salt and pepper; toss to mix. Serve at room temperature. This is a great summer lunch recipe. Yield: 10 servings.

Approx Per Serving: Cal 369; Prot 27 g; Carbo 19 g; Fiber 6 g; T Fat 21 g; 51% Calories from Fat; Chol 61 mg; Sod 67 mg.

Cantaloupe, papaya, or a large peach or nectarine makes a delicious bowl for chicken or seafood salad. Just cut a thin slice off its bottom to stabilize it.

Zucchini-Shrimp Vinaigrette

2 pounds small zucchini, cut into ¹/₄-inch diagonal slices
¹/₂ teaspoon dillseed
1 cup boiling water
1   7-ounce can small shrimp, drained
¹/₂ teaspoon salt
6 tablespoons oil
2 tablespoons wine vinegar
1 tablespoon each minced parsley, chives and dillweed
1 clove of garlic, crushed
Freshly ground pepper to taste

Cook zucchini with dillseed in boiling water for 5 minutes or until tender-crisp; drain. Combine with shrimp in large salad bowl. Mix salt, oil, vinegar, parsley, chives, dillweed, garlic and pepper in small bowl. Pour over zucchini mixture, tossing to coat. Chill overnight. Serve on lettuce-lined plates. This is a great use for all the zucchini from the garden. Yield: 8 servings.

Approx Per Serving: Cal 138; Prot 7 g; Carbo 4 g; Fiber 1 g; T Fat 11 g; 69% Calories from Fat; Chol 43 mg; Sod 178 mg.

Make your own flavored vinegars. Put fresh herbs in a bottle of vinegar; age for 3 weeks. Use for salads or cooking.

Vegetable Crunch Salad

2 cups broccoli flowerets
2 cups cauliflowerets
1 cup sliced celery
1 cup cherry tomato halves
1 cup sliced zucchini
1/4 cup sliced carrot
3/4 cup sliced green onions
1/2 cup sliced black olives
1 cup Italian salad dressing
3 ounces bacon, crisp-fried, crumbled

Combine broccoli, cauliflower, celery, tomatoes, zucchini, carrot, green onions and black olives in salad bowl. Add salad dressing; mix well. Marinate, covered, in refrigerator for 4 hours to overnight, stirring occasionally. Add bacon at serving time; toss gently. Garnish with additional cherry tomatoes. May add spinach if desired. Yield: 8 servings.

Approx Per Serving: Cal 199; Prot 3 g; Carbo 9 g; Fiber 3 g; T Fat 22 g; 81% Calories from Fat; Chol 3 mg; Sod 302 mg.

For a vinaigrette dressing with a smooth consistency, try whisking some heavy cream, about 1/3 the quantity of oil used, together with the seasonings before adding the vinegar and the remaining oil.

Hot Salad Dressing

1 1/2 tablespoons flour　2 tablespoons sugar
1/4 teaspoon salt　Pepper to taste
3/4 cup milk　1 egg, beaten
2 1/2 tablespoons vinegar
1/2 teaspoon prepared mustard

Mix flour, sugar, salt and pepper in saucepan. Add milk and egg gradually, mixing until smooth. Cook until thickened, stirring constantly. Stir in vinegar and mustard. Serve over salad of lettuce or dandelion greens; garnish salad with crisp-fried bacon. Yield: 6 servings.

Approx Per Serving: Cal 56; Prot 2 g; Carbo 8 g; Fiber <1 g; T Fat 2 g; 31% Calories from Fat; Chol 40 mg; Sod 119 mg.

Basil Salad Dressing

1/2 cup cider vinegar
2 medium cloves of garlic, crushed
1 cup extra-virgin olive oil
1 tablespoon chopped basil
2 tablespoons chopped parsley　2 tablespoons water
Salt to taste　1 teaspoon pepper

Mix all ingredients in jar with tight-fitting lid. Store in refrigerator for up to 1 week. Yield: 6 servings.

Approx Per Serving: Cal 323; Prot <1 g; Carbo 2 g; Fiber <1 g; T Fat 36 g; 98% Calories from Fat; Chol 0 mg; Sod 1 mg.

Depot Bleu Cheese Dressing

4 ounces bleu cheese, crumbled   1 quart mayonnaise
1/4 cup vinegar · 1/4 cup lemon juice
2 1/2 tablespoons sugar
2 tablespoons Worcestershire sauce   1 teaspoon MSG
1 teaspoon seasoned salt   1 teaspoon salt
1/2 teaspoon white pepper

Combine all ingredients in bowl; mix well. Store in refrigerator. Serve on salad of lettuce; garnish with crumbled crisp-fried bacon and garlic croutons. Yield: 24 servings.

Approx Per Serving: Cal 287; Prot 1 g; Carbo 3 g; Fiber <1 g;
T Fat 31 g; 94% Calories from Fat; Chol 25 mg; Sod 608 mg.

Ginger Dressing Benihana

3 1/2-inch pieces fresh gingerroot, chopped
1 small onion, chopped   1 1/2 cups soybean oil
1/2 cup vinegar   1/2 cup water   1/4 cup soy sauce
1 stalk celery, sliced   1 tablespoon tomato paste
Juice of 1 lemon   Salt to taste

Combine gingerroot, onion, oil, vinegar, water, soy sauce, celery, tomato paste, lemon juice and salt in blender container; process at medium speed for 2 minutes or until smooth. Yield: 16 servings.

Approx Per Serving: Cal 189; Prot <1 g; Carbo 2 g; Fiber <1 g;
T Fat 21 g; 95% Calories from Fat; Chol 0 mg; Sod 260 mg.

Mustard Vinaigrette

2 teaspoons chopped green onion
1 tablespoon (or more) Dijon mustard
2 tablespoons white wine vinegar
1 teaspoon (scant) salt   1/2 teaspoon ground pepper
1/2 cup olive oil   1/4 teaspoon lemon juice

Process first 5 ingredients in food processor until smooth. Let stand for several minutes to dissolve salt. Add oil gradually, processing until smooth. Add lemon juice. Store in refrigerator; dressing will thicken. Serve on salad Niçoise, spinach salad or fruit salad. Yield: 8 servings.

Approx Per Serving: Cal 123; Prot <1 g; Carbo <1 g; Fiber < g;
T Fat 14 g; 98% Calories from Fat; Chol 0 mg; Sod 317 mg.

Dressing for Spinach Salad

1/3 cup chopped scallions   1/4 cup chopped parsley
2 cups mayonnaise   1 cup sour cream
1/4 cup tarragon vinegar   2 tablespoons lemon juice
4 ounces bleu cheese, crumbled   Salt and pepper to taste

Combine scallions, parsley, mayonnaise and sour cream in blender container; process until smooth. Combine with remaining ingredients in refrigerator container; mix well. Store in refrigerator for up to 2 weeks. Yield: 24 servings.

Approx Per Serving: Cal 170; Prot 2 g; Carbo 1 g; Fiber <1 g;
T Fat 18 g; 93% Calories from Fat; Chol 19 mg; Sod 176 mg.

Philadelphia Green

The Pennsylvania Horticultural Society's Philadelphia Green is the nation's largest and most comprehensive greening program. Working with the Society's staff, citizens turn trash-strewn vacant lots into community gardens and transform ugly urban roadways into blooming vistas.

The Society's partnerships with neighborhood leaders and business groups ensure that the greening process, once started, will continue. The formerly deteriorated Azalea Garden near the Philadelphia Museum of Art is now a showpiece of beauty and a hub of activity. Millions of black-eyed susans carry a 'Ribbon of Gold' throughout the city, along major thoroughfares and atop the raised terrace walls of the historically certified Eastern State Penitentiary.

Against all odds, skeptics watched the Pennsylvania Horticultural Society's 26th Street Gateway Project transform a major city and highway intersection (highlighted by billboards and massive oil storage tanks) into a tree-lined boulevard with low maintenance wildflowers and native grasses.

Funding for Philadelphia Green's successful projects come from combined revenues from the Philadelphia Flower Show, generous foundation and corporate contributions, and from caring individuals.

Like all activities of the Pennsylvania Horticultural Society, Philadelphia Green accomplishes so much by combining the efforts of staff members with those of volunteers. Whether they are distributing seeds to community gardens or pruning newly planted street trees, the staff, the volunteers and the gardening public develop mutual respect that keeps the system running smoothly.

Thanks to hundreds of hours of volunteer cleanup and planting, the Azalea Garden in Fairmount Park is now a favorite place for recreation and relaxation. – Photography by Ira Beckoff

A Garden Party Dinner

Flower-Glazed Cheeses *(page 13)*   Rosemary Pizza *(page 24)*
Marinated Brussels Sprouts *(page 29)*

Cranberry Chicken *(page 102)*   Never-Fail Wild Rice *(page 151)*

Minted Peas in Cream *(page 138)*

Garden Lettuces and Spiced Peaches
(topped with equal amounts of orange marmalade and mayonnaise)

Almond-Apple Cheesecake *(page 209)*   or   Lemon Snow *(page 213)*   or
Amber Pudding *(page 214)*

Cover a flowerpot with sheet moss tied with green thread or thin green wire. Place dry floral foam in the pot. Fill with bunches of rye or wheat tied with raffia. Add moss to the rim of the pot.

Beef Brisket

3 pounds beef brisket, trimmed
1/4 cup catsup
2 tablespoons brown sugar
2 tablespoons vinegar
5 sprigs of fresh parsley
1 large Bermuda or Spanish onion, sliced into rings
2 cups hot water
6 potatoes, peeled

Sear brisket in roasting pan in 400-degree oven for 5 minutes on each side; reduce oven temperature to 300 degrees. Combine catsup, brown sugar and vinegar in bowl; brush over lean side of meat. Top with parsley and onion rings. Pour water around brisket. Roast, covered, for 2 hours or until tender. Place potatoes around brisket. Roast for 1 hour longer. Yield: 6 servings.

Approx Per Serving: Cal 481; Prot 46 g; Carbo 43 g; Fiber 3 g; T Fat 13 g; 25% Calories from Fat; Chol 128 mg; Sod 198 mg.

For roasting a *Perfect Filet Mignon*, preheat oven to 500 degrees and roast for 10 minutes. Reduce oven temperature to 325 degrees and roast for 45 to 50 minutes for medium-rare and 55 to 60 minutes for medium. Let stand for 5 to 10 minutes and season with garlic powder, salt and pepper.

Beef Burgundy

6 slices bacon, cut into 1-inch pieces
3 pounds beef chuck, cubed
1 large carrot, sliced
2 cloves of garlic, mashed
1 14-ounce can beef broth
1/4 cup flour
1 teaspoon salt
Pepper to taste
1/2 teaspoon thyme
1 bay leaf
2 cups Burgundy
1 6-ounce can tomato paste
8 ounces mushrooms
1 medium onion, sliced

Brown bacon in large saucepan until crisp; drain, reserving pan drippings. Brown beef cubes in reserved pan drippings. Add carrot and garlic. Sauté until lightly browned. Add broth. Mix flour, salt, pepper, thyme and bay leaf with wine in small bowl. Stir wine mixture and tomato paste into saucepan. Simmer, covered, for 1 1/2 hours, stirring frequently. Add mushrooms and onion. Cook for 30 minutes longer. Discard bay leaf before serving. Garnish with bacon. Yield: 6 servings.

Approx Per Serving: Cal 463; Prot 48 g; Carbo 16 g; Fiber 3 g; T Fat 17 g; 33% Calories from Fat; Chol 133 mg; Sod 770 mg.

Grilled Marinated Flank Steak

1 cup tomato juice
1/4 cup minced onion
1/4 cup minced green bell pepper
1/2 cup minced celery
1/4 cup olive oil
1 tablespoon vinegar
1/4 teaspoon salt
1 tablespoon chili powder
1 to 2 cloves of garlic, minced
1   2-pound flank steak, tenderized

Combine tomato juice, onion, green pepper, celery, oil, vinegar, salt, chili powder and garlic in saucepan. Bring to a boil; reduce heat. Simmer, covered, for 15 minutes; cool. Place flank steak in shallow glass dish. Pour cooled marinade over steak. Marinate in refrigerator for 1 hour, turning occasionally. Drain, reserving marinade. Grill 4 inches from hot coals for 3 to 4 minutes on each side, basting with reserved marinade. Yield: 4 servings.

Approx Per Serving: Cal 442; Prot 43 g; Carbo 6 g; Fiber 2 g; T Fat 27 g; 55% Calories from Fat; Chol 128 mg; Sod 449 mg.

Make a good *Flank Steak Marinade* from 1/2 cup corn oil, 1/2 cup wine vinegar, 2 crushed cloves of garlic, 2 teaspoons Worcestershire sauce, 2 teaspoons dry mustard, 1 teaspoon salt and 1/4 teaspoon pepper.

Filet Mignon in Cognac Cream

1/4 cup olive oil
4   2-inch thick filet mignon
3 bay leaves
3 tablespoons Cognac
1/4 cup butter
1/2 teaspoon paprika
1/2 cup chopped onion
1/4 cup dark beer
1 teaspoon Worcestershire sauce
1/4 cup snipped fresh parsley
1/4 cup heavy cream

Heat oil in large skillet over high heat. Sauté steaks with bay leaves until steaks are done to taste. Remove steaks to warmed platter; discard bay leaves. Drain oil from skillet. Pour in Cognac. Cook over medium heat, stirring to deglaze skillet. Add butter and paprika, stirring until butter is melted. Add onion; cook until tender. Add beer, Worcestershire sauce, parsley and juice from steaks on platter. Bring to a boil, stirring constantly; remove from heat. Stir in cream. Pour over steaks. Serve over rice. Yield: 4 servings.

Approx Per Serving: Cal 776; Prot 65 g; Carbo 7 g; Fiber 1 g; T Fat 52 g; 62% Calories from Fat; Chol 242 mg; Sod 261 mg.

Flemish Beef

2 pounds onions, sliced
2 tablespoons butter
4 pounds beef, cubed
2 tablespoons flour
1 tablespoon sugar
1 teaspoon thyme
2 teaspoons salt
2 tablespoons vinegar
2 cups beer
2 bay leaves
10 carrots, cut into 1¹/₂-inch pieces
8 potatoes, cubed

Sauté onions in butter in large skillet until tender; remove and set aside. Add beef cubes to skillet. Cook for 1 to 2 minutes or until brown; remove and set aside. Add flour, sugar, thyme, salt and vinegar to pan drippings. Simmer until thickened. Stir in onions, beef cubes, beer and bay leaves. Spoon into 4-quart casserole. Bake, covered, at 350 degrees for 1¹/₂ hours. Add carrots and potatoes; discard bay leaves. Bake for 30 to 35 minutes longer or until vegetables are tender. Yield: 8 servings.

Approx Per Serving: Cal 583; Prot 48 g; Carbo 57 g; Fiber 7 g; T Fat 16 g; 26% Calories from Fat; Chol 135 mg; Sod 671 mg.

Busy-Day Stew

2 pounds lean beef cubes
1   10-ounce can cream of mushroom soup
¹/₂ soup can Burgundy
1 clove of garlic, crushed
2 cups sliced onions
³/₄ cup chopped green or red bell pepper
2 tablespoons prepared horseradish
Chopped parsley to taste

Combine beef, soup, wine, garlic, onions and bell pepper in Dutch oven. Bake, covered, at 300 degrees for 3 hours. Stir in horseradish and parsley. May add flour or cornstarch to thicken sauce. Yield: 4 servings.

Approx Per Serving: Cal 424; Prot 45 g; Carbo 12 g; Fiber 1 g; T Fat 19 g; 39% Calories from Fat; Chol 128 mg; Sod 654 mg.

 Never cook stews at a boil. The ingredients may toughen if cooked at a boil.

Beef Stew in-a-Pumpkin

2 pounds beef cubes   2 tablespoons butter
1 clove of garlic, chopped
2 medium onions, chopped
2 large tomatoes, chopped
2 large green bell peppers, chopped
1¹/₂ teaspoons salt   ¹/₂ teaspoon pepper
¹/₄ teaspoon garlic powder
1 teaspoon sugar
8 dried peach halves   6 small whole potatoes
3 small sweet potatoes, cubed
2 cups beef broth
2   10-ounce packages frozen corn
¹/₂ cup Madeira   1 medium pumpkin
1 tablespoon melted butter
Salt to taste

Brown beef cubes in butter in 5-quart saucepan. Add garlic, onions, tomatoes, green peppers, salt, pepper, garlic powder and sugar. Simmer for 30 minutes, stirring occasionally. Add peaches, potatoes, sweet potatoes and beef broth. Simmer, covered, for 30 minutes longer. Stir in corn and wine; remove from heat. Slice top from pumpkin and set aside; scoop out seeds and center of pumpkin. Brush inside with melted butter; sprinkle with salt. Place on baking sheet. Pour stew mixture inside pumpkin; replace top. Bake at 325 degrees for 1 hour or until pumpkin is tender. Yield: 8 servings.

Approx Per Serving: Cal 474; Prot 29 g; Carbo 64 g; Fiber 11 g;
  T Fat 12 g; 22% Calories from Fat; Chol 76 mg; Sod 688 mg.

Oven-Baked Short Ribs

6 pounds meaty short ribs
1 lemon, sliced
3 medium onions, thickly sliced
1 cup vinegar
¹/₂ cup tomato juice
1 cup catsup
1 cup tomato sauce
¹/₂ cup melted margarine
1 cup packed brown sugar
2 tablespoons prepared horseradish
1 teaspoon pepper
2 cloves of garlic, crushed
1 tablespoon lemon juice

Place ribs in 4-quart baking dish. Arrange lemon slices and onions over ribs. Bake, covered, at 350 degrees for 1¹/₂ hours. Combine vinegar, tomato juice, catsup, tomato sauce, margarine, brown sugar, horseradish, pepper, garlic and lemon juice in bowl; mix well. Remove ribs from oven; drain. Pour sauce over ribs. Bake, covered, for 45 to 60 minutes longer or until tender. Yield: 8 servings.

Approx Per Serving: Cal 821; Prot 40 g; Carbo 52 g; Fiber 2 g;
  T Fat 51 g; 55% Calories from Fat; Chol 156 mg; Sod 870 mg.

If you want to save seeds from year to year, keep them in a tightly sealed plastic bag in the refrigerator.

Bobotie

1½ cups coarsely chopped onions
1 tablespoon olive oil
2 tablespoons curry powder
1 cup bread crumbs
½ cup raisins
½ cup roasted unsalted peanuts
⅓ cup mango chutney
3 tablespoons lemon juice
1 teaspoon salt
¼ teaspoon pepper
2 pounds ground round
4 eggs   2 bay leaves
2 cups milk
½ teaspoon salt
¼ teaspoon pepper

Sauté onions in oil in large skillet until golden brown. Add curry powder. Cook for 1 minute. Combine with bread crumbs, raisins, peanuts, chutney, lemon juice, 1 teaspoon salt and ¼ teaspoon pepper in large bowl. Add ground beef and 2 beaten eggs. Spoon into greased 2½-quart baking dish. Top with bay leaves. Bake at 350 degrees for 25 minutes. Remove from oven; discard bay leaves. Beat milk, ½ teaspoon salt, ¼ teaspoon pepper and remaining 2 eggs in bowl. Pour over beef mixture. Bake for 25 to 30 minutes longer or until golden brown. Yield: 8 servings.

Approx Per Serving: Cal 480; Prot 31 g; Carbo 28 g; Fiber 3 g; T Fat 28 g; 52% Calories from Fat; Chol 189 mg; Sod 678 mg.

Apple Meat Loaf

1 large onion, chopped
2 cups chopped apples
2 tablespoons butter, softened
2½ pounds ground beef
1½ cups herb-seasoned stuffing mix
3 eggs, beaten
1 tablespoon mustard
¼ cup catsup
½ cup red wine or sherry

Combine onion, apples, butter, ground beef, stuffing mix, eggs, mustard and catsup in bowl; mix well. Shape into loaf. Place in greased loaf pan. Bake at 350 degrees for 45 minutes. Pour wine over loaf. Bake for 15 minutes longer. Let stand at room temperature for 15 minutes before slicing. Yield: 8 servings.

Approx Per Serving: Cal 437; Prot 31 g; Carbo 19 g; Fiber 1 g; T Fat 26 g; 54% Calories from Fat; Chol 180 mg; Sod 421 mg.

For meat loaf in a hurry, shape it into miniature individual loaves or bake it in a ring mold and fill the center with a hot vegetable or cold salad.

Swedish Meatballs

2 cups cubed white bread, crusts trimmed
6 tablespoons heavy cream
1 medium onion, finely chopped
1 teaspoon butter
2 pounds ground beef
1 pound ground veal
2 teaspoons salt
1/2 teaspoon pepper
1/4 teaspoon each allspice and nutmeg
2 eggs, beaten
2   10-ounce jars lingonberries
1 cup beef broth
2 teaspoons dry mustard

Soak bread cubes in cream in bowl until cream is absorbed. Sauté onion in butter in skillet until tender. Combine with ground beef, ground veal, salt, pepper, allspice, nutmeg, eggs and bread cubes in large bowl; mix well. Shape into 1-inch balls. Place on baking sheet. Bake at 350 degrees for 20 minutes or until done to taste. Combine lingonberries, beef broth and mustard in large saucepan; mix well. Add meatballs. Simmer until warmed through. May substitute one 16-ounce can whole berry cranberry sauce for lingonberries. Yield: 10 servings.

Approx Per Serving: Cal 363; Prot 31 g; Carbo 15 g; Fiber 2 g; T Fat 20 g; 49% Calories from Fat; Chol 162 mg; Sod 638 mg.

Creole Hamburger Pie

1 pound ground beef
1/4 cup olive oil
1/4 cup chopped green bell pepper
1 clove of garlic, minced
1 medium onion, chopped
1 cup chopped celery
1   16-ounce can whole tomatoes
1 1/2 teaspoons salt
1/4 teaspoon pepper
1/2 teaspoon each basil and chili powder
1 1/4 cups flour
1   8-ounce can tomato sauce
1/3 cup shortening
2 tablespoons cold water

Brown ground beef in olive oil in skillet, stirring until crumbly. Add green pepper, garlic, onion and celery. Cook until tender. Add tomatoes, 1 teaspoon salt, pepper, basil and chili powder; mix well. Stir in 1/4 cup flour and tomato sauce. Simmer for several minutes, stirring occasionally. Combine remaining 1 cup flour and remaining 1/2 teaspoon salt in bowl for crust; cut in shortening until crumbly. Add water, stirring until dough forms a ball. Roll on floured surface; fit into 2-quart casserole. Spoon ground beef mixture into pastry-lined casserole. Bake at 425 degrees for 30 to 35 minutes. Yield: 6 servings.

Approx Per Serving: Cal 468; Prot 19 g; Carbo 29 g; Fiber 3 g; T Fat 32 g; 60% Calories from Fat; Chol 49 mg; Sod 947 mg.

Ham Loaf Supreme

1 pound ground smoked ham
2 pounds ground pork shoulder
1 green bell pepper, finely chopped
2 eggs, beaten
1 cup fine bread crumbs
1 cup milk
1 tablespoon Worcestershire sauce
1/2 cup heavy cream
3 tablespoons horseradish
2 to 4 tablespoons sugar
1/2 teaspoon salt
1/2 teaspoon dry mustard

Combine ground ham, ground pork, green pepper, eggs, bread crumbs, milk and Worcestershire sauce in bowl; mix well. Shape into loaf. Place in 9x13-inch baking dish sprayed with nonstick cooking spray. Bake at 350 degrees for 45 to 60 minutes. Beat heavy cream in mixer bowl until stiff peaks form. Fold in horseradish, sugar, salt and mustard. Serve with ham loaf. Yield: 6 servings.

Approx Per Serving: Cal 576; Prot 57 g; Carbo 25 g; Fiber 1 g; T Fat 27 g; 42% Calories from Fat; Chol 248 mg; Sod 1220 mg.

Wah-Tu-Do Lamb Chops

4 medium lamb chops
Meat tenderizer, as needed
2 tablespoons soy sauce
2 tablespoons Chinese duck sauce
2 tablespoons Chinese mustard

Pound lamb chops with meat tenderizer. Combine soy sauce, duck sauce and mustard in plastic bag. Add lamb chops. Marinate in refrigerator for 1 hour to overnight; drain. Grill over hot coals or broil for 4 minutes on each side. Yield: 2 servings.

Approx Per Serving: Cal 349; Prot 44 g; Carbo 7 g; Fiber <1 g; T Fat 14 g; 38% Calories from Fat; Chol 133 mg; Sod 1393 mg.

Make a delicious *Lamb Sauce* by heating 1/2 cup chili sauce, 1/2 cup mint sauce and 1/2 cup red currant jelly.

Grilled Shish Kabob

½ cup olive oil
½ cup red wine
1 teaspoon salt
½ teaspoon coarse pepper
1 medium onion, thinly sliced
1 4-pound leg of lamb, boned, cubed
2 to 3 green bell peppers, cut into 1-inch squares
6 cherry tomatoes

Combine olive oil, wine, salt, pepper and onion in shallow bowl; mix well. Add cubed lamb, tossing to coat. Marinate in refrigerator for 24 hours, stirring occasionally; drain. Place lamb cubes on skewers alternately with green pepper and tomatoes. Grill 3 to 4 inches from medium-hot coals for 5 to 6 minutes. Yield: 5 servings.

Approx Per Serving: Cal 652; Prot 61 g; Carbo 6 g; Fiber 2 g; T Fat 40 g; 57% Calories from Fat; Chol 195 mg; Sod 580 mg.

Make a *Marinade for Shish Kabob* by mixing ¼ cup oil, 5 ounces soy sauce, 1 minced clove of garlic, 1 tablespoon sugar and 1 teaspoon each ginger and dry mustard. Mix ingredients 24 hours in advance and marinate meat for 2 hours or longer.

Marinated Broiled Lamb

1 medium onion, sliced
½ cup soy sauce
½ cup oil
Juice of 1 lemon
1 4-pound leg of lamb, boned, cubed
1 green bell pepper, cut into 1-inch pieces
1 red bell pepper, cut into 1-inch pieces
1 to 2 onions, cut into 1-inch pieces
4 ounces fresh whole mushrooms

Make marinade by processing sliced onion, soy sauce, oil and lemon juice in blender until puréed. Place lamb, bell peppers, onion pieces and mushrooms in shallow pan. Pour marinade over all, stirring to coat. Marinate for 1 hour; drain. Place on skewers or on baking sheet. Broil for 5 minutes on each side. Yield: 4 servings.

Approx Per Serving: Cal 840; Prot 79 g; Carbo 16 g; Fiber 3 g; T Fat 50 g; 54% Calories from Fat; Chol 243 mg; Sod 2248 mg.

A good *Basting Sauce for Lamb* can be made from equal parts of orange juice and apple cider. The gravy will be delicious.

Roast Leg of Lamb

1/2 teaspoon ground thyme
1 clove of garlic, crushed
1 tablespoon soy sauce
1/2 cup Dijon mustard
1/4 cup olive oil
1 4-pound leg of lamb, trimmed, boned
Garlic salt to taste
1/2 cup sliced carrots
1/2 cup sliced onion
2 tablespoons cornstarch
2 cups beef broth

Combine thyme, garlic, soy sauce and mustard in small bowl. Whisk in oil gradually until mixture thickens; reserve 3 tablespoons. Sprinkle lamb with garlic salt. Spread mustard mixture over bottom of lamb. Place on rack in roasting pan; arrange carrots and onion around lamb. Brush top of lamb with mustard mixture. Bake at 350 degrees for 1 to 1½ hours or until done to taste; do not overcook. Remove to warm serving platter; let stand for 20 minutes. Blend cornstarch with small amount of beef broth in saucepan. Add remaining broth and reserved mustard mixture. Simmer until thickened, stirring frequently. Serve with lamb. Yield: 4 servings.

Approx Per Serving: Cal 726; Prot 79 g; Carbo 8 g; Fiber 1 g;
T Fat 40 g; 51% Calories from Fat; Chol 244 mg; Sod 1637 mg.

Pine Nut-Parmesan Lamb Roast

1/2 cup pine nuts
2 ounces Parmesan cheese, cubed
1 slice whole wheat bread, torn into small pieces
2 teaspoons Dijon mustard
1 large clove of garlic, sliced
1/2 teaspoon crumbled dried rosemary
1/4 teaspoon salt
Freshly ground pepper to taste
1 egg white
1 3½-pound leg of lamb, trimmed, boned
Salt to taste

Process pine nuts, cheese, bread, mustard, garlic, rosemary, salt and pepper in food processor until puréed. Add egg white. Pulse for 4 seconds. Season lamb with salt and pepper. Place in roasting pan. Spread pine nut mixture over lamb, pressing gently. Roast at 450 degrees for 15 minutes; reduce oven temperature to 375 degrees. Roast until done to taste; do not overcook. Let stand at room temperature for 10 to 15 minutes before slicing. Yield: 6 servings.

Approx Per Serving: Cal 424; Prot 49 g; Carbo 5 g; Fiber 1 g;
T Fat 23 g; 49% Calories from Fat; Chol 148 mg; Sod 439 mg.

Roast lamb for 30 minutes per pound or to 175 to 180 degrees on meat thermometer for well done. Roast to 160 to 165 degrees for rarer lamb.

Sarma

2 pounds ground lamb
3/4 cup uncooked rice
1/2 bunch Italian parsley, chopped
3 tablespoons onion powder
1 teaspoon allspice
1 teaspoon dillweed
3/4 teaspoon celery salt
1   8-ounce can tomato sauce
1   8-ounce jar grape leaves
1   10-ounce can beef broth

Combine ground lamb, rice, parsley, onion powder, allspice, dillweed, celery salt and tomato sauce in bowl; mix well. Place 1 heaping teaspoon of lamb mixture on stem end of each grape leaf, shiny side down. Fold up sides to enclose filling. Layer filled grape leaves in large deep saucepan lined with additional grape leaves. Pour beef broth over all. Bring to a boil; reduce heat. Simmer, covered, for 45 minutes. May cook in pressure cooker for 12 minutes. Serve hot. Yield: 8 servings.

Approx Per Serving: Cal 268; Prot 28 g; Carbo 19 g; Fiber 1 g; T Fat 8 g; 29% Calories from Fat; Chol 80 mg; Sod 504 mg. Nutritional information does not include grape leaves.

Bourbon Pork Chops

8   1-inch thick pork chops
2 teaspoons oil
1 small clove of garlic, crushed
2 ounces bourbon
1 ounce soy sauce

Brown pork chops in hot oil in large skillet. Add mixture of garlic, bourbon and soy sauce. Simmer, covered, for 15 to 20 minutes. Drain, reserving pan drippings to serve over chops. Yield: 8 servings.

Approx Per Serving: Cal 257; Prot 32 g; Carbo <1 g; Fiber <1 g; T Fat 12 g; 40% Calories from Fat; Chol 98 mg; Sod 280 mg.

Make a delicious *Soy Sauce Marinade* for pork from 1 cup soy sauce, 1/2 cup white wine, 2 teaspoons brown sugar, 1/2 teaspoon ground ginger and 1/4 teaspoon garlic powder. Marinate for 24 hours.

Pork Roast with Fennel

6 cloves of garlic, minced
2 tablespoons fennel seed
2 teaspoons coarse salt
Ground pepper to taste
1 4-pound boneless pork roast, tied
1 to 2 teaspoons fruity olive oil

Mash garlic, fennel seed, salt and pepper in small bowl until paste forms. Untie roast and spread open. Spread half the garlic paste on inside of roast; roll up and secure with string. Spread remaining paste on outside of roast; sprinkle with half the olive oil. Place on rack in roasting pan; insert meat thermometer. Roast at 350 degrees for 2 hours or until meat thermometer registers 170 degrees. Let stand to cool. Slice into 1/4-inch slices; drizzle with remaining olive oil. Yield: 6 servings.

Approx Per Serving: Cal 450; Prot 60 g; Carbo 1 g; Fiber <1 g; T Fat 21 g; 44% Calories from Fat; Chol 185 mg; Sod 857 mg.

The leaves and seed of fennel are especially good with fattier meats; they impart a slightly vigorous flavor to the meat.

Pork Tenderloin Supreme

2 pounds pork tenderloin, cut into 1-inch cubes
2 tablespoons butter
1 10-ounce can cream of asparagus soup
1/2 cup milk
1/2 teaspoon salt
1/4 teaspoon pepper
1/4 teaspoon curry powder
1 4-ounce can sliced mushrooms, drained
1 small onion, thinly sliced

Brown pork in butter in heavy skillet. Combine soup, milk, salt, pepper, curry, mushrooms and onion in small bowl; mix well. Pour over pork. Simmer, covered, for 45 minutes or until tender. Serve over rice. Yield: 4 servings.

Approx Per Serving: Cal 460; Prot 48 g; Carbo 11 g; Fiber 2 g; T Fat 24 g; 48% Calories from Fat; Chol 161 mg; Sod 559 mg.

Curry powder is a mixture of herbs and spices. Commercial curry powder usually contains coriander, turmeric, cumin, fenugreek, ginger, salt, pepper, cloves, celery seed, allspice, cayenne pepper, caraway seed, mace and garlic powder.

Viennese Roast Pork

1   3-pound boned pork roast
2 cloves of garlic
2 teaspoons salt
2 tablespoons Hungarian sweet paprika
2 tablespoons caraway seed
1   14-ounce can beef broth
2 to 3 tablespoons flour

Rub roast with garlic cloves. Slice garlic; place in slits cut in roast. Place roast in roasting pan. Sprinkle with salt, paprika and caraway seed. Pour half the broth in pan. Roast at 350 degrees for 2½ to 3 hours, basting with remaining beef broth occasionally. Let stand for several minutes before slicing. Drain pan drippings into saucepan. Stir in flour. Cook over medium heat until thickened, stirring constantly. Boil for 1 minute, adding water if needed for desired consistency. Serve with roast. Yield: 6 servings.

Approx Per Serving: Cal 358; Prot 47 g; Carbo 6 g; Fiber 1 g; T Fat 16 g; 40% Calories from Fat; Chol 139 mg; Sod 1037 mg.

Hungarian paprika is made from mild tetragonna peppers which have been seeded before grinding. Buy paprika in small quantities because it loses flavor on the shelf.

Sausage and Sauerkraut

1   2x2-inch cube salt pork   2 tablespoons margarine
2 carrots, chopped   2 stalks celery and leaves, chopped
1 onion, chopped   1 clove of garlic, minced
2   16-ounce packages sauerkraut, rinsed, well drained
¾ cup low-salt chicken broth
¾ cup dry white wine   Half of 1 bay leaf
1 cinnamon stick   5 whole cloves   ½ teaspoon thyme
3 to 4 juniper berries or 2 tablespoons
Freshly ground pepper to taste
8 ounces each ham, fresh pork, bockwurst, knockwurst,
bratwurst and ham hock, cut into bite-sized pieces

Cook salt pork in margarine in stainless steel kettle over low heat for 5 minutes. Add carrots, celery, onion and garlic. Cook for 5 to 6 minutes or until vegetables are tender. Add sauerkraut. Cook for 5 to 6 minutes longer. Add broth, wine, bay leaf half, cinnamon stick, cloves, thyme, juniper berries and pepper. Simmer, covered, for 45 minutes, stirring occasionally. Bring water to a boil in large saucepan. Add ham, pork and sausages. Poach for 3 to 12 minutes or just until tender. Remove meats with slotted spoon; reserve liquid. Add meats to sauerkraut mixture. Chill sauerkraut mixture and reserved liquid overnight. Skim fat from liquid. Add small amount of liquid to sauerkraut mixture. Simmer for 20 to 30 minutes, stirring occasionally. May substitute 2 ounces gin for juniper berries and may use any variety of sausages. Yield: 8 servings.

Approx Per Serving: Cal 362; Prot 24 g; Carbo 10 g; Fiber 3 g; T Fat 24 g; 62% Calories from Fat; Chol 54 mg; Sod 1507 mg.

Hot Antipasto

1½ pounds Italian sausage
1   12-ounce jar red bell peppers
2 zucchini, sliced
8 ounces fresh mushrooms, sliced
2   14-ounce cans artichoke hearts, drained,
cut into fourths
1   8-ounce can black olives, cut into halves
Salt and pepper to taste
2 tablespoons olive oil
1 cup Italian-seasoned bread crumbs
½ cup melted margarine

Brown sausage in skillet, stirring until crumbly; drain and set aside. Sprinkle all vegetables with salt, pepper and olive oil. Layer red peppers, zucchini, mushrooms, artichoke hearts, olives and sausage in 2-quart baking dish. Top with mixture of bread crumbs and margarine. Bake at 350 degrees for 45 minutes. Yield: 8 servings.

Approx Per Serving: Cal 416; Prot 14 g; Carbo 21 g; Fiber 3 g; T Fat 33 g; 68% Calories from Fat; Chol 32 mg; Sod 1641 mg.

Antipasto, in Italian, refers to the course that comes after the pasta course in a meal. It is a good way to use garden vegetables in season.

Sausage and Potato Stew

1 slice bacon, chopped
1 carrot, finely chopped
1 stalk celery, finely chopped
1 onion, finely chopped
1 clove of garlic, minced
6 to 8 fresh basil leaves
1   28-ounce can plum tomatoes
6 potatoes, cubed
1 pound Italian sausage, cut into 2-inch pieces
Salt and pepper to taste

Fry bacon in large saucepan until crisp. Add carrot, celery, onion, garlic and basil. Sauté in pan drippings until onion is lightly browned. Add tomatoes, potatoes and sausage. Bring to a boil; reduce heat to low. Simmer for 1 hour, stirring occasionally, adding water for desired consistency. Season with salt and pepper. May also add cubed zucchini, squash or more potatoes. Yield: 6 servings.

Approx Per Serving: Cal 278; Prot 12 g; Carbo 37 g; Fiber 4 g; T Fat 10 g; 32% Calories from Fat; Chol 29 mg; Sod 577 mg.

Serve additional basil with Italian recipes in a bouquet of sprigs in a small vase of water, as they do in Italy.

Blackened Veal with Salmon

1   4-pound veal ribeye roast
16 ounces salmon filets, split lengthwise
12 ounces fresh spinach, blanched
6 ounces sole filets
3 ounces scallops
4 ounces heavy cream
Salt and black pepper to taste
Cognac to taste
Paprika, cayenne pepper, thyme
and garlic salt to taste

Butterfly veal; pound to 1½-inch thickness. Turn inside out. Place salmon filets over veal. Process spinach, sole, scallops, cream, salt, pepper and Cognac in food processor until puréed. Spread over salmon. Roll up veal, securing with string. Combine equal amounts of paprika, cayenne pepper, black pepper, thyme and garlic salt in small bowl. Place in hot skillet. Add veal, turning to coat. Sear until blackened. Place on rack in roasting pan. Roast at 350 degrees for 20 minutes. Let stand at room temperature for 10 minutes before slicing. Yield: 6 servings.

Approx Per Serving: Cal 570; Prot 85 g; Carbo 3 g; Fiber 2 g;
T Fat 22 g; 36% Calories from Fat; Chol 343 mg; Sod 289 mg.

Ginger-Flavored Veal Loaf

2 pounds ground lean veal
Salt and pepper to taste
¾ cup finely chopped onion
¾ cup finely chopped celery
1 teaspoon minced garlic
1 tablespoon margarine
2 cups bread cubes
½ cup milk
1 egg, beaten
1 tablespoon minced fresh ginger

Combine veal, salt and pepper in large bowl; set aside. Sauté onion, celery and garlic in margarine in skillet until tender; cool. Combine bread cubes, milk, egg and ginger in small bowl. Let stand until bread is soft. Combine with veal and sautéed vegetables; mix well. Pack into 6-cup loaf pan; insert meat thermometer. Bake at 425 degrees for 40 minutes or until thermometer registers 150 degrees. Let stand at room temperature for 15 to 20 minutes before serving. May add chopped green peppers or pickles and top with mustard or tomato sauce. Yield: 6 servings.

Approx Per Serving: Cal 287; Prot 40 g; Carbo 9 g; Fiber 1 g;
T Fat 9 g; 29% Calories from Fat; Chol 194 mg; Sod 204 mg.

Osso Buco

1-pound veal shanks, sliced 1 inch thick
Salt and pepper to taste
1/2 cup olive oil
1 ounce onion, chopped
1 ounce tomato, chopped
1 ounce carrot, chopped
1 ounce celery, chopped
1/2 ounce garlic, minced
1/2 to 1 teaspoon flour
1 ounce tomato sauce
1 cup demiglacé or chicken stock
1 cup white wine

Tie veal shanks with string; sprinkle with salt and pepper. Brown in olive oil in large skillet; remove to warm platter. Sauté onion, tomato, carrot, celery and garlic in pan drippings. Stir in flour, tomato sauce, demiglacé and wine. Add veal shanks. Simmer, covered, until tender. Serve with saffron rice pilaf garnished with lemon zest and chopped fresh thyme. Yield: 1 serving.

Approx Per Serving: Cal 1686; Prot 96 g; Carbo 14 g; Fiber 3 g; T Fat 122 g; 65% Calories from Fat; Chol 368 mg; Sod 1223 mg.

 Houseplants generally need less water when they're not in bloom.

Rosemary Veal with Marsala

1 pound thinly sliced veal
1 egg, beaten
1 tablespoon lemon juice
Salt and pepper to taste
1/2 cup (about) flour
Olive oil for browning
1 cup Marsala
2 cups chicken broth
1 tablespoon ground rosemary
2 tablespoons each chopped fresh parsley and chives
2 tablespoons butter

Pound veal with meat mallet. Dip in mixture of egg, lemon juice, salt and pepper; coat with flour. Brown each side in hot oil in skillet for 1 1/2 minutes; drain. Remove to covered warming dish. Add Marsala to skillet. Cook until reduced by half. Add broth, rosemary, parsley and chives. Simmer until heated through. Return veal to skillet. Stir in butter. Serve hot. Yield: 4 servings.

Approx Per Serving: Cal 361; Prot 28 g; Carbo 20 g; Fiber 1 g; T Fat 11 g; 28% Calories from Fat; Chol 161 mg; Sod 517 mg. Nutritional information does not include olive oil for browning.

 Houseplants like to take showers too!

Veal and Pepper

2 large onions, chopped
1 large green bell pepper, chopped
1/4 cup margarine
1 1/2 pounds cubed veal
1   16-ounce can stewed tomatoes
Salt and pepper to taste

Sauté onions and green pepper in margarine in covered skillet for 5 minutes. Add veal cubes, tomatoes, salt and pepper. Simmer, covered, for 1 hour. Serve over noodles. Yield: 6 servings.

Approx Per Serving: Cal 234; Prot 24 g; Carbo 11 g; Fiber 1 g; T Fat 11 g; 41% Calories from Fat; Chol 92 mg; Sod 390 mg.

Try *Horseradish and Beet Relish* with meats. Combine 1 grated uncooked beet with 1 grated tart apple, horseradish and salt to taste and several drops of lemon juice and olive oil.

Veal Scallopini alla Genovese

1 small clove of garlic
3 tablespoons butter
1 pound thinly sliced veal scallops
1 tablespoon sifted flour
1 teaspoon each salt and pepper
Sage and nutmeg to taste
1 teaspoon capers
1 small onion, thinly sliced
1/2 cup dry white wine
4 ounces mushrooms, thinly sliced
1 tablespoon thinly sliced stuffed green olives

Sauté garlic in 2 tablespoons butter in skillet for 5 minutes; discard garlic. Brown veal scallops in skillet over medium-high heat. Sprinkle with flour, salt, pepper, sage, nutmeg and capers; add onion and wine. Simmer, covered, for 20 minutes, turning occasionally. Sauté mushrooms in remaining 1 tablespoon butter in small skillet until tender. Add mushrooms and olives to veal mixture. Simmer, covered, for 7 to 8 minutes longer. Yield: 4 servings.

Approx Per Serving: Cal 243; Prot 23 g; Carbo 5 g; Fiber 1 g; T Fat 12 g; 45% Calories from Fat; Chol 115 mg; Sod 697 mg
Nutritional information does not include capers.

Veal with White Wine

1 clove of garlic, crushed
2 tablespoons olive oil
1 tablespoon butter
1 pound veal tenderloin, thinly sliced
1/4 cup flour
8 ounces mushrooms, sliced
1/2 cup dry white wine
1 tablespoon minced flat-leaf Italian parsley

Sauté garlic in mixture of oil and butter in large skillet. Dust veal with flour. Brown on both sides in skillet. Add mushrooms and wine. Cook until liquid is reduced and slightly thickened. Remove to serving platter; top with parsley. Yield: 2 servings.

Approx Per Serving: Cal 540; Prot 48 g; Carbo 18 g; Fiber 3 g; T Fat 26 g; 43% Calories from Fat; Chol 199 mg; Sod 170 mg.

The cork of the wine bottle can be used in cooking meats. Add the cork to a stew dish because it will release enzymes which tenderize meat. It can also reduce the harsh taste of game.

Almond Eggplant with Chicken

2 pounds eggplant, peeled, cut into 1-inch cubes
2 cups lightly packed bread cubes
2 cloves of garlic, crushed
2/3 cup sliced green onions
1 1/2 teaspoons thyme
1 1/2 teaspoons basil
2 eggs, slightly beaten
3/4 cup diced cooked chicken
1/4 cup chopped parsley
3/4 cup chopped almonds
1/4 cup grated Parmesan cheese
Salt and pepper to taste

Sauté eggplant in nonstick skillet. Place in buttered 8-inch baking dish. Sauté bread cubes and garlic in nonstick skillet. Spread over eggplant. Layer green onions, thyme, basil, eggs and chicken over bread cubes. Top with parsley, almonds, cheese, salt and pepper. Place baking dish in pan filled with 1 inch hot water. Bake at 375 degrees for 30 minutes. This recipe is Armenian in origin. Yield: 6 servings.

Approx Per Serving: Cal 361; Prot 19 g; Carbo 42 g; Fiber 9 g; T Fat 15 g; 35% Calories from Fat; Chol 91 mg; Sod 386

Chicken and Artichoke Buffet

4 tablespoons butter
4 cups cooked wild rice
10 medium mushrooms, sliced
10 scallions, chopped
2   10-ounce cans cream of chicken soup
1/2 cup heavy cream
1/2 cup sherry
1 teaspoon salt
4 cups chopped cooked chicken breast filets
2   14-ounce cans artichoke hearts, drained,
cut into quarters
10 slices crisp-fried bacon, crumbled
2 cups carrots, cut into 1-inch julienne strips, blanched
3 cups shredded mozzarella cheese
1/4 cup grated Parmesan cheese

Grease 9x13-inch baking pan with 2 tablespoons butter. Spread rice in prepared pan. Sauté mushrooms and scallions in remaining 2 tablespoons butter in skillet until tender. Add soup, cream, sherry and salt; mix well. Combine mushroom mixture, chicken, artichokes, bacon, carrots and mozzarella cheese in bowl; mix well. Spread over rice. Sprinkle with Parmesan cheese. Bake, covered, at 350 degrees for 30 minutes. Bake, uncovered, for 15 minutes longer. Yield: 10 servings.

Approx Per Serving: Cal 500; Prot 34 g; Carbo 28 g; Fiber 3 g;
T Fat 26 g; 47% Calories from Fat; Chol 108 mg; Sod 1223 mg.

Barbecued Chicken

6 chicken breast filets
6 chicken thighs
1 cup dry vermouth
2 cups mayonnaise
2 teaspoons hot pepper sauce
5 teaspoons Worcestershire sauce
1 teaspoon steak sauce
5 tablespoons sugar
1/2 teaspoon salt
1/2 teaspoon pepper

Rinse chicken and pat dry. Place in large non-metallic bowl. Combine vermouth, mayonnaise, hot pepper sauce, Worcestershire sauce, steak sauce, sugar, salt and pepper in blender container. Process until blended. Pour over chicken. Marinate, covered, in refrigerator for 4 to 24 hours. Drain chicken, reserving marinade. Grill chicken over hot coals or bake in 350-degree oven for 35 minutes or until tender. Pour reserved marinade over chicken in skillet. Heat until warm. Serve immediately. Yield: 12 servings.

Approx Per Serving: Cal 434; Prot 20 g; Carbo 8 g; Fiber <1 g;
T Fat 34 g; 73% Calories from Fat; Chol 82 mg; Sod 379 mg.

 Always rinse uncooked chicken well to guard against salmonella contamination.

Chicken Alberghetti

1 cup Marinara sauce
1/2 cup half and half
2 whole chicken breasts, split, boned
2 eggs, beaten
1/4 cup bread crumbs
6 tablespoons butter
2 tablespoons oil
4 slices mozzarella cheese
4 slices Swiss cheese
1/3 cup grated Parmesan cheese

Combine Marinara sauce and half and half in bowl; mix well. Spread 1/2 of mixture in baking dish. Rinse chicken and pat dry. Dip in eggs; roll in bread crumbs. Sauté in mixture of 2 tablespoons butter and oil in skillet until light brown. Arrange in prepared pan. Place one slice each of mozzarella cheese and Swiss cheese on chicken breasts. Pour remaining Marinara mixture over cheese. Sprinkle with Parmesan cheese. Dot with remaining 4 tablespoons butter. Bake at 325 degrees for 1 hour. Yield: 4 servings.

Approx Per Serving: Cal 716; Prot 49 g; Carbo 14 g; Fiber <1 g; T Fat 51 g; 65% Calories from Fat; Chol 290 mg; Sod 999 mg.

Chicken Cape Cod

6 chicken breast filets
1/2 cup pesto   1 red bell pepper, chopped
1 small onion, chopped
1/2 cup chopped mushrooms
1/2 cup pine nuts   1 clove of garlic, crushed
2 tablespoons butter   1/4 cup chicken broth
1 teaspoon coarsely ground black pepper
1/4 cup light mayonnaise
1/4 cup honey mustard

Rinse chicken and pat dry. Pound as thin as possible between sheets of waxed paper. Spread with pesto. Sauté bell pepper, onion, mushrooms, 1/4 cup pine nuts and garlic in butter in skillet until onion is tender. Spoon sautéed mixture over prepared chicken breasts. Roll from narrow side to enclose filling; secure with wooden picks. Place in baking dish. Add chicken broth and any remaining sauté mix. Sprinkle with pepper. Bake at 325 degrees for 20 minutes or until chicken is tender. Combine mayonnaise and mustard in bowl. Place a spoonful on plate; top with chicken breast. Sprinkle with remaining 1/4 cup toasted pine nuts. Yield: 6 servings.

Approx Per Serving: Cal 427; Prot 33 g; Carbo 16 g; Fiber 3 g; T Fat 28 g; 56% Calories from Fat; Chol 91 mg; Sod 404 mg.

Chicken Czardas

3 whole chicken breasts
1¹/2 teaspoons salt
1 tablespoon reduced-calorie margarine
1 medium onion, chopped
8 ounces mushrooms, sliced
¹/4 cup sherry
2 teaspoons arrowroot
2 tablespoons cold water
1 cup plain low-fat yogurt
1¹/2 teaspoons paprika

Cut chicken into strips, discarding skin and bones. Rinse and pat dry. Sprinkle with salt. Cook chicken in margarine in skillet over medium heat for 3 minutes, stirring constantly. Add onion and mushrooms. Cook for 2 minutes, stirring constantly. Add sherry. Cook, covered, for 4 minutes. Stir in mixture of arrowroot and cold water. Cook until thickened, stirring constantly. Stir in yogurt and paprika, stirring until heated. Do not boil. May substitute cornstarch for arrowroot. Yield: 6 servings.

Approx Per Serving: Cal 206; Prot 30 g; Carbo 7 g; Fiber 1 g;
   T Fat 5 g; 20% Calories from Fat; Chol 75 mg; Sod 648 mg.

Chicken with Lemon and Bulgur

1¹/2 to 2 pounds chicken breast filets
4 teaspoons oil   Salt to taste
Ground black pepper to taste
3 medium onions, chopped
2 cloves of garlic, minced
1¹/2 cups bulgur
¹/2 teaspoon ground cardamom
¹/2 teaspoon ground coriander
¹/2 teaspoon ground cumin
Juice and grated rind of 2 lemons
3 cups boiling chicken broth

Rinse chicken and pat dry. Pound between sheets of waxed paper. Brown chicken in 2 teaspoons oil in skillet. Sprinkle with salt and pepper. Place in baking dish. Sauté onions and garlic in remaining 2 teaspoons oil in skillet. Cook until translucent, stirring constantly. Stir in bulgur. Cook until light brown. Add spices, lemon juice and lemon rind; mix well. Spoon over chicken breasts. Pour boiling chicken broth over top. Bake, covered, at 350 degrees for 30 minutes or until chicken is tender. Yield: 8 servings.

Approx Per Serving: Cal 313; Prot 33 g; Carbo 30 g; Fiber 7 g;
   T Fat 6 g; 19% Calories from Fat; Chol 73 mg; Sod 357 mg.

Chicken with Lemon and Lime

6 chicken breast filets
Salt and pepper to taste
1/2 cup chopped parsley
1/2 cup chopped dill
1/2 cup chopped mint
2 cloves of garlic, minced
3 lemons, sliced
3 limes, sliced
1/4 cup margarine

Rinse chicken and pat dry. Arrange in single layer in baking dish. Season with salt and pepper. Sprinkle with mixture of parsley, dill, mint and garlic. Top with lemon and lime slices. Dot with margarine. Bake, covered with foil, at 350 degrees for 35 minutes or until chicken is tender. Yield: 6 servings.

Approx Per Serving: Cal 233; Prot 27 g; Carbo 8 g; Fiber 1 g; T Fat 11 g; 41% Calories from Fat; Chol 72 mg; Sod 156 mg.

 Prune the mint in your garden to have bushy tops for use in recipes and beverages. It is wise to confine it with edgings to keep it from invading the less sturdy herbs.

Chicken Pizza

1 recipe pizza pastry
1 10-ounce can pizza sauce with cheese
2 whole chicken breasts, boned
1 large onion, sliced into rings
8 ounces mushrooms, sliced
1/2 cup black olives, sliced   1/4 cup oil
1 teaspoon garlic salt   1 teaspoon oregano
1/4 cup grated Parmesan cheese
2 cups shredded mozzarella cheese

Line pizza pan with pizza pastry. Spread with pizza sauce. Cut chicken into 1-inch pieces. Rinse and pat dry. Cook chicken, onion, mushrooms, and olives in oil in skillet for 5 minutes or until chicken is tender. Spread in prepared pan. Sprinkle with garlic salt, oregano and Parmesan cheese. Top with mozzarella cheese. Bake at 425 degrees for 15 to 20 minutes or until light brown. Yield: 4 servings.

Approx Per Serving: Cal 713; Prot 48 g; Carbo 44 g; Fiber 2 g; T Fat 38 g; 48% Calories from Fat; Chol 120 mg; Sod 1741 mg.

Lettuce doesn't grow well if the soil's too acidic.

Chicken with Sauerkraut

6 whole chicken breasts, split, boned
1   27-ounce can sauerkraut, drained
6 slices Swiss cheese
1½   8-ounce bottles of Thousand Island dressing

Rinse chicken and pat dry. Place skin side down in buttered baking dish. Spread sauerkraut over chicken breasts. Top with Swiss cheese. Pour dressing over top. Bake at 325 degrees for 2¼ hours or until chicken is tender. Yield: 12 servings.

Approx Per Serving: Cal 313; Prot 31 g; Carbo 8 g; Fiber 1 g; T Fat 17 g; 50% Calories from Fat; Chol 92 mg; Sod 721 mg.

Make a delicious **Barbecue Sauce for Chicken** by combining 1 small minced onion, ½ cup oil, 2 cups tomato juice, ⅓ cup lemon juice, 2 tablespoons water, 1 tablespoon brown sugar, 2 teaspoons salt, cayenne pepper to taste and 1 teaspoon each chili powder, dry mustard and paprika.

Grilled Chicken Rouget

50   6-ounce chicken breast filets
6 cups olive oil
Salt and pepper to taste
1⅔   cups lemon juice
1   4-ounce jar pimentos, diced
6 large tomatoes, chopped
1⅓   cups chopped fresh chives
1⅓   cups chopped fresh tarragon
1⅓   cups chopped fresh basil

Rinse chicken and pat dry. Rub with olive oil. Sprinkle with salt and pepper. Grill over hot coals for 2 minutes or until grill marks appear on chicken breasts. Place on baking sheet. Bake at 350 degrees for 5 to 10 minutes or until chicken is tender. Cut into bite-sized pieces. Combine chicken, lemon juice, pimentos, tomatoes and herbs in bowl. Season with additional salt and pepper. Yield: 50 servings.

Approx Per Serving: Cal 447; Prot 40 g; Carbo 2 g; Fiber <1 g; T Fat 31 g; 62% Calories from Fat; Chol 108 mg; Sod 96 mg.

For a long lasting indoor arrangement, let ivy or pachysandra root in dampened floral foam; just change the accent flowers.

Chicken and Seafood Stroganoff

2 tablespoons lemon juice
1 tablespoon soy sauce
2 teaspoons thyme
1 teaspoon instant chicken bouillon
8   8-ounce boneless chicken breasts
1/2 cup butter
1 pound peeled deveined medium shrimp
1 pound bay scallops
1 cup Chablis
1   10-ounce can cream of mushroom soup
1 tablespoon chopped parsley
12 ounces mushrooms, chopped
4 cups cooked rice

Combine lemon juice, soy sauce, thyme and chicken bouillon in saucepan. Cook until blended, stirring constantly. Set aside. Rinse chicken and pat dry. Sauté chicken breasts in butter in skillet for 3 to 4 minutes on each side. Remove from skillet. Add shrimp and scallops to skillet. Cook until shrimp turn pink and scallops are tender. Return chicken breasts to skillet. Add wine, stirring to deglaze skillet. Stir in soup, parsley and mushrooms. Simmer for 5 to 7 minutes or until heated through. Arrange chicken breasts over rice. Top with seafood mixture. May substitute white cream sauce or celery soup for mushroom soup. Yield: 8 servings.

Approx Per Serving: Cal 661; Prot 76 g; Carbo 32 g; Fiber 1 g; T Fat 22 g; 31% Calories from Fat; Chol 284 mg; Sod 918 mg.

Crab-Stuffed Chicken Breasts

6 whole chicken breasts, boned, skinned
Salt and pepper to taste
1/2 cup chopped onion
1/2 cup chopped celery
5 tablespoons butter
5 tablespoons dry white wine
1   7-ounce can crab meat, drained, flaked
1/2 cup herb stuffing mix
2 tablespoons flour   1/2 teaspoon paprika
1 envelope Hollandaise sauce mix
3/4 cup milk
1/2 cup shredded Swiss cheese

Rinse chicken and pat dry. Pound between sheets of waxed paper. Sprinkle with salt and pepper. Cook onion and celery in 3 tablespoons butter in skillet until tender. Remove from heat. Stir in 3 tablespoons wine, crab meat and stuffing mix. Spread on chicken breasts. Roll chicken to enclose filling; secure with skewers. Roll in mixture of flour and paprika. Place in baking dish. Drizzle with remaining 2 tablespoons melted butter. Bake at 375 degrees for 1 hour. Remove to serving platter. Combine sauce mix and milk in saucepan. Cook until thickened, stirring constantly. Add remaining 2 tablespoons wine and cheese; mix well. Cook until cheese melts. Spoon 1/2 of the mixture over chicken breasts; serve with remaining sauce. Yield: 6 servings.

Approx Per Serving: Cal 525; Prot 65 g; Carbo 12 g; Fiber 1 g; T Fat 21 g; 38% Calories from Fat; Chol 212 mg; Sod 644 mg.

Cranberry Chicken

8 chicken breast filets
4 tablespoons sesame oil
1 16-ounce can whole berry cranberry sauce
1/4 teaspoon ginger
1/2 teaspoon orange zest
1/2 teaspoon lemon zest

Rinse chicken and pat dry. Arrange in baking pan greased with 1 tablespoon sesame oil. Melt cranberry sauce in saucepan over low heat. Stir in remaining 3 tablespoons sesame oil, ginger, orange zest and lemon zest. Pour over chicken breasts. Bake at 325 degrees for 1 hour. Yield: 8 servings.

Approx Per Serving: Cal 287; Prot 27 g; Carbo 22 g; Fiber 1 g;
T Fat 10 g; 31% Calories from Fat; Chol 72 mg; Sod 80 mg.

Make *Champagne Sauce* by sautéing 1 minced shallot in 1 tablespoon butter or margarine. Add 1/2 cup Champagne or sparkling white wine and bring to a boil. Boil for 5 minutes; reduce heat to medium. Stir in 1 cup heavy cream and 1/8 teaspoon salt. Cook for 2 minutes.

Herb Chicken in Phyllo

2 tablespoons minced watercress
1 1/2 teaspoons minced fresh tarragon
1/2 cup plus 6 tablespoons butter, softened
8 chicken breast filets
8 sheets fresh or frozen phyllo
Salt and pepper to taste

Combine watercress, 1 1/2 teaspoons tarragon and 1/2 cup butter in bowl; mix well. Chill, covered, in refrigerator. Rinse chicken and pat dry. Pound 1/2 inch thick between sheets of waxed paper. Slice crosswise almost to edge to form pocket. Place 1 tablespoon watercress and butter mixture in each pocket; press to seal. Brush each phyllo sheet with part of the remaining melted butter; fold into halves, forming rectangle. Place chicken in center of rectangle; sprinkle with salt and pepper. Fold dough over to enclose chicken, pressing edges together to form a ruffled edge on top. Place on baking sheet. Brush with remaining melted butter. Bake at 400 degrees for 20 minutes or until golden brown. Garnish with fresh tarragon sprigs. Serve with Champagne Sauce (this page). Yield: 8 servings.

Approx Per Serving: Cal 379; Prot 29 g; Carbo 14 g; Fiber 1 g;
T Fat 23 g; 55% Calories from Fat; Chol 127 mg; Sod 309 mg.

Herb French Chicken

2 whole chicken breasts, split, boned
Salt and pepper to taste
4 tablespoons unsalted butter
1 cup dry white wine
4 large shallots, minced
1 cup chicken stock
2 tablespoons flour
1 tablespoon lemon juice
1 tablespoon finely chopped parsley
2 teaspoons dried chervil
2 teaspoons dried tarragon or
1 tablespoon fresh tarragon

Rinse chicken and pat dry. Sprinkle with salt and pepper. Sauté chicken breasts in 3 tablespoons butter in skillet until brown on both sides. Remove to warm serving platter. Add wine and shallots to pan juices. Simmer until juices are reduced by half. Stir in chicken stock. Boil until reduced by half. Melt remaining 1 tablespoon butter in saucepan. Stir in flour until smooth. Cook for 3 minutes or until bubbly. Stir in wine mixture. Add lemon juice, parsley, chervil and tarragon. Simmer for 1 minute. Pour sauce over chicken. Yield: 4 servings.

Approx Per Serving: Cal 363; Prot 30 g; Carbo 17 g; Fiber 1 g; T Fat 15 g; 37% Calories from Fat; Chol 104 mg; Sod 365 mg.

Yogurt-Herbed Chicken

6 chicken breast filets
1 cup fat-free yogurt
1 cup wheat germ cereal
2 tablespoons dried rosemary, minced
2 tablespoons dried lemon verbena, minced
1 10-ounce can Italian tomato soup

Rinse chicken and pat dry. Spread both sides with yogurt. Dip in mixture of cereal, rosemary and lemon verbena. Place in greased baking pan. Bake at 325 degrees for 25 minutes or until brown. Top each chicken breast with 1/4 cup soup. Pour remaining soup around chicken. Bake for 10 minutes. Yield: 6 servings.

Approx Per Serving: Cal 253; Prot 32 g; Carbo 19 g; Fiber 2 g; T Fat 5 g; 17% Calories from Fat; Chol 73 mg; Sod 440 mg.

Balsamic and herb-flavored vinegars enhance the flavor of poached chicken without adding salt. They can also be used to deglaze skillets; try them with sautéed chicken.

Spinach Chicken

6 10-ounce packages spinach
5 whole chicken breasts, split
1/2 cup flour
Salt and white pepper to taste
1 cup melted butter
10 mushrooms, chopped
Garlic powder to taste
1 tablespoon Maggi seasoning
1 quart heavy cream
1 cup grated Parmesan cheese

Cook spinach using package directions; drain. Spread in buttered baking dish. Rinse chicken and pat dry. Roll in mixture of flour, salt and white pepper. Dip in mixture of butter and mushrooms. Arrange over spinach. Sprinkle liberally with garlic powder. Pour mixture of Maggi seasoning and heavy cream over chicken. Top with Parmesan cheese. Bake, covered, at 350 degrees for 15 minutes. Bake, uncovered, for 40 to 45 minutes longer or until tender. Yield: 10 servings.

Approx Per Serving: Cal 733; Prot 38 g; Carbo 15 g; Fiber 6 g; T Fat 60 g; 72% Calories from Fat; Chol 259 mg; Sod 539 mg. Nutritional information does not include Maggi seasoning.

Chicken Supreme

1 cup cooked white rice
1 cup cooked wild rice
6 cups chopped cooked chicken
1 cup sliced almonds
3 cups sautéed sliced mushrooms
1 8-ounce can water chestnuts, sliced
1 cup chopped onions
1 cup chopped celery
1/2 cup butter
1/2 cup flour
6 cups chicken broth
1/4 cup chopped parsley
1 4-ounce jar chopped pimentos
Salt to taste
1/2 teaspoon pepper

Layer white rice, wild rice, chicken, almonds, mushrooms and water chestnuts in buttered baking pan. Sauté onions and celery in butter in skillet until tender. Add flour and broth; mix well. Stir in parsley, pimentos, salt and pepper. Cook until slightly thickened. Pour over chicken mixture. Bake at 350 degrees for 45 minutes. May be frozen. Do not preheat oven for frozen casserole; bake for 1 1/2 hours or until bubbly. Yield: 12 servings.

Approx Per Serving: Cal 352; Prot 27 g; Carbo 19 g; Fiber 3 g; T Fat 19 g; 48% Calories from Fat; Chol 86 mg; Sod 534 mg.

Special Avocado Chicken

2 tablespoons flour
2 tablespoons melted butter
1/2 cup milk
2 cups chopped cooked chicken
1/2 cup light cream
1/2 teaspoon Worcestershire sauce
1 teaspoon salt
Cayenne pepper to taste
1 tablespoon sherry
3 avocados

Blend flour into butter in saucepan. Cook for several minutes. Stir in milk. Cook until thickened, stirring constantly. Add chicken, cream, Worcestershire sauce, salt and cayenne pepper. Simmer for 3 minutes. Stir in sherry. Peel avocados and cut into halves lengthwise; place on baking sheet. Spoon chicken mixture into cavities. Broil just until golden brown. Serve immediately. May omit sherry if preferred. Yield: 6 servings.

Approx Per Serving: Cal 336; Prot 17 g; Carbo 11 g; Fiber 10 g; T Fat 26 g; 67% Calories from Fat; Chol 62 mg; Sod 459 mg.

Nasturtiums are easy to grow, high in vitamin C and taste as bright as they look in salads, in pasta dishes or with fish.

Tarragon Chicken

1 pound chicken breast filets
2 cloves of garlic, slivered
2 tablespoons olive oil
1/2 cup white wine
Juice of 1/2 lemon
1/4 cup chopped fresh tarragon
2 tablespoons chopped fresh parsley
2 tablespoons chopped fresh chives
Grated zest of 1/2 lemon
Salt and pepper to taste

Cut chicken into bite-sized pieces; rinse and pat dry. Sauté chicken and garlic in olive oil in skillet or wok until chicken is tender. Add wine and lemon. Cook for several minutes. Stir in tarragon, parsley, chives, lemon zest, salt and pepper. Cook for 2 to 3 minutes longer, stirring frequently. Serve with rice and sliced tomatoes; garnish with fresh herbs. May drizzle with olive oil. Yield: 4 servings.

Approx Per Serving: Cal 225; Prot 27 g; Carbo 1 g; Fiber <1 g; T Fat 10 g; 39% Calories from Fat; Chol 72 mg; Sod 66 mg.

To keep mint in bounds, plant it in PVC piping sunk into the ground 10 or 12 inches.

Chicken Veronique

1 pound seedless white grapes
1½ cups dry white wine   1 cup water
3 tablespoons oil   2 teaspoons garlic salt
Juice of ½ lemon
5 whole chicken breasts, split, boned
1 medium onion, sliced
1 to 1½ cups shredded Swiss cheese
¼ cup butter   2 tablespoons flour
⅔ cup light cream   2 chicken bouillon cubes
Tabasco sauce to taste   2 egg yolks

Cook grapes in ½ cup wine and 1 cup water in saucepan until tender. Drain; set aside. Place 1 tablespoon oil, garlic salt, remaining 1 cup wine and lemon juice in skillet; mix well. Rinse chicken and pat dry. Add chicken and onion to skillet. Bring to a boil. Simmer for 20 minutes. Remove chicken, reserving broth and discarding onions. Slice chicken. Place in greased baking dish. Sprinkle with half the cheese. Top with grapes. Melt butter in skillet. Add remaining 2 tablespoons oil; mix well. Stir in flour and reserved broth. Cook until thickened, stirring constantly. Remove from heat. Add cream, bouillon cubes and Tabasco sauce. Simmer until heated through, stirring constantly. Stir a small amount of hot mixture into egg yolks; stir egg yolks into hot mixture. Pour cream sauce over casserole. Sprinkle with remaining cheese. Chill overnight. Bake at 350 degrees for 20 to 25 minutes or until bubbly. Yield: 8 servings.

Approx Per Serving: Cal 481; Prot 41 g; Carbo 16 g; Fiber 1 g; T Fat 25 g; 49% Calories from Fat; Chol 186 mg; Sod 997 mg.

Howerton Brunswick Stew

2 3-pound chickens, cut up   1 cup flour
Salt and pepper to taste   ½ cup oil
4 large onions   2 tablespoons butter
2 16-ounce cans tomatoes   ½ teaspoon thyme
2 tablespoons chopped parsley
3 chicken bouillon cubes   1 2-ounce jar pimento
½ slice country ham, chopped
4 cups lima beans   2 tablespoons Worcestershire sauce
1   cup (8 ounces) frozen okra   1 8-ounce can corn
Chopped parsley to taste

Rinse chicken and pat dry. Coat with mixture of flour, salt and pepper. Brown chicken in oil in skillet; drain. Cut onions into halves lengthwise; slice medium thin. Cook in butter in covered heavy saucepan over medium heat for 15 to 20 minutes. Cook, uncovered, for 30 to 45 minutes or until brown. Place chicken and onions in large stockpot. Add chopped undrained tomatoes, thyme, parsley, bouillon cubes, pimento, ham and enough boiling water to cover. Simmer, covered, over medium-low heat for 1 to 1½ hours or until chicken is tender. Remove chicken. Cut into pieces, discarding skin and bone. Chill overnight. Add lima beans to stew. Simmer for 30 minutes or until partially done. Stir in Worcestershire sauce. Add okra, simmering until okra and beans are tender. Cool slightly. Chill overnight. Combine stew, chicken and corn in large stockpot. Cook until heated through. Ladle into soup bowls; sprinkle with chopped parsley. Yield: 20 servings.

Approx Per Serving: Cal 380; Prot 31 g; Carbo 38 g; Fiber 12 g; T Fat 12 g; 29% Calories from Fat; Chol 65 mg; Sod 386 mg.

Chicken Marengo

1 3-pound chicken, cut up
1/3 cup flour
1 teaspoon salt   1/4 teaspoon pepper
1/4 cup olive oil
1 clove of garlic, crushed
3 tablespoons chopped onion
4 tomatoes, cut into quarters
1 cup white wine   1/2 bay leaf
4 sprigs of parsley
1/2 teaspoon thyme
4 ounces mushrooms
2 tablespoons butter
1/2 cup sliced olives
1/2 cup consommé
2 tablespoons flour
3 cups cooked noodles

Rinse chicken and pat dry. Shake chicken in mixture of 1/3 cup flour, salt and pepper in plastic bag. Brown in olive oil in skillet. Add garlic, onion, tomatoes, wine and herbs. Simmer, covered, for 30 minutes. Sauté mushrooms in butter in skillet until tender. Add mushrooms and olives to chicken mixture; mix well. Remove chicken to platter. Stir mixture of consommé and 2 tablespoons flour into skillet gradually. Boil until thickened. Return chicken to skillet; simmer for 10 minutes. Remove bay leaf half. Serve over noodles. Yield: 5 servings.

Approx Per Serving: Cal 650; Prot 47 g; Carbo 38 g; Fiber 5 g; T Fat 31 g; 45% Calories from Fat; Chol 164 mg; Sod 852 mg.

Cornell Barbecued Chicken

4 chicken breasts, skinned
1/2 cup oil
1/2 cup wine vinegar
1/2 cup lemon juice
2 teaspoons salt
1 1/2 teaspoons poultry seasoning
1/4 teaspoon white pepper
1/2 teaspoon oregano
1/2 teaspoon dry mustard
1/2 teaspoon Worcestershire sauce
1 egg

Rinse chicken and pat dry. Place in 2 1/2-quart bowl. Combine oil, wine vinegar, lemon juice, salt, poultry seasoning, white pepper, oregano, dry mustard, Worcestershire sauce and egg in blender container. Process until smooth. Pour over chicken. Marinate in refrigerator for 8 to 10 hours. Drain, reserving marinade. Grill chicken over hot coals for 45 to 60 minutes or until tender, basting frequently with reserved marinade. Yield 4 servings.

Approx Per Serving: Cal 416; Prot 28 g; Carbo 5 g; Fiber <1 g; T Fat 32 g; 68% Calories from Fat; Chol 125 mg; Sod 1095 mg.

When roasting a bird, bake it breast down for 2/3 of the baking time to insure a juicy breast. Turn it over during the remaining 1/3 of the baking time for even browning.

Orange-Rosemary Chicken

1   3½-pound roasting chicken
2 teaspoons dried rosemary
½ cup butter, softened
2 tablespoons English-style orange marmalade
Salt and ground pepper to taste

Rinse chicken and pat dry. Crush rosemary in mortar with pestle. Combine rosemary with butter, orange marmalade, salt and pepper in bowl; mix well. Separate chicken skin from the breast. Spread half of the butter mixture under skin, covering chicken breast. Spread remaining butter mixture over the outside of chicken. Place on rack in shallow roasting pan. Roast at 400 degrees for 20 minutes. Reduce oven temperature to 350 degrees. Roast for 1 hour longer or until chicken is tender, basting with pan juices. Cool for 20 minutes. Serve with deglazed pan juices. May serve cold. Yield: 5 servings.

Approx Per Serving: Cal 485; Prot 46 g; Carbo 6 g; Fiber <1 g; T Fat 30 g; 57% Calories from Fat; Chol 191 mg; Sod 292 mg.

Rosemary Roasted Chickens

2   3-pound chickens
15 large cloves of garlic
3 tablespoons olive oil
Juice of 1 lemon
2 tablespoons dried rosemary
Salt and pepper to taste

Cut chickens into 16 pieces. Rinse and pat dry. Place in large baking pan. Arrange garlic around chicken. Drizzle with olive oil and lemon juice. Sprinkle with rosemary, salt and pepper. Roast, covered, at 325 degrees for 1 hour. Roast, uncovered, at 350 degrees for 20 to 30 minutes longer or until skin is brown and crisp. Yield: 16 servings.

Approx Per Serving: Cal 189; Prot 25 g; Carbo 1 g; Fiber <1 g; T Fat 9 g; 43% Calories from Fat; Chol 76 mg; Sod 73 mg.

Make a *Delicious Marinade for Chicken* by combining ½ cup olive oil, ½ cup vinegar, 1 egg or egg substitute, ¾ teaspoon pepper and 2 teaspoons each salt and poultry seasoning. Marinate chicken for 3 hours or longer and grill over hot coals.

Chicken South Philly

1 3-pound chicken, cut up
1/2 cup butter
1 envelope onion soup mix
6 ounces barbecue sauce

Rinse chicken and pat dry. Melt butter in baking dish. Stir in soup mix and barbecue sauce. Place chicken in baking dish, turning to coat both sides. Cook, covered, at 350 degrees for 1 hour or until chicken is tender. Yield: 8 servings.

Approx Per Serving: Cal 279; Prot 25 g; Carbo 3 g; Fiber <1 g; T Fat 18 g; 60% Calories from Fat; Chol 107 mg; Sod 421 mg.

Curried Turkey Dijonnaise

1 envelope chicken-Dijonnaise sauce mix
1 1/2 tablespoons curry powder
4 cups chopped cooked turkey
4 cups cooked white rice

Prepare sauce mix using package directions in saucepan. Stir in curry powder. Add turkey; mix well. Cook until heated through. Spoon over rice. Yield: 8 servings.

Approx Per Serving: Cal 288; Prot 23 g; Carbo 30 g; Fiber 1 g; T Fat 8 g; 26% Calories from Fat; Chol 54 mg; Sod 320 mg.

Moussaka Sandwiches

1 pound ground turkey
2 tablespoons olive oil
Salt and pepper to taste
1 to 2 cloves of garlic, chopped
2 cups diced eggplant
1/2 cup chopped onion
2 medium tomatoes, peeled, seeded, chopped
1/3 cup chili sauce
Basil and oregano to taste
8 ounces mushrooms, sliced, sautéed
4 1-inch slices Italian or French bread
2 tablespoons grated Parmesan cheese
8 ounces shredded mozzarella cheese

Brown turkey in olive oil in skillet. Stir in salt, pepper and garlic. Push aside. Add eggplant and onion to skillet. Cook for 5 minutes, stirring occasionally. Stir in tomatoes, chili sauce, basil, oregano and mushrooms. Cook over medium heat for 30 minutes, stirring occasionally. Spread on bread slices; sprinkle with cheeses. Place on baking sheet. Broil until cheese melts. Yield: 4 servings.

Approx Per Serving: Cal 575; Prot 40 g; Carbo 34 g; Fiber 5 g; T Fat 31 g; 49% Calories from Fat; Chol 117 mg; Sod 846 mg.

Turkey Devonshire

18 slices smoked bacon
1 cup flour
4 cups low-fat milk
1 pound low-fat sharp Cheddar cheese, shredded
1 tablespoon dry mustard
1 teaspoon Worcestershire sauce
1/2 teaspoon Tabasco sauce
6 slices white bread, toasted
6 1/2-inch thick tomato slices
6 1/4 to 1/2-inch thick slices turkey breast
1/4 cup grated Parmesan cheese

Fry bacon in skillet until crisp. Drain, reserving 3/4 cup bacon drippings. Combine bacon drippings and flour in saucepan. Cook over medium heat for 2 to 3 minutes, stirring constantly. Add milk; mix well. Cook over medium heat until mixture begins to boil, stirring constantly. Remove from heat. Add cheese, dry mustard, Worcestershire sauce and Tabasco sauce, stirring until cheese melts; mix well. Place toast in 9x13-inch baking pan sprayed with nonstick cooking spray. Arrange bacon, tomato slices and turkey over toast. Pour cheese sauce over turkey. Sprinkle with Parmesan cheese. Bake at 350 degrees for 10 to 15 minutes or until hot and bubbly. May be baked in 6 ramekins. May substitute rye bread for white bread. Yield: 6 servings.

Approx Per Serving: Cal 929; Prot 57 g; Carbo 43 g; Fiber 2 g; T Fat 59 g; 57% Calories from Fat; Chol 281 mg; Sod 1326 mg.

Turkey Empañadas

1 cup chopped cooked turkey
1 4-ounce can chopped green chilies, drained
1/4 cup chopped green bell pepper
1 tablespoon minced onion
1 teaspoon cumin
1 cup shredded Cheddar cheese
1/2 cup taco sauce
1 cup flour
5 tablespoons yellow cornmeal
1/3 cup shortening
1/4 cup ice water
1 tablespoon milk

Combine turkey, green chilies, green pepper, onion, cumin, cheese and taco sauce in bowl; mix well. Set aside. Combine flour and 4 tablespoons cornmeal in bowl; mix well. Cut in shortening until crumbly. Add ice water, stirring until mixture holds together. Divide into 2 portions. Roll each portion into 11-inch circle on lightly floured surface. Spoon half the filling on half of 1 circle. Fold dough over to enclose filling. Seal edges with fork. Repeat with remaining circle and filling. Place on lightly greased baking sheet. Brush with milk; sprinkle with remaining 1 tablespoon cornmeal. Bake at 400 degrees for 20 minutes or until light brown. Cool for 10 minutes. Spoon 1/4 cup heated taco sauce over empañadas. Yield: 8 servings.

Approx Per Serving: Cal 250; Prot 11 g; Carbo 19 g; Fiber 1 g; T Fat 15 g; 53% Calories from Fat; Chol 29 mg; Sod 266 mg.

Wild Duck with Grand Marnier

1   2 to 3-pound wild duck
Salt to taste
1 medium onion
2 stalks celery
1/2 cup melted butter
1/2 cup dry white wine
1/4 cup Grand Marnier

Rinse duck inside and out; pat dry. Salt cavity. Place onion and celery in cavity; truss. Place in baking pan. Baste with mixture of butter, wine and Grand Marnier. Roast at 325 degrees for 1 hour or until duck tests done. Cool for 10 minutes before carving. Yield: 2 servings.

Approx Per Serving: Cal 1267; Prot 61 g; Carbo 18 g; Fiber 2 g; T Fat 98 g; 74% Calories from Fat; Chol 396 mg; Sod 619 mg.

When cooking whole poultry, a chicken or turkey yields about 1/2 its weight in edible meat. A duck has only about 1/5 its total weight in edible meat.

Pheasant with Cream Sauce

3 tablespoons chopped onion
1 cup chopped mushrooms
6 tablespoons peanut oil
1   2 to 3-pound pheasant, cut into pieces
1/2 cup flour
1 teaspoon salt
1/2 teaspoon pepper
1 teaspoon paprika
1/2 teaspoon garlic salt
1/2 cup heavy cream

Sauté onion and mushrooms in 2 tablespoons peanut oil in skillet until tender. Rinse pheasant and pat dry. Coat with mixture of flour, salt, pepper, paprika and garlic salt. Brown in remaining 4 tablespoons peanut oil in skillet for 15 minutes. Place in large heavy saucepan. Spoon onion and mushroom mixture over top. Pour in cream; mix well. Cook, covered, over medium-low heat for 15 minutes. Cook, uncovered, for 15 minutes longer, turning pieces 1 or 2 times. Remove pheasant, onion and mushrooms to a warm platter. May make gravy with pan drippings. Yield: 4 servings.

Approx Per Serving: Cal 653; Prot 41 g; Carbo 14 g; Fiber 1 g; T Fat 47 g; 66% Calories from Fat; Chol 168 mg; Sod 870 mg.

Sautéed Catfish with Peppers

1¹/2 cups dry white wine
2 shallots, minced
¹/4 cup heavy cream
3 cups unsalted butter
Salt and pepper to taste
4   8-ounce catfish filets
¹/3 cup flour
2 each red and green bell peppers,
cut into thin 2-inch strips

Combine wine and shallots in small saucepan. Cook until wine is reduced to 1 tablespoon. Stir in cream. Cook until liquid is reduced by half; remove from heat. Whisk in 2 cups chopped butter gradually. Season with salt and pepper; keep warm. Melt remaining 1 cup butter in saucepan, skimming foam from surface. Pour clarified butter into skillet carefully, discarding milky sediment. Sprinkle catfish with salt and pepper; coat with flour. Sauté in clarified butter in skillet; remove to warm platter. Drain skillet, reserving ¹/2 tablespoon drippings. Sauté peppers in reserved drippings. Place catfish and peppers on serving plates; top with butter sauce. Yield: 4 servings.

Approx Per Serving: Cal 1460; Prot 38 g; Carbo 20 g; Fiber 2 g; T Fat 151 g; 93% Calories from Fat; Chol 498 mg; Sod 150 mg.

Fantastic Fish

2 pounds 1-inch haddock filets
¹/4 cup flour
Salt to taste
¹/4 teaspoon pepper
1 cup milk
2 cups soft coarse bread crumbs
¹/4 cup butter
1 cup sour cream
1 teaspoon dried dillseed or dillweed

Cut fish into 6 portions; coat with mixture of flour, salt and pepper. Arrange in single layer in 9x13-inch baking dish. Pour milk over filets. Bake at 350 degrees for 45 minutes. Sauté bread crumbs lightly in butter in skillet. Spoon mixture of sour cream and dillseed over fish; top with bread crumbs. Bake for 10 minutes longer. Serve with baked parslied new potatoes or baked tomatoes and spinach salad. Garnish with lemon and parsley. May roll thin filets for this recipe. Yield: 6 servings.

Approx Per Serving: Cal 373; Prot 37 g; Carbo 15 g; Fiber <1 g; T Fat 19 g; 45% Calories from Fat; Chol 133 mg; Sod 284 mg.

Dill butter is delicious with any broiled or grilled fish dish. Dill mayonnaise is especially good with chilled salmon.

Flounder and Spinach Casserole

2 cups sour cream
3 tablespoons flour
1/2 cup chopped green onions with tops
2 tablespoons lemon juice
2 teaspoons salt
4   10-ounce packages frozen chopped spinach
2 pounds flounder

Combine sour cream, flour, green onions, lemon juice and salt in bowl; mix well. Cook spinach using package directions; drain and press to remove moisture. Combine spinach with half the sour cream mixture in bowl; mix well. Spread in 9x13-inch baking dish. Arrange fish over spinach mixture; top with remaining sour cream sauce. Bake at 350 degrees for 1 hour. Garnish with paprika and parsley. Yield: 8 servings.

Approx Per Serving: Cal 282; Prot 29 g; Carbo 13 g; Fiber 4 g; T Fat 14 g; 43% Calories from Fat; Chol 87 mg; Sod 781 mg.

The use of lemon, wine, vinegar, ginger, green onions or garlic in marinating or cooking fish reduces fishy taste and odor.

Quick Delicious Flounder

4 medium thick flounder filets
2 medium onions, sliced
1/3 cup mayonnaise
1 teaspoon Dijon mustard
1/4 cup freshly grated Parmesan cheese

Arrange fish in broiler pan lined with oiled foil; place onions over fish. Combine mayonnaise, mustard and Parmesan cheese in bowl; mix well. Spread over onions. Broil, covered with foil, at 500 degrees for 20 minutes. Broil, uncovered, for 5 minutes or until brown. Yield: 4 servings.

Approx Per Serving: Cal 289; Prot 25 g; Carbo 7 g; Fiber 1 g; T Fat 18 g; 56% Calories from Fat; Chol 77 mg; Sod 328 mg.

Oven-poached fish is both nutritious and delicious. Place filets in a buttered shallow pan; pour wine over filets and add seasonings. Cover with foil and place in a preheated 350-degree oven. When wine reaches a boil, cook the fish for about 10 minutes per inch of thickness.

Teriyaki Mahi-Mahi

1/2 cup pineapple juice   9 1/3 tablespoons oil
7 1/2 tablespoons soy sauce   2 teaspoons dry sherry
1 packet sugar substitute   1/3 teaspoon ground ginger
Salt and pepper to taste
4   6-ounce mahi-mahi filets
4 teaspoons chili sauce
2 teaspoons dry sherry
4 teaspoons pineapple juice
10 2/3 tablespoons butter
1/3 cup chopped fresh parsley
1 tablespoon flour
2 tablespoons (or more) bread crumbs

Combine 1/2 cup pineapple juice, 5 1/3 tablespoons oil, 6 1/3 tablespoons soy sauce, 2 teaspoons wine, sugar substitute, ginger, salt and pepper in shallow dish. Remove skin from fish; add to marinade. Marinate in refrigerator for 3 hours or longer. Combine chili sauce, remaining 4 teaspoons soy sauce, 2 teaspoons wine and 4 teaspoons pineapple juice in saucepan; mix well. Bring to a boil; remove from heat. Mix in butter gradually. Add parsley; keep warm. Drain fish; coat with mixture of flour and bread crumbs. Brown on both sides in remaining 4 tablespoons oil in skillet. Serve with heated butter sauce. Yield: 4 servings.

Approx Per Serving: Cal 771; Prot 35 g; Carbo 14 g; Fiber 1 g;
T Fat 64 g; 75% Calories from Fat; Chol 209 mg; Sod 2483 mg.
Nutritional information includes entire amount of marinade.

Redfish with Seafood Sauce

8   6-ounce redfish filets
1/4 cup flour
2 tablespoons butter
1/4 cup white wine
1/4 cup fish stock
1/2 cup shredded fresh fennel
1/4 cup chopped yellow onion
1 cup heavy cream
8 ounces lump crab meat
8 ounces fresh shrimp, peeled, chopped

Coat fish with flour. Sauté in butter in skillet until brown. Remove to platter in warm oven. Add wine, fish stock, fennel and onion to drippings in skillet, stirring to deglaze skillet. Cook until reduced by one third. Strain into saucepan. Stir in cream. Simmer for 5 minutes. Stir in crab meat and shrimp. Simmer for 10 minutes. Spoon over fish. Yield: 8 servings.

Approx Per Serving: Cal 367; Prot 43 g; Carbo 4 g; Fiber <1 g;
T Fat 18 g; 46% Calories from Fat; Chol 188 mg; Sod 303 mg.
Nutritional information does not include fennel.

Sour cream or mayonnaise spread on fish to be baked, broiled or grilled helps keep it moist and flavorful as it cooks.

Roughy with Basil Sauce

1/4 onion, chopped   2 cloves of garlic, chopped
5 tablespoons butter
1/4 cup chopped basil
1/4 cup chopped celery leaves
1/4 cup skim milk   1 egg yolk
1/2 teaspoon instant chicken bouillon
White pepper to taste
1 each red and green bell pepper, julienned
2 carrots, julienned
1/4 small red head cabbage, shredded
2 pounds orange roughy filets

Sauté onion and 1 clove of chopped garlic in 1 tablespoon butter in skillet for 2 minutes. Add basil and celery leaves. Cook, covered, for 3 minutes, stirring occasionally. Combine with skim milk, egg yolk, chicken bouillon and white pepper in food processor container; process until smooth. Return to saucepan; set aside. Sauté peppers, carrots, remaining 1 clove of minced garlic and cabbage in 2 tablespoons butter in saucepan for 7 minutes or until tender; keep warm. Sauté fish filets in remaining 2 tablespoons butter in skillet for 3 1/2 minutes on each side or until fish flakes easily. Cook basil sauce until bubbly, stirring constantly. Spoon immediately onto 4 serving plates. Arrange fish in sauce; top with vegetables. Yield: 4 servings.

Approx Per Serving: Cal 472; Prot 36 g; Carbo 8 g; Fiber 2 g; T Fat 32 g; 61% Calories from Fat; Chol 138 mg; Sod 436 mg.

Grilled Danish Salmon

4   6 to 7-ounce salmon filets with skin
1 tablespoon kosher salt
2 tablespoons water
2 tablespoons aquavit
1 cup unsalted butter
2 tablespoons chopped dill
Salt and freshly ground pepper to taste

Place fish on grill rack over hot coals; sprinkle with kosher salt. Grill for 10 minutes without turning. Bring water and aquavit to a boil in small saucepan. Add butter 1 tablespoon at a time, whisking until smooth. Season with chopped dill and salt and pepper to taste. Place fish on serving plates; garnish with sprigs of fresh dill. Serve with dilled butter sauce. Yield: 4 servings.

Approx Per Serving: Cal 717; Prot 38 g; Carbo <1 g; Fiber <1 g; T Fat 61 g; 78% Calories from Fat; Chol 243 mg; Sod 1696 mg.

A good *Chutney Sauce for Fish* can be made by mixing chutney with mayonnaise and adding lime juice, honey, garlic powder, ginger and curry powder.

Dilled Salmon

1½ cups sour cream
½ cup mayonnaise
1 teaspoon grated onion
1½ tablespoons chopped fresh dill or
1 tablespoon dried dillweed
½ teaspoon salt
¼ teaspoon pepper
8 7-ounce salmon filets
¼ cup melted butter

Combine sour cream, mayonnaise, onion, dill, salt and pepper in bowl; mix well. Chill, covered, overnight. Brush salmon filets with melted butter. Grill on oiled grill for 4 to 5 minutes. Brush salmon with butter and turn. Grill for 2 to 3 minutes longer or until fish flakes easily. Serve with dill sauce. Yield: 8 servings.

Approx Per Serving: Cal 585; Prot 45 g; Carbo 2 g; Fiber <1 g;
T Fat 43 g; 67% Calories from Fat; Chol 181 mg; Sod 388 mg.

Green Goddess salad dressing or zesty Italian salad dressing makes a good marinade for fish. A generous coating of lemon pepper lends a delicious flavor to grilled fish.

Salmon with Oyster Sauce

2 tablespoons mayonnaise-type salad dressing
1 tablespoon Chinese oyster sauce
1 pound salmon steaks or filets
2 sprigs of fresh dill, chopped

Combine salad dressing and oyster sauce in small bowl. Brush on both sides of salmon; place on rack in broiler pan. Broil for 12 minutes or until fish flakes easily; do not turn. Sprinkle with fresh dill. May use salmon filet or other fish. May serve cold. Yield: 3 servings.

Approx Per Serving: Cal 305; Prot 33 g; Carbo 4 g; Fiber 0 g;
T Fat 17 g; 50% Calories from Fat; Chol 108 mg; Sod 166 mg.
Nutritional information does not include Chinese oyster sauce.

Make *Cucumber Sauce* to serve with salmon. Combine ¾ cup sour cream, ¼ teaspoon salt and ⅛ teaspoon paprika. Add 1 cucumber, peeled, seeded and chopped and 2 teaspoons chopped chives or dill.

San Francisco Salmon

6 1-inch salmon steaks
3 tablespoons grated fresh ginger
1 cup chopped cilantro
Juice and rind of 3 lemons
1 cup white wine

Arrange salmon in 7x12-inch baking dish. Sprinkle with ginger and cilantro; drizzle with lemon juice. Cut rind of lemons into strips. Add to baking dish. Pour wine over fish. Bake at 350 degrees for 10 minutes or until fish flakes easily. May substitute water for wine. Yield: 6 servings.

Approx Per Serving: Cal 252; Prot 25 g; Carbo 7 g; Fiber 1 g; T Fat 11 g; 38% Calories from Fat; Chol 79 mg; Sod 87 mg.

Cilantro is the fresh leaves of the coriander plant. It is also known as Chinese parsley, Kothamille in Mexico and Dhuma in India. Remove the stems and use the leaves only.

Stuffed Snapper

3/4 cup chopped celery   1/2 cup chopped onion
1/4 cup oil   4 cups dry bread cubes
1/2 cup sour cream   1/4 cup chopped peeled lime
3 tablespoons grated lime rind
1 teaspoon each paprika and salt
1 3 to 4-pound whole snapper
Salt to taste   2 tablespoons oil

Sauté celery and onion in 1/4 cup oil in skillet; remove from heat. Stir in bread cubes, sour cream, lime, lime rind, paprika and 1 teaspoon salt. Rinse fish inside and out. Pat dry and sprinkle with salt to taste. Stuff with bread cube mixture; secure with wooden picks. Place in greased baking dish. Bake at 350 degrees for 40 to 60 minutes or until fish flakes eaily, brushing with 2 tablespoons oil during baking time. Garnish with parsley and fresh lime. Yield: 6 servings.

Approx Per Serving: Cal 555; Prot 67 g; Carbo 18 g; Fiber 1 g; T Fat 23 g; 37% Calories from Fat; Chol 122 mg; Sod 783 mg.

Use fresh borage for a cucumber-like flavor in fish sauces.

Baked Sole Primavera

1 pound asparagus spears
Salt to taste
1 pound sole filets
1/2 teaspoon grated lemon rind
1/8 teaspoon pepper
3 tablespoons melted butter
2 tablespoons lemon juice
1 tablespoon finely chopped shallot
1 tablespoon chopped red bell pepper
1 teaspoon Dijon mustard

Cut asparagus into 2 to 3-inch lengths. Cook in lightly salted water in saucepan for 5 minutes; drain. Sprinkle skin side of fish with lemon rind, salt and pepper. Arrange asparagus spears at 1 end of fish filets; roll filets to enclose asparagus and secure with wooden picks. Arrange in buttered baking dish. Combine butter, lemon juice, shallot, bell pepper and mustard in bowl; mix well. Pour over fish. Bake at 400 degrees for 15 to 20 minutes or until fish flakes easily, basting twice. Yield: 4 servings.

Approx Per Serving: Cal 213; Prot 26 g; Carbo 5 g; Fiber 2 g; T Fat 11 g; 43% Calories from Fat; Chol 85 mg; Sod 203 mg.

 Keep the flavor of your mustard fresh by placing a thin slice of lemon under the lid of the jar.

Grilled Swordfish Steaks

1/4 cup butter
2 teaspoons Pick-A-Peppa sauce
1/2 teaspoon garlic sauce
1/2 teaspoon instant minced onion
1/2 teaspoon Worcestershire sauce
1/4 teaspoon hot pepper sauce
2 pounds swordfish steaks

Melt butter in small saucepan. Stir in Pick-A-Peppa sauce, garlic sauce, onion, Worcestershire sauce and hot pepper sauce. Brush over swordfish steaks; place on heated grill. Grill for 7 to 10 minutes on each side or until fish flakes easily, basting occasionally with remaining sauce. Yield: 6 servings.

Approx Per Serving: Cal 256; Prot 31 g; Carbo <1 g; Fiber <1 g; T Fat 14 g; 50% Calories from Fat; Chol 81 mg; Sod 216 mg.

The flesh of swordfish is firm and delicious but it can become dry during grilling without a butter-based basting sauce.

Luxurious Crab Cakes

5 tablespoons chopped parsley
2 tablespoons fresh dill   1 green onion
1 cup plus 1 tablespoon mayonnaise
3 tablespoons cracker crumbs
Grated rind of 1 lemon
3 tablespoons chopped green onions
1 teaspoon Dijon mustard
1 teaspoon Worcestershire sauce
1 teaspoon Old Bay seasoning
1½ pounds lump crab meat   2 eggs, slightly beaten
Juice of 1 lemon   1 cup fresh bread crumbs
½ cup melted butter   ¼ cup oil

Combine ¼ cup parsley, dill and 1 green onion in food processor container; process until smooth. Mix with ½ cup mayonnaise in serving bowl; chill until serving time. Combine cracker crumbs, remaining 9 tablespoons mayonnaise, lemon rind, 3 tablespoons green onions, remaining 1 tablespoon parsley, mustard, Worcestershire sauce and seasoning in bowl; mix well. Fold in crab meat gently. Chill in refrigerator. Beat eggs with lemon juice in small bowl. Shape crab meat mixture into patties. Dip into egg mixture; coat with bread crumbs. Fry in mixture of butter and oil in skillet for 3 to 5 minutes on each side. Serve with dill-mayonnaise mixture. This is best made with homemade mayonnaise. Yield: 6 servings.

Approx Per Serving: Cal 679; Prot 27 g; Carbo 8 g; Fiber 1 g; T Fat 61 g; 81% Calories from Fat; Chol 208 mg; Sod 808 mg.

Crab Cakes with Dill Sauce

10 tablespoons chopped fresh dill
2 tablespoons lemon juice
1 cup plus 2 tablespoons butter, softened
Salt and pepper to taste
1 cup fish stock
4 ounces scallops
1 cup heavy cream
1 pound lump crab meat
3 tablespoons chopped red or
green bell pepper

Process ½ cup dill and lemon juice in blender until finely chopped. Add 1 cup butter, salt and pepper; process until smooth. Cook fish stock in saucepan until reduced by ½. Whisk in dill butter until smooth; set aside. Purée scallops with salt and pepper in food processor or blender. Add cream; process until of consistency of mousse. Combine with crab meat, remaining 2 tablespoons dill and bell pepper in bowl; mix gently. Shape into cakes. Fry in remaining 2 tablespoons butter in skillet until brown on both sides. Place in baking dish. Bake at 400 degrees for 10 minutes. Serve with dill sauce. Yield: 6 servings.

Approx Per Serving: Cal 549; Prot 21 g; Carbo 3 g; Fiber <1 g; T Fat 51 g; 82% Calories from Fat; Chol 230 mg; Sod 678 mg.

Scalloped Oysters

3 pints oysters
1/4 cup vodka
1/2 cup heavy cream
2 cups stuffing mix, crushed
1/2 cup each chopped celery, onion and parsley
1 tablespoon Dijon mustard
1 tablespoon Worcestershire sauce
1/4 teaspoon each cayenne pepper, paprika
and Old Bay seasoning
1 teaspoon white pepper
1/2 cup melted butter
1/2 cup grated Parmesan cheese

Drain oysters in colander over bowl for 45 minutes. Pour vodka over oysters; drain for 15 minutes longer. Reserve 1/2 cup drained liquid. Combine reserved liquid with cream; set aside. Combine stuffing mix, celery, onion, parsley, mustard, Worcestershire sauce and seasonings in bowl; mix well. Grease 2-quart baking dish with a small amount of the melted butter. Add remaining butter to stuffing mixture; mix well. Alternate layers of stuffing mixture, oysters, Parmesan cheese and cream mixture in prepared dish until all ingredients are used, ending with stuffing mixture and cheese. Bake at 375 degrees for 30 minutes. Yield: 6 servings.

Approx Per Serving: Cal 632; Prot 35 g; Carbo 24 g; Fiber 16 g; T Fat 245 g; 90% Calories from Fat; Chol 1139 mg; Sod 1125 mg.

Broiled Scallops

2 pounds scallops
3/4 cup melted butter
2 large cloves of garlic, minced
3 tablespoons minced scallions
3 tablespoons finely chopped parsley
1/2 teaspoon salt
1/4 teaspoon freshly ground pepper

Rinse scallops and pat dry. Arrange in single layer in baking dish. Combine butter, garlic, scallions, parsley, salt and pepper in bowl; mix well. Pour over scallops. Marinate in refrigerator for 2 to 3 hours. Drain; place scallops in broiler pan. Broil for 3 to 4 minutes on each side or until cooked through. Yield: 4 servings.

Approx Per Serving: Cal 514; Prot 42 g; Carbo 6 g; Fiber <1 g; T Fat 36 g; 63% Calories from Fat; Chol 173 mg; Sod 916 mg.

Shellfish such as mussels, clams and oysters may be cooked in the microwave. Arrange them in a single layer around the edge of a shallow dish. Microwave on High until the shell opens.

Seviche

1 pound fresh pompano filets
3/4 cup plus 1/3 cup lime juice
1 large onion, chopped
1 4-ounce can chopped green chilies
1/2 cup tomato juice
1 large tomato, peeled, chopped
1 1/2 cloves of garlic, minced
1 tablespoon chopped parsley
1/2 teaspoon dried thyme or
2 chopped sprigs of fresh thyme
1 tablespoon finely chopped coriander leaves
1/2 teaspoon oregano
1 teaspoon pepper
1/3 cup olive oil

Slice pompano into 1/2 to 1 1/2-inch strips. Combine with 3/4 cup lime juice in glass dish. Marinate in refrigerator for several hours or until fish appears opaque. Rinse and drain fish. Combine onion, green chilies, remaining 1/3 cup lime juice, tomato juice, tomato, garlic, parsley, thyme, coriander, oregano and pepper in bowl; mix well. Add fish and olive oil; mix gently. Chill overnight. Serve with tortilla chips, party pumpernickel or pita bread; garnish with parsley and lime twists. May substitute scallops, flounder, haddock, red snapper or sierra for pompano; the important element is to use very fresh fish which has not been frozen. Yield: 4 servings.

Approx Per Serving: Cal 295; Prot 23 g; Carbo 14 g; Fiber 2 g; T Fat 29 g; 64% Calories from Fat; Chol 58 mg; Sod 385 mg. Nutritional information includes entire amount of marinade.

Shrimp and Vegetables

1 3/4 cups chicken broth
1 7-ounce package long grain and wild rice mix
2 tablespoons butter
1/4 to 1/2 teaspoon red pepper flakes
1 pound medium shrimp, peeled, deveined
1 15-ounce can artichoke hearts, drained, chopped
1 4-ounce can sliced mushrooms
1/4 cup sour cream
2 to 4 tablespoons chopped parsley

Combine chicken broth, rice and seasoning packet, butter and red pepper flakes in 10-inch skillet. Bring to a boil; add shrimp. Simmer, covered, for 5 minutes or until liquid has evaporated. Add artichokes and mushrooms. Cook until heated through. Let stand, covered, for 5 minutes. Stir in sour cream; sprinkle with parsley. Serve with lemon wedges. Yield: 4 servings.

Approx Per Serving: Cal 403; Prot 26 g; Carbo 48 g; Fiber 1 g; T Fat 11 g; 26% Calories from Fat; Chol 178 mg; Sod 964 mg.

When selecting clams, mussels and oysters be sure the shells are tightly closed. Be sure to not overcook them as they will toughen. They are cooked when the shells open.

Scampi in Ten Minutes

1 cup olive oil
1/2 cup melted butter
6 tablespoons bread crumbs
2 tablespoons lemon juice
2 tablespoons minced garlic
1 teaspoon oregano
Salt and pepper to taste
2 pounds peeled shrimp

Combine olive oil, butter, bread crumbs, lemon juice, garlic, oregano, salt and pepper in bowl; mix well. Add shrimp. Marinate in refrigerator for 1 hour or longer. Drain shrimp and arrange in single layer in broiler pan. Broil for 5 to 6 minutes or until cooked through. Serve over rice. Yield: 8 servings.

Approx Per Serving: Cal 455; Prot 20 g; Carbo 5 g; Fiber <1 g; T Fat 40 g; 78% Calories from Fat; Chol 208 mg; Sod 335 mg. Nutritional information includes entire amount of marinade.

Make **Dilled Scallops** by poaching in 1/2 cup dry white wine, 2 tablespoons lemon juice and 2 tablespoons chopped fresh dill. Cook, covered, for 5 to 8 minutes.

Shrimp and Sausage Paella

1 1/2 pounds smoked sausage
1 1/2 cups chopped onion
2 cloves of garlic, chopped
6 tablespoons butter
1 1/2 pounds peeled shrimp
3 cups chicken stock
1/2 teaspoon cayenne pepper
1/2 teaspoon salt
8 ounces uncooked rice
3 saffron stamens
1 avocado, peeled, chopped
2 tomatoes, peeled, chopped

Brown sausage with onion and garlic in butter in large skillet. Add shrimp, chicken stock, cayenne pepper and salt. Stir in rice and saffron. Bring to a boil, stirring occasionally. Simmer, covered, for 20 minutes. Simmer, uncovered, until all liquid is absorbed. Fold in avocado and tomatoes. Yield: 8 servings.

Approx Per Serving: Cal 473; Prot 28 g; Carbo 30 g; Fiber 4 g; T Fat 27 g; 51% Calories from Fat; Chol 183 mg; Sod 1252 mg.

Paella is one of the Spanish national dishes and typically includes chicken, seafood, sausage, rice and saffron.

Shrimp Delight

3 tablespoons butter   1/4 cup rosé
2 tablespoons lemon juice
1 tablespoon sugar   1 1/2 tablespoons cornstarch
1 tablespoon chopped chives
1 pound medium shrimp, peeled

Place butter in 7x11-inch glass dish. Microwave on Medium until melted. Add wine, lemon juice, sugar, cornstarch and chives; mix well. Add shrimp; toss to coat well. Microwave, covered with waxed paper, on High for 4 minutes. Let stand, covered, for 2 minutes. Mix well before serving. Yield: 4 servings.

Approx Per Serving: Cal 191; Prot 17 g; Carbo 7 g; Fiber <1 g; T Fat 10 g; 48% Calories from Fat; Chol 179 mg; Sod 253 mg.

In buying shrimp, 2 to 2 1/2 pounds of shrimp in the shell gives about 1 pound of cooked peeled shrimp or about 2 cups.

Grilled Scampi

1/2 cup butter
1/2 cup olive oil
1 tablespoon lemon juice
1/4 cup finely chopped scallions
1 tablespoon finely chopped garlic
1 teaspoon salt
Freshly ground pepper to taste
24 large shrimp, peeled, deveined
1/4 cup chopped parsley

Melt butter in skillet. Stir in olive oil, lemon juice, scallions and garlic. Cook for 2 minutes, stirring occasionally. Season with salt and pepper. Pour over shrimp in 9x13-inch baking dish, stirring to coat well. Broil 3 to 4 inches from heat source for 10 minutes, turning after 5 minutes. Remove shrimp to serving plates; spoon sauce over top. Sprinkle with parsley. Garnish with lemon quarters. Yield: 6 servings.

Approx Per Serving: Cal 389; Prot 19 g; Carbo 1 g; Fiber <1 g; T Fat 34 g; 79% Calories from Fat; Chol 215 mg; Sod 685 mg.

In center of table place a round or long narrow mirror. Place various sizes and shapes of bottles on mirror. Fill with individual stems of flowers, such as roses, daffodils, tulips, or whatever is available.

Shrimp New Orleans

1/2 cup chopped onion
1/2 cup chopped green bell pepper
2 tablespoons margarine
2 10-ounce cans tomato soup
1 15-ounce can tomatoes
1 8-ounce can whole kernel corn
1/4 teaspoon nutmeg
1 teaspoon lemon pepper
Salt to taste
1/3 cup cooking sherry
1 1/2 pounds peeled shrimp, cooked
2 cups rice, cooked
1/3 cup slivered almonds

Sauté onion and green pepper lightly in margarine in skillet. Stir in soup, tomatoes, corn, nutmeg, lemon pepper and salt. Simmer for 20 minutes, adding water if necessary for desired consistency. Add wine and shrimp. Cook just until heated through. Spoon servings over rice; sprinkle with almonds. May substitute chicken for some or all of the shrimp or wild rice for part of the rice.
Yield: 6 servings.

Approx Per Serving: Cal 516; Prot 28 g; Carbo 74 g; Fiber 3 g; T Fat 11 g; 19% Calories from Fat; Chol 177 mg; Sod 1256 mg.

Seafood Melt

1 7-ounce can shrimp
1 7-ounce can crab meat
1 large stalk celery, finely chopped
2 or 3 scallions with 2 inches green stems, sliced
1 cup shredded Swiss cheese
3/4 cup (about) mayonnaise
1 teaspoon Worcestershire sauce
1/2 cup sliced mushrooms
Hot sauce to taste
Pepper to taste
4 English muffins, split, toasted

Combine shrimp, crab meat, celery, scallions, cheese, mayonnaise, Worcestershire sauce, mushrooms, hot sauce and pepper in bowl; mix well. Spread on muffin halves; place on baking sheet. Bake at 350 degrees until bubbly. May substitute ham for seafood. Yield: 4 servings.

Approx Per Serving: Cal 649; Prot 33 g; Carbo 30 g; Fiber 2 g; T Fat 43 g; 60% Calories from Fat; Chol 167 mg; Sod 2014 mg.

If sautéed slowly, onions become mild and sweet. A quick sauté over high heat produces a more robust onion flavor.

Party Seafood Casserole

1 pound sea scallops   1 cup dry white wine
1 small onion, chopped
1 tablespoon chopped parsley
2 teaspoons lemon juice   1/2 teaspoon salt
6 tablespoons flour
5 tablespoons melted butter   1 cup light cream
1/2 cup shredded sharp Cheddar cheese
1   6-ounce can crab meat, drained
6 ounces cooked peeled shrimp
1   4-ounce can mushrooms, drained
1 1/2 cups soft bread crumbs

Combine scallops, wine, onion, parsley, lemon juice and salt in saucepan. Simmer for 5 minutes. Drain, reserving 1 1/2 cups liquid. Blend flour into 4 tablespoons melted butter in saucepan. Cook for several minutes. Stir in cream and reserved liquid. Cook until thickened, stirring constantly. Stir in cheese until melted. Add crab meat, scallops mixture, shrimp and mushrooms; mix gently. Spoon into baking dish. Sauté bread crumbs in remaining 1 tablespoon butter in skillet. Sprinkle over casserole. Bake at 350 degrees for 25 to 30 minutes or until heated through. Serve over rice or noodles. Yield: 6 servings.

Approx Per Serving: Cal 396; Prot 32 g; Carbo 18 g; Fiber 1 g; T Fat 19 g; 47% Calories from Fat; Chol 158 mg; Sod 751 mg.

Seafood Casserole

1/2 cup chopped green bell pepper
1/2 cup chopped onion
1/2 cup butter
1/2 cup sifted flour
1 cup milk
1 teaspoon dry mustard
1/2 teaspoon MSG
1 cup shredded Cheddar cheese
1   28-ounce can tomatoes, drained
2 teaspoons Worcestershire sauce
2 teaspoons salt
1 pound cooked peeled shrimp

Sauté green pepper and onion in butter in heavy saucepan until tender. Blend flour, milk, dry mustard and MSG in double boiler. Cook until thickened, stirring constantly. Stir in cheese until melted. Combine with tomatoes, Worcestershire sauce, salt, sautéed vegetables and shrimp in bowl; mix well. Spoon into baking dish. Bake at 350 degrees for 30 minutes. Serve with rice. May substitute crab meat for shrimp. Yield: 6 servings.

Approx Per Serving: Cal 380; Prot 25 g; Carbo 17 g; Fiber 2 g; T Fat 24 g; 57% Calories from Fat; Chol 214 mg; Sod 1732 mg.

The City Gardens Contest

The City Gardens Contest is more than the name suggests. City gardeners can enter with just about anything that grows, whether it's in a painted tire outside the front door, in a hanging basket or in the ground.

Sometimes neighbors on a city block enter their newly planted street trees. One gardener submitted the 'front of his house' to the contest, impressing the judges with a rowhouse covered with flowers and greenery cascading from extra large homemade window boxes.

Every year a new version of the same story pops up: it's about neighbors who didn't know each other, how they come together with the help of the Pennsylvania Horticultural Society, create a community vegetable garden or sitting park, enter the City Gardens contest and finally become friends and proud partners in their prize winning venture.

Throughout July and August, hundreds of volunteer judges visit the contestants, marveling at the ingenuity of city gardeners. Creative solutions abound, such as the gardener who glued reflective foil to the side of his house to bring more light to the tomatoes he planted in a dark, tight space surrounded by tall buildings.

The City Gardens Contest Awards ceremony in October, complete with prize money and gift certificates, is just one of the many events hosted by the Pennsylvania Horticultural Society to honor the city's gardeners. Other activities include dedication ceremonies and celebrations for newly acclaimed Greene Countrie Townes and a Gardeners' Gala Brunch at the Philadelphia Flower Show.

What was once vacant houses, then a vacant lot, became the pride of the block when neighbors joined with The Pennsylvania Horticultural Society to create an outstanding vegetable garden. – Photography by Ira Beckoff

City Gardens Neighborhood Dinner

Have several neighbors make the same recipe and each family bring a candle in a holder so that every person feels part of the action.

Cheesy Green Chili Tart *(page 14)*

Armenian Cucumber Soup *(page 42)*   or   Icy Cold Gazpacho *(page 44)*

Lemon-Pepper Pasta *(page 192)*   Grilled Marinated Flank Steak *(page 80)*

Mesclun Salad with Fresh Herbs *(page 64)*
or
Chicory Salad *(page 58)*

Strawberry-Basil Parfait *(page 216)*

Dried flower topiary (page 129)

Vegetables

129

Phony Artichoke Hearts

12 ounces fresh Brussels sprouts
¹/₃ cup Italian salad dressing

Cook Brussels sprouts in a small amount of water until tender; drain. Slice each into halves. Place in shallow bowl with salad dressing, tossing to coat. Marinate, covered, overnight. Serve cut side up. Yield: 4 servings.

Approx Per Serving: Cal 128; Prot 3 g; Carbo 10 g; Fiber 4 g; T Fat 12 g; 68% Calories from Fat; Chol 0 mg; Sod 117 mg.

Brussels Sprouts with Chestnuts

10 ounces Brussels sprouts
¹/₄ cup milk   Salt to taste
4 ounces chestnuts
2 tablespoons melted butter
Pepper to taste

Trim and core Brussels sprouts; cut into halves. Combine with milk, salt to taste and water to cover in saucepan. Cook until tender; drain. Cook chestnuts in water in saucepan until tender; drain. Break chestnuts into small pieces. Stir into butter in saucepan. Add Brussels sprouts. Cook until heated through. Season with salt and pepper to taste. Yield: 2 servings.

Approx Per Serving: Cal 242; Prot 7 g; Carbo 28 g; Fiber 8 g; T Fat 13 g; 46% Calories from Fat; Chol 35 mg; Sod 153 mg.

Green Beans and Sunchokes

1 10-ounce package frozen green beans, thawed, cut up
8 ounces large sunchokes from garden
Juice of 1 lemon
¹/₄ cup butter
1 tablespoon peanut oil
Salt to taste

Steam green beans in steamer for 6 minutes; rinse under cold water. Drain and chill. Scrub choke knobs thoroughly. Scrape bumps off knobs; slice off stems and top ends. Slice each knob into 4 thin slivers. Soak in mixture of lemon juice and water to cover in small bowl for several minutes; drain. Combine with green beans. Heat butter and oil in wok over high heat. Add beans, chokes and salt. Stir-fry for 2 minutes. Serve in warmed bowl. Yield: 6 servings.

Approx Per Serving: Cal 131; Prot 2 g; Carbo 10 g; Fiber 2 g; T Fat 10 g; 66% Calories from Fat; Chol 21 mg; Sod 72 mg.

How about a dried flower topiary? Fill flowerpot with plaster of Paris. Before the plaster of Paris is hard, insert a birch or beech 'stem.' Using floral foam or styrofoam ball, insert dried flowers until the surface is covered, then carefully place the decorated topiary ball onto the top of the stem. Tie wired ribbon at the base of the ball. Hydrangea flowers inserted in the ball make a great "head" and last forever!

Roasted Green Beans

2 small red onions, sliced
1 pound green beans, trimmed
4 cloves of garlic, sliced
3 tablespoons extra-virgin olive oil
Salt and pepper to taste
3 tablespoons Balsamic vinegar

Toss onions, green beans and garlic with olive oil, salt and pepper in bowl. Spoon into baking pan. Bake at 350 degrees for 30 minutes, stirring every 10 minutes. Sprinkle with vinegar, stirring to mix. Serve hot or chilled, garnished with crumbled feta cheese. Yield: 4 servings.

Approx Per Serving: Cal 151; Prot 3 g; Carbo 14 g; Fiber 4 g; T Fat 10 g; 58% Calories from Fat; Chol 0 mg; Sod 8 mg.

For better tasting green vegetables, add 1/2 teaspoon baking soda per gallon to reduce acidity and improve color. Use lots of water in a rolling boil. When vegetables are *al dente* (crisp/tender), remove and immerse in very cold water to stop the cooking process. Once chilled, toss with olive oil. Reheat the vegetables just prior to serving, tossing frequently over moderate heat. Season to taste and serve.

Beets in Orange Sauce

1/2 cup sugar   11/2 tablespoons cornstarch
11/4 teaspoons salt
1/4 teaspoon ground ginger
1/8 teaspoon pepper   1/3 cup vinegar
2/3 cup orange juice
2 tablespoons lemon juice
2 tablespoons butter   12 beets, sliced, cooked

Combine sugar, cornstarch, 1/2 teaspoon salt, ginger, pepper and vinegar in saucepan. Cook over medium heat until thickened, stirring constantly. Add orange juice, lemon juice and butter; mix well. Stir in beets and remaining 3/4 teaspoon salt. Cook over low heat until heated through. Yield: 6 servings.

Approx Per Serving: Cal 151; Prot 1 g; Carbo 29 g; Fiber 2 g; T Fat 4 g; 23% Calories from Fat; Chol 10 mg; Sod 526 mg.

For a quick and easy flavor boost, add herbs, spices, wine or chicken stock to the water of steamed vegetables.

Oven-Cooked Beets

8 medium beets
1/2 cup cranberry juice
1 tablespoon fresh lemon juice
1/2 teaspoon grated lemon zest
2 tablespoons sugar
2 tablespoons flour
1/4 teaspoon salt
2 tablespoons butter

Peel beets and cut into thin slices; place in baking dish. Combine cranberry juice, lemon juice, lemon zest, sugar, flour and salt in bowl; mix until smooth. Pour over beets; dot with butter. Bake, covered, at 350 degrees for 1 hour or until tender. May substitute orange juice for cranberry juice. Yield: 6 servings.

Approx Per Serving: Cal 93; Prot 1 g; Carbo 14 g; Fiber 1 g; T Fat 3 g; 37% Calories from Fat; Chol 10 mg; Sod 154 mg.

When boiling whole beets, leave a portion of the stem intact until beets are cooked to prevent bleaching of color.

Carrot Ring

1 cup butter, softened
1/2 cup sugar
1 egg
1 1/4 cups sifted flour
1 teaspoon baking powder
1 teaspoon baking soda
1 cup grated carrots
2 teaspoons lemon juice

Cream butter and sugar in mixer bowl. Beat in egg. Sift flour, baking powder and baking soda together. Add to creamed mixture, mixing well. Stir in carrots and lemon juice. Spoon into buttered ring mold. Bake at 350 degrees for 45 minutes. Yield: 4 servings.

Approx Per Serving: Cal 667; Prot 6 g; Carbo 56 g; Fiber 2 g; T Fat 48 g; 64% Calories from Fat; Chol 177 mg; Sod 703 mg.

For dramatically improved color and flavor in cooked carrots do not cut, peel and boil as usual. Instead, boil carrots whole and rinse under cold water and scrape off the skin using the back of a knife. Slice and add sweet butter, white pepper and a dash of sugar.

Winter Carrot Casserole

1½ pounds carrots, thinly sliced
½ cup mayonnaise
2 tablespoons chopped onion
2 tablespoons prepared horseradish
¼ teaspoon salt
Pepper to taste
8 crackers, crushed
2 teaspoons melted butter

Cook carrots in boiling water for 10 minutes; drain. Place in 1-quart baking dish. Combine mayonnaise, onion, horseradish, salt and pepper in small bowl. Spoon over carrots. Top with mixture of cracker crumbs and melted butter. Bake at 350 degrees for 30 minutes.
Yield: 6 servings.

Approx Per Serving: Cal 211; Prot 2 g; Carbo 16 g; Fiber 4 g; T Fat 17 g; 68% Calories from Fat; Chol 16 mg; Sod 300 mg.

 Add a sprig of fresh rosemary the next time you make cooked carrots. Mint-flavored carrots are especially good when served with lamb.

Pine Nutty Cauliflower

2 tablespoons raisins
1 small head cauliflower, leaves and stalk removed
4 quarts water
2 teaspoons minced garlic
¼ cup extra-virgin olive oil
2 tablespoons pine nuts
¼ teaspoon salt
⅛ teaspoon freshly ground pepper
2 tablespoons chopped fresh parsley

Soak raisins in water to cover for 15 minutes; drain and set aside. Cook cauliflower in 4 quarts boiling water for 6 to 7 minutes or until tender-crisp; drain. Break into flowerets. Sauté garlic in oil in large skillet until tender. Add raisins, cauliflowerets, pine nuts, salt and pepper. Cook, covered, over low heat for 8 to 10 minutes or until cauliflowerets are tender, stirring occasionally. Sprinkle with parsley. Yield: 6 servings.

Approx Per Serving: Cal 121; Prot 2 g; Carbo 6 g; Fiber 2 g; T Fat 11 g; 76% Calories from Fat; Chol 0 mg; Sod 99 mg.

Add 1 tablespoon vinegar to water when cooking cauliflower to help it retain its white color.

Creamed Cauliflower

1 cup water
1/2 teaspoon salt
Flowerets of 1 head cauliflower
2 tablespoons oil
2 tablespoons flour
1/2 teaspoon ground nutmeg
Pepper to taste
1 cup chicken broth
1 egg yolk, beaten
2 tablespoons chopped parsley
Paprika to taste

Bring water and salt to a boil in large saucepan; add cauliflower. Cook, covered, over medium heat for 20 minutes or until tender; drain. Combine oil, flour, nutmeg and pepper in small heavy saucepan. Cook over low heat until bubbly, stirring constantly; remove from heat. Stir in chicken broth. Bring to a boil, stirring constantly. Stir a small amount of the hot sauce into egg yolk. Add egg yolk to sauce, stirring constantly. Stir in parsley. Pour sauce over cauliflower in serving bowl; sprinkle with paprika. Yield: 6 servings.

Approx Per Serving: Cal 83; Prot 3 g; Carbo 6 g; Fiber 2 g; T Fat 6 g; 61% Calories from Fat; Chol 36 mg; Sod 363 mg.

Celery-Almond Casserole

4 cups 1-inch celery slices
1 10-ounce can cream of chicken soup
1/4 cup chopped pimento
1 8-ounce can sliced water chestnuts, drained
1/2 cup bread cubes
2 teaspoons melted butter
1/3 cup slivered almonds

Cook celery in boiling water in saucepan for 8 minutes; drain. Stir in soup, pimento and water chestnuts. Spoon into 1-quart baking dish. Sprinkle with mixture of bread cubes and butter. Top with almonds. Bake at 350 degrees for 35 minutes or until bubbly. Yield: 8 servings.

Approx Per Serving: Cal 107; Prot 3 g; Carbo 11 g; Fiber 3 g; T Fat 6 g; 49% Calories from Fat; Chol 5 mg; Sod 368 mg.

Make *Easy Corn Fritters* by mixing 1 undrained can corn, 2 beaten eggs, 1 cup flour, 1/4 cup sugar and 1 teaspoon salt and add enough milk to make of desired consistency. Brown on both sides on oiled skillet.

Corn Soufflé Fritters

4 ears of corn   2 eggs yolks, beaten
1/4 teaspoon salt   1/2 teaspoon sugar
Pepper to taste   2 egg whites, stiffly beaten

Cut down center of each row of kernels with sharp knife; scrape ears to extract juice and pulp. Mix with egg yolks, salt, sugar and pepper in bowl. Fold in egg whites. Drop by tablespoonfuls onto hot skillet as for pancakes. Cook until light brown and puffed, turning once. Yield: 4 servings.

Approx Per Serving: Cal 122; Prot 6 g; Carbo 20 g; Fiber 3 g; T Fat 4 g; 25% Calories from Fat; Chol 106 mg; Sod 175 mg.

Corn Puddin'

2   16-ounce cans cream-style corn   4 eggs, beaten
1 1/2 teaspoons nutmeg
1   4-ounce can evaporated milk   3/4 to 1 cup sugar
1 1/2 teaspoons vanilla extract
1 1/2 tablespoons cornstarch   1/4 cup warm milk

Combine first 6 ingredients in bowl; mix well. Dissolve cornstarch in warm milk in small bowl. Add to corn mixture, stirring well. Pour into 9x13-inch baking pan. Bake for 1 1/4 hours or until firm and edges are golden brown. Serve hot or cold. Yield: 10 servings.

Approx Per Serving: Cal 198; Prot 5 g; Carbo 39 g; Fiber 2 g; T Fat 4 g; 16% Calories from Fat; Chol 89 mg; Sod 301 mg.

Mexican Eggplant Casserole

1 large eggplant
1/4 cup oil
1   15-ounce can tomato sauce
2   4-ounce cans chopped green chilies, drained
1/2 cup thinly sliced green onions
1   2-ounce can sliced black olives, drained
1/2 teaspoon ground cumin
1/4 teaspoon garlic powder
1 1/2 cups shredded Cheddar cheese
1/2 cup sour cream

Cut unpeeled eggplant into 1/2-inch slices; brush with oil. Place on baking sheet. Bake at 450 degrees for 15 minutes or until tender; set aside. Combine tomato sauce, green chilies, green onions, olives, cumin and garlic powder in bowl; mix well. Layer eggplant, sauce and cheese 1/2 at a time in 2-quart baking dish. Bake at 350 degrees for 20 to 25 minutes or until cheese is melted. Serve with sour cream. Yield: 6 servings.

Approx Per Serving: Cal 298; Prot 10 g; Carbo 13 g; Fiber 3 g; T Fat 25 g; 71% Calories from Fat; Chol 38 mg; Sod 956 mg.

Male eggplants have fewer seeds and are less likely to be bitter. To differentiate between male and female eggplant, inspect the flower end. The male has a small round and smooth end, the female is irregular and less smooth.

Eggplant for Dinner

1 medium eggplant, peeled, sliced 1/2 inch thick
2 to 3 onions, sliced
2 to 3 tomatoes, peeled, sliced 1/2 inch thick
1/2 teaspoon basil
1/2 teaspoon each salt and pepper
8 ounces mozzarella cheese, sliced
2 tablespoons grated Parmesan cheese
3/4 cup bread crumbs
1/4 cup melted butter

Layer eggplant, onions and tomatoes in greased 9x13-inch baking dish. Sprinkle with basil, salt and pepper. Bake, covered, at 450 degrees for 20 minutes. Cover with mozzarella cheese and mixture of Parmesan cheese and bread crumbs. Drizzle with butter. Bake for 10 minutes longer or until cheese is melted and browned. Yield: 8 servings.

Approx Per Serving: Cal 213; Prot 9 g; Carbo 17 g; Fiber 3 g; T Fat 13 g; 53% Calories from Fat; Chol 39 mg; Sod 387 mg.

To avoid a watery eggplant casserole, remove excess moisture by salting eggplant slices and draining them on a rack prior to using. Rub slices with lemon juice to prevent discoloration.

Poireaux au Gratin

3 pounds small leeks, trimmed
2 tablespoons butter
Salt and freshly ground pepper to taste
1/8 teaspoon freshly grated nutmeg
1 cup heavy cream
1/2 cup freshly grated Parmesan cheese

Slice off green part of leeks, leaving a 7-inch stem. Slice lengthwise; cut into 1 1/2-inch lengths. Rinse in cold water; drain. Place in heavy skillet with butter, salt, pepper and nutmeg. Cook over medium heat for 1 minute, stirring frequently. Add cream. Simmer, covered, for 15 minutes. Spoon into baking dish. Top with Parmesan cheese. Broil until golden brown. Serve hot. Yield: 6 servings.

Approx Per Serving: Cal 340; Prot 7 g; Carbo 33 g; Fiber 5 g; T Fat 21 g; 54% Calories from Fat; Chol 70 mg; Sod 219 mg.

Poireaux is the name for leeks in France where they are so plentiful that they are known as the asparagus of the poor. They can be cooked in the same manner as asparagus.

Braised Lentils

6 slices bacon, chopped
1/2 onion, chopped
1 carrot, chopped
1 1/4 cups dried lentils
3 cups chicken stock
1 bay leaf
2 tablespoons butter
2 tablespoons white wine vinegar
Salt and pepper to taste

Fry bacon in large saucepan until crisp; drain, reserving 2 tablespoons pan drippings. Sauté onion and carrot in pan drippings until tender-crisp. Add lentils, chicken stock, bay leaf, butter and vinegar; mix well. Simmer, covered, for 1 hour. Remove bay leaf. Season to taste; sprinkle with bacon. Yield: 4 servings.

Approx Per Serving: Cal 416; Prot 24 g; Carbo 39 g; Fiber 8 g; T Fat 19 g; 41% Calories from Fat; Chol 66 mg; Sod 865 mg.

If you are fortunate enough to come into possession of a fresh truffle, savor its flavor even before it's cooked by nestling it in a bowl of fresh eggs for a few days. The flavor will be absorbed into the eggs. Scramble the eggs for a real taste treat.

Deep-Fried Day Lilies

1 1/2 cups day lily roots
Salt to taste
2 cups flour
1 tablespoon garlic powder
2 eggs, beaten
2 cups Italian-seasoned bread crumbs
Oil for deep frying

Clean day lily roots thoroughly; soak for 10 minutes in salted water to cover in bowl. Drain and rinse. Parboil, covered, in water to cover in saucepan for 5 minutes; drain. Trim into 3/4-inch pieces. Coat with mixture of flour and garlic powder. Dip in beaten eggs; roll in bread crumbs. Deep-fry in hot oil until golden brown; drain. Yield: 3 servings.

Approx Per Serving: Cal 616; Prot 21 g; Carbo 112 g; Fiber 5 g; T Fat 8 g; 12% Calories from Fat; Chol 145 mg; Sod 538 mg. Nutritional information does not include day lily roots or oil for deep frying.

To remove garden soil from beneath your fingernails, soak your hands in a fizzy denture-cleaning tablet which has been dissolved. This also softens cuticles.

Marinated Mushrooms

2 to 3 quarts water
2 tablespoons vinegar
1 pound fresh mushrooms
1 onion, finely chopped
1/2 cup butter
1 teaspoon each dried sweet basil and crushed oregano
1/2 teaspoon each crushed thyme, garlic salt and salt
1/2 teaspoon hot pepper sauce
2 teaspoons fresh lime juice
1/2 cup dry sherry

Bring water to a boil in stainless steel saucepan. Add vinegar and mushrooms. Boil for 10 minutes; drain. Sauté onion in butter in large skillet until tender. Add mushrooms, stirring to coat. Stir in basil, oregano, thyme, garlic salt, salt, pepper sauce, lime juice and sherry. Simmer, covered, over low heat for 1 to 1 1/2 hours or until liquid has evaporated. Place mixture in covered container; chill overnight. Serve hot or at room temperature. Yield: 4 servings.

Approx Per Serving: Cal 289; Prot 3 g; Carbo 9 g; Fiber 3 g; T Fat 24 g; 75% Calories from Fat; Chol 64 mg; Sod 753 mg.

Cruciferous vegetables are members of the botanical mustard family, the Cruciferae. Included are mustard greens, horseradish, cabbage, turnips, watercress, radishes and broccoli. Flowers of these plants are cross-shaped, hence the name.

Mushroom Casserole

2 chicken bouillon cubes
1/4 cup water
2 tablespoons flour
1/2 cup heavy cream
1/2 cup herb-seasoned stuffing mix
1/2 cup melted butter
Grated Parmesan cheese to taste
1 pound fresh mushrooms, sliced

Dissolve bouillon cubes in boiling water in saucepan. Stir in flour and cream. Toss stuffing mix with melted butter; add to bouillon mixture. Stir in Parmesan cheese; remove from heat. Arrange mushrooms in small baking dish. Cover with stuffing mixture. Bake, covered, at 350 degrees for 30 minutes. May top with additional cheese and bake until melted. Yield: 6 servings.

Approx Per Serving: Cal 257; Prot 3 g; Carbo 11 g; Fiber 2 g; T Fat 23 g; 79% Calories from Fat; Chol 69 mg; Sod 601 mg.

A good way to prepare fresh mushrooms is to cook them in a double boiler over low heat with butter, salt, pepper and your choice of herbs for 30 minutes. Serve on toast.

Mushrooms in Oyster Sauce

22 shiitake mushrooms   1¹/2 cups chicken broth
1 tablespoon chicken fat   1 tablespoon cornstarch
2 tablespoons oyster sauce

Soak mushrooms in warm water for 30 minutes. Remove stems; drain well. Combine with broth and chicken fat in saucepan. Simmer, covered, for 30 minutes or longer. Dissolve cornstarch in a small amount of water and oyster sauce in bowl. Stir into mushroom mixture. Simmer for 3 minutes longer, stirring frequently. Yield: 4 servings.

Approx Per Serving: Cal 121; Prot 4 g; Carbo 20 g; Fiber 7 g; T Fat 4 g; 27% Calories from Fat; Chol 3 mg; Sod 318 mg.

Parsnips and Carrots Glacé

1¹/4 cups chicken broth   1/4 cup butter
3 tablespoons sugar   4 cups sliced carrots
4 cups sliced parsnips   Salt and nutmeg to taste

Combine broth, butter and sugar in saucepan. Bring to a boil. Add carrots. Cook over medium heat for 1 minute. Add parsnips. Cook, covered, for 4 to 5 minutes or until tender. Strain vegetables, reserving liquid. Boil liquid until reduced to 1/3 cup. Pour over vegetables in serving bowl. Season with salt and nutmeg. Yield: 8 servings.

Approx Per Serving: Cal 140; Prot 2 g; Carbo 20 g; Fiber 4 g; T Fat 6 g; 38% Calories from Fat; Chol 16 mg; Sod 189 mg.

Minted Peas in Cream

3 tablespoons melted butter   1¹/2 teaspoons sugar
1/4 teaspoon salt   1/8 teaspoon pepper
2 cups cooked peas   1 teaspoon flour
1/2 teaspoon dried mint   1/2 cup heavy cream

Combine butter, sugar, salt and pepper in saucepan; mix well. Stir in peas. Cook until heated through. Stir in flour; add mint and cream. Bring to a boil. Cook until sauce is thickened, stirring constantly. Garnish with fresh mint; serve immediately. Yield: 4 servings.

Approx Per Serving: Cal 254; Prot 5 g; Carbo 15 g; Fiber 4 g; T Fat 20 g; 69% Calories from Fat; Chol 64 mg; Sod 219 mg.

Roasted Red Peppers

10 to 12 red bell peppers   1/2 teaspoon garlic powder
1/3 cup fresh lemon juice   1/2 cup olive oil
1 teaspoon salt

Slice bell peppers lengthwise into 3 sections. Place skin side up on baking sheet lined with foil. Broil 3 inches from heat source until skin is evenly blackened. Place in covered pan to cool. Remove skins. Combine with remaining ingredients in bowl, tossing to coat. Marinate in refrigerator for 24 hours. Serve at room temperature. Yield: 6 servings.

Approx Per Serving: Cal 198; Prot 1 g; Carbo 9 g; Fiber 2 g; T Fat 19 g; 80% Calories from Fat; Chol 0 mg; Sod 359 mg.

Mashed Potato Casserole

5 pounds potatoes, peeled, chopped
8 ounces cream cheese, softened
1 cup half and half
3/4 cup butter
1 teaspoon each onion salt and salt
1/4 teaspoon white pepper
Paprika to taste

Cook potatoes in water to cover in saucepan until tender; drain. Beat cream cheese and half and half in mixer bowl until smooth. Add potatoes. Beat until smooth. Stir in 1/2 cup butter, onion salt, salt and pepper. Spoon into greased 2-quart baking dish. Brush top with remaining 1/4 cup melted butter; sprinkle with paprika. Bake at 350 degrees for 30 minutes. Yield: 12 servings.

Approx Per Serving: Cal 357; Prot 5 g; Carbo 39 g; Fiber 3 g; T Fat 21 g; 51% Calories from Fat; Chol 59 mg; Sod 481 mg.

Make *Parsnips with Bacon* by sautéing 1 chopped onion in 1 tablespoon olive oil. Add 2 pounds chopped parsnips and 1/2 cup water. Steam for 15 minutes or until parsnips are tender. Serve with crumbled crisp-fried bacon.

Buffet Potato Casserole

1 32-ounce package frozen hashed brown potatoes
1/2 cup melted butter
2 cups sour cream
1 10-ounce can cream of chicken soup
1/2 cup chopped onion
2 cups shredded Cheddar cheese
1 teaspoon salt
1/2 teaspoon pepper
2 cups cornflake crumbs
1/2 cup melted butter

Combine potatoes and 1/2 cup butter in large bowl. Stir in sour cream, soup, onion, cheese, salt and pepper. Spoon into greased 9x13-inch baking dish. Sprinkle with mixture of cornflake crumbs and remaining 1/2 cup butter. Bake, covered with foil, at 350 degrees for 20 minutes. Bake, uncovered, for 20 minutes longer. Yield: 12 servings.

Approx Per Serving: Cal 420; Prot 10 g; Carbo 36 g; Fiber 2 g; T Fat 34 g; 73% Calories from Fat; Chol 64 mg; Sod 771 mg.

Potatoes and onions should not be stored together. The high moisture content in potatoes causes the onions to sprout prematurely.

Special Potato Pancakes

3 large potatoes, chopped
1 large carrot, sliced
1 small onion, sliced
2 eggs, beaten
2 tablespoons cracker meal
1 teaspoon salt
1/4 cup chopped fresh parsley
Peanut oil for browning

Combine half the potatoes, carrot, onion, eggs, cracker meal and salt in food processor container. Process with steel blade until crumbly but not smooth. Add remaining potatoes and parsley. Process until crumbly. Drop by tablespoonfuls into hot oil in skillet. Brown on both sides; drain. Serve with applesauce. Yield: 12 (1-pancake) servings.

Approx Per Serving: Cal 60; Prot 2 g; Carbo 11 g; Fiber 1 g; T Fat 1 g; 15% Calories from Fat; Chol 36 mg; Sod 194 mg. Nutritional information does not include oil for browning.

Remove a thin strip of peel from around the centers of new potatoes. This prevents the skin from bursting.

Prosciutto Potatoes Florentine

1/2 cup butter
1/2 cup flour
2 cups milk
2 cups chicken broth
12 ounces Provolone cheese, shredded
Salt to taste
1/2 teaspoon pepper
5 large potatoes, peeled, sliced 1/8 inch thick
1 large onion, thinly sliced
4 ounces sliced prosciutto
1   10-ounce package frozen chopped spinach, thawed, drained
1/2 cup grated Parmesan cheese

Melt butter in saucepan; blend in flour. Cook until bubbly, stirring frequently. Add milk and chicken broth. Cook until smooth and thickened, stirring constantly. Add cheese, salt and pepper. Cook until cheese is melted, stirring constantly. Layer 1/3 of the potatoes, 1/2 of the onion, 1/2 of the prosciutto, 1/2 of the spinach and 1/3 of the cheese sauce in 9x13-inch casserole. Repeat layers. Top with remaining potatoes and cheese sauce. Bake, covered, at 375 degrees for 30 minutes. Bake, uncovered, for 1 hour. Sprinkle with Parmesan cheese. Bake for 5 minutes longer. Let stand for 10 minutes before serving. Yield: 6 servings.

Approx Per Serving: Cal 639; Prot 32 g; Carbo 46 g; Fiber 4 g; T Fat 37 g; 52% Calories from Fat; Chol 108 mg; Sod 1341 mg.

Scalloped Potatoes

3 tablespoons butter
1 tablespoon flour
1 1/2 cups milk
1/2 cup grated Parmesan cheese
2 tablespoons chopped chives
1/4 cup chopped parsley
2 teaspoons dillweed
Salt to taste
6 large potatoes, peeled, sliced
1 onion, thinly sliced

Melt butter in saucepan. Stir in flour. Cook for several minutes. Add milk. Cook until thickened and smooth, stirring constantly. Stir in cheese, chives, parsley, dillweed and salt. Toss potatoes with onion in bowl. Add cheese sauce; mix gently. Spoon into buttered baking dish. Bake at 375 degrees for 1 hour or until potatoes are tender and casserole is golden brown. May increase recipe to serve more. Yield: 6 servings.

Approx Per Serving: Cal 279; Prot 8 g; Carbo 40 g; Fiber 3 g; T Fat 10 g; 32% Calories from Fat; Chol 29 mg; Sod 209 mg.

For creamier fresh corn, score the kernels by slicing through the middle of each row and then remove the kernels by holding the cob vertically over a wide shallow bowl and cutting down the cob with a very sharp knife.

Aunt Kootzie's Sauerkraut

1 1-pound package sauerkraut, drained
1 16-ounce jar chunky applesauce
2 to 3 tablespoons caraway seed
1 to 2 tablespoons dry mustard
1 to 2 tablespoons dark brown sugar
1 cup dry white wine

Combine sauerkraut, applesauce, caraway seed, mustard, brown sugar and wine in bowl; mix well. Spoon into large baking dish. Bake at 350 degrees for 1 to 1 1/2 hours or until bubbly. May add additional caraway seed, mustard and brown sugar to taste. Yield: 10 servings.

Approx Per Serving: Cal 85; Prot 1 g; Carbo 16 g; Fiber 2 g; T Fat 1 g; 11% Calories from Fat; Chol 0 mg; Sod 304 mg.

Make an easy *Spinach Casserole* by combining 4 packages cooked frozen spinach with 1 cup sour cream and 1 envelope onion soup mix and place in baking dish. Top with cracker crumbs and Parmesan cheese and dot with butter. Bake at 350 degrees for 45 minutes.

Malfatti di Ricotta

2 cups chopped cooked spinach
2 cups grated Parmesan cheese
1/2 cup flour
1 cup ricotta cheese
2 eggs, beaten
Freshly grated nutmeg, salt and
freshly ground pepper to taste
3 ounces butter, melted

Combine spinach with 1/2 cup Parmesan cheese, 1/4 cup flour, ricotta cheese, eggs, nutmeg, salt and pepper in bowl; mix well. Shape mixture into small ovals. Roll ovals in remaining 1/4 cup flour. Drop a few at a time into boiling water in saucepan. Cook until ovals float to surface; drain. Place in serving dish. Drizzle with melted butter; sprinkle with remaining 1 1/2 cups Parmesan cheese. May also use as filling for ravioli. This recipe is from the Abruzzi region of Italy. Yield: 6 servings.

Approx Per Serving: Cal 359; Prot 21 g; Carbo 14 g; Fiber 2 g; T Fat 25 g; 62% Calories from Fat; Chol 136 mg; Sod 716 mg.

Épinards en branches Parmesan

6 10-ounce packages frozen chopped spinach
6 tablespoons butter   8 ounces cream cheese
2 tablespoons flour   1/4 teaspoon cayenne pepper
1 teaspoon dry mustard
1/4 teaspoon each salt and black pepper
3/4 cup grated Parmesan cheese   1/4 cup sour cream

Cook spinach using package directions; drain well and set aside. Combine butter, cream cheese, flour, cayenne pepper, mustard, salt and black pepper in saucepan. Simmer over medium heat until thickened, stirring constantly. Stir in Parmesan cheese gradually; add sour cream. Simmer for 5 minutes, stirring frequently. Add spinach. Simmer until heated through. Spoon into serving bowl. Yield: 12 servings.

Approx Per Serving: Cal 194; Prot 8 g; Carbo 10 g; Fiber 4 g; T Fat 15 g; 66% Calories from Fat; Chol 42 mg; Sod 367 mg.

Make *Spinach and Rice Casserole* by combining 1 package frozen spinach, cooked, 1 cup cooked rice, 1 cup cheese, 2 beaten eggs, 1/3 cup milk, 3 tablespoons melted margarine, 2 tablespoons chopped onion, 1/2 teaspoon Worcestershire sauce and 1/2 teaspoon rosemary and bake at 350 degrees for 25 minutes.

Acorn Squash with Applesauce

3 acorn squash
2 cups applesauce
1/3 cup packed brown sugar
1/3 cup raisins
1/4 cup chopped walnuts
1 tablespoon lemon juice
2 tablespoons butter

Cut squash into halves lengthwise; discard seed and fibers. Place cut side up in 9x13-inch baking dish; add 1 inch boiling water. Combine applesauce, brown sugar, raisins, walnuts and lemon juice in bowl; mix well. Spoon into centers of squash. Dot with butter. Bake, covered, at 350 degrees for 25 minutes. Bake, uncovered, for 25 minutes longer or until squash is tender. Yield: 6 servings.

Approx Per Serving: Cal 330; Prot 4 g; Carbo 70 g; Fiber 8 g; T Fat 7 g; 19% Calories from Fat; Chol 10 mg; Sod 52 mg.

Make *Vegetables Provençale* by simmering 4 sliced small zucchini, 2½ cups chopped eggplant, 1 chopped onion, 2 minced cloves of garlic, one 16-ounce can tomatoes, 1 teaspoon salt and ½ teaspoon oregano for 10 to 15 minutes or until tender-crisp.

Spiced Acorn Squash

4 acorn squash
1/3 cup packed brown sugar
1 teaspoon cinnamon
1/4 teaspoon ground cloves
1/2 teaspoon each grated nutmeg and salt
1/4 cup melted butter
1/2 cup real maple syrup
2 slices bacon, cut into 8 pieces

Cut squash into halves lengthwise; discard seed and fibers. Place cut side up in shallow baking pan; add 1 inch boiling water. Combine brown sugar, cinnamon, cloves, nutmeg, salt and butter in bowl; mix well. Spoon into centers of squash. Drizzle with maple syrup; top with bacon. Bake at 350 degrees for 30 minutes or until squash is tender. Yield: 8 servings.

Approx Per Serving: Cal 267; Prot 3 g; Carbo 54 g; Fiber 6 g; T Fat 7 g; 21% Calories from Fat; Chol 17 mg; Sod 224 mg.

Acorn squash is a hard-skinned squash available in the market from fall to early spring. Because of its bland flavor, it is ideal to stuff.

Courgettes au Gratin

2 pounds yellow squash, thinly sliced
¹/₄ cup grated onion   ¹/₂ cup water
1 bay leaf
¹/₈ teaspoon dried thyme
2 teaspoons salt   3 tablespoons butter
2 tablespoons flour
Cayenne pepper to taste
1 cup half and half   2 egg yolks
¹/₂ cup shredded Gruyère cheese
3 tablespoons dry bread crumbs

Combine squash, onion, water, bay leaf, thyme and 1 teaspoon salt in saucepan. Bring to a boil; reduce heat. Simmer, covered, for 10 minutes or until squash is tender-crisp; discard bay leaf. Melt butter in small saucepan. Blend in flour, cayenne pepper and remaining 1 teaspoon salt. Stir in half and half gradually. Bring to a boil, stirring constantly; reduce heat to low. Cook for 5 minutes, stirring frequently. Whisk a small amount of the hot sauce into egg yolks; stir egg yolks into sauce. Add squash and half the cheese. Spoon into buttered 9x13-inch baking dish. Sprinkle with mixture of remaining cheese and bread crumbs. Bake at 325 degrees for 30 minutes. Garnish with parsley sprigs and tomato slices. Yield: 6 servings.

Approx Per Serving: Cal 217; Prot 8 g; Carbo 13 g; Fiber 3 g; T Fat 16 g; 63% Calories from Fat; Chol 112 mg; Sod 836 mg.

Spaghetti Squash

¹/₂ cup finely chopped onion
¹/₄ cup unsalted butter
1 cup small cauliflowerets
1   14-ounce can plum tomatoes, drained, seeded, chopped
¹/₂ cup chicken stock
Salt and pepper to taste
1   3-pound spaghetti squash
¹/₂ cup freshly grated Parmesan cheese

Sauté onion in 2 tablespoons butter in saucepan over low heat until tender. Add cauliflower. Simmer for 2 minutes, stirring frequently. Add tomatoes, chicken stock, salt and pepper to taste. Simmer for 15 minutes, stirring occasionally. Cut squash into halves lengthwise, discarding seed; place cut side down on greased baking sheet. Bake at 350 degrees for 1 hour, or microwave in glass dish on High for 7 minutes. Scoop out squash into bowl; toss with remaining 2 tablespoons butter and half the Parmesan cheese. Spoon onto serving plates. Top with tomato sauce and remaining Parmesan cheese. Yield: 4 servings.

Approx Per Serving: Cal 234; Prot 8 g; Carbo 18 g; Fiber 7 g; T Fat 16 g; 57% Calories from Fat; Chol 39 mg; Sod 483 mg.

 You may substitute zucchini for summer squash in any squash recipe.

Sweet Potato Casserole

2 pounds sweet potatoes, peeled, cubed
1 cup packed brown sugar
1/2 cup sherry
1/4 cup bourbon
1/2 cup butter
1/2 teaspoon each nutmeg and cinnamon

Cook sweet potatoes in boiling water in saucepan until tender; drain. Mash in bowl with remaining ingredients. Spoon into greased baking dish. Bake at 350 degrees for 45 minutes. Yield: 6 servings.

Approx Per Serving: Cal 511; Prot 2 g; Carbo 82 g; Fiber 5 g; T Fat 16 g; 30% Calories from Fat; Chol 41 mg; Sod 171 mg.

Curried Green Tomatoes

1 onion, chopped
1/4 cup butter
4 green tomatoes, cut into bite-sized pieces
2 tablespoons curry powder

Cook onion in butter in skillet for 10 minutes or until golden brown; remove from heat. Add tomatoes; sprinkle with curry powder. Cook, covered, over low heat for 5 minutes or until tomatoes are tender. Yield: 6 servings.

Approx Per Serving: Cal 103; Prot 2 g; Carbo 7 g; Fiber 1 g; T Fat 8 g; 67% Calories from Fat; Chol 21 mg; Sod 77 mg.

Tomatoes with Basil and Garlic

2 large cloves of garlic
Salt to taste
1 tablespoon extra-virgin olive oil
3 to 4 large ripe tomatoes, sliced 1/2 inch thick
1/4 to 1 teaspoon sugar
Juice of 1 lime
5 to 10 basil leaves, chopped

Mash garlic with salt and olive oil with pestle in mortar until creamy paste forms. Layer tomato slices in large shallow bowl. Sprinkle with salt, sugar, lime juice, basil; add garlic paste. Mix gently. Let stand for 30 minutes, stirring occasionally. Reserve leftover juices for delicious salad dressing. Yield: 6 servings.

Approx Per Serving: Cal 41; Prot 1 g; Carbo 5 g; Fiber 1 g; T Fat 2 g; 48% Calories from Fat; Chol 0 mg; Sod 7 mg.

Make something different; try **Tomato Dumplings**. Wrap small peeled and cored tomatoes in flattened crescent roll dough and bake at 400 degrees for 20 to 25 minutes. Serve with heated sauce of 1 can Cheddar cheese soup and 3 tablespoons milk; sprinkle with chopped green onions and crumbled crisp-fried bacon.

Turnips Dauphinois

2 pounds turnips, peeled, thinly sliced
3/4 cup chopped scallions
2 large cloves of garlic, minced   1 1/2 teaspoons salt
1/2 teaspoon pepper   3/4 cup milk
3/4 cup heavy cream   1/2 cup shredded Gruyère cheese

Mix first 5 ingredients in buttered 1 1/2-quart baking dish. Bring milk and heavy cream to a boil in saucepan. Pour over turnip mixture; sprinkle with cheese. Bake at 400 degrees for 45 minutes or until tender. Yield: 8 servings.

Approx Per Serving: Cal 154; Prot 5 g; Carbo 10 g; Fiber 3 g; T Fat 11 g; 65% Calories from Fat; Chol 41 mg; Sod 519 mg.

Baseball Bat Zucchini

1 very large zucchini, shredded
1 large red onion, chopped   1 clove of garlic, minced
2 tablespoons olive oil   1 cup sour cream
1 to 2 teaspoons dried tarragon
Freshly ground pepper to taste

Drain zucchini for 15 to 20 minutes. Sauté onion and garlic in olive oil in skillet until tender. Add zucchini. Simmer until liquid is evaporated. Stir in remaining ingredients. Garnish with fresh tarragon leaves. Yield: 6 servings.

Approx Per Serving: Cal 141; Prot 2 g; Carbo 6 g; Fiber 1 g; T Fat 13 g; 78% Calories from Fat; Chol 17 mg; Sod 23 mg.

Summer Squash Purée

3 large onions, thinly sliced
6 tablespoons butter   1/4 cup water
6 pounds zucchini, thinly sliced
2 green bell peppers, thinly sliced
3 cloves of garlic, crushed
2 1/4 teaspoons salt   1/2 teaspoon pepper
1 cup chopped parsley
1 cup chopped fresh basil leaves
1/2 cup chopped cilantro

Sauté onions in butter in 8-quart saucepan for 10 minutes or until tender. Add water, zucchini, green peppers, garlic, salt and pepper. Simmer, covered, for 3 minutes. Simmer, uncovered, for 15 minutes longer; remove from heat. Stir in parsley, basil and cilantro. Purée a small amount at a time in blender. Cool to room temperature. Spoon into six 1-pint freezer containers. Freeze until firm. To make a 4-serving casserole, combine 1 pint purée with 2 eggs in baking dish; top with Parmesan cheese. Bake at 350 degrees for 30 to 35 minutes. Yield: 24 servings.

Approx Per Serving: Cal 55; Prot 2 g; Carbo 6 g; Fiber 2 g; T Fat 3 g; 47% Calories from Fat; Chol 8 mg; Sod 229 mg. Nutritional information is for purée only.

Make *Green and Gold Purée* by substituting yellow squash and yellow bell peppers for half the zucchini and green peppers in the recipe above.

Golden Vegetable Purée

1¹/₄ pounds carrots, cut into 1-inch slices
1 pound rutabagas, peeled, cubed
1¹/₄ pounds sweet potatoes, peeled, cubed
2 tablespoons salt   3 tablespoons butter
2 tablespoons brown sugar   ¹/₄ teaspoon nutmeg

Cook vegetables in salted water to cover in saucepan for 20 minutes or until tender; drain. Put through food mill. Stir in remaining ingredients. Yield: 10 servings.

Approx Per Serving: Cal 142; Prot 2 g; Carbo 26 g; Fiber 4 g; T Fat 4 g; 24% Calories from Fat; Chol 9 mg; Sod 1346 mg.

Summer Garden Surprise

1 onion, thinly sliced   2 cloves of garlic, minced
2 green bell peppers, chopped
Marjoram, parsley, thyme, chives and basil to taste
2 tablespoons olive oil   2 potatoes, cubed
1 small eggplant, cubed   6 ripe plum tomatoes, sliced
1 zucchini, sliced   1 cup fresh green beans, trimmed

Sauté first 8 ingredients in olive oil in skillet. Add potatoes, eggplant and tomatoes. Simmer, covered, for 10 to 15 minutes. Add zucchini and beans. Simmer until tender. Spoon into serving dish. Garnish with grated cheese. Yield: 8 servings.

Approx Per Serving: Cal 106; Prot 3 g; Carbo 17 g; Fiber 4 g; T Fat 4 g; 30% Calories from Fat; Chol 0 mg; Sod 13 mg.

Ratatouille

1 cup sliced onions   1 cup sliced green bell pepper
2 to 3 cloves of garlic, minced
3 tablespoons olive oil   1 eggplant, peeled, cubed
2 zucchini, cubed
3 tomatoes, peeled, chopped
1 teaspoon chopped thyme
Parsley, salt and pepper to taste

Sauté onions, green pepper and garlic in oil in large skillet until tender. Remove with slotted spoon to warm plate. Brown eggplant and zucchini in skillet. Add onion mixture, tomatoes, thyme, parsley, salt and pepper. Simmer, covered, for 15 minutes, stirring occasionally. Simmer, uncovered, until liquid has evaporated.
Yield: 4 servings.

Approx Per Serving: Cal 165; Prot 4 g; Carbo 17 g; Fiber 6 g; T Fat 11 g; 54% Calories from Fat; Chol 0 mg; Sod 15 mg.

Place leftover tomato paste into ice cube trays measured in quantities of 1 tablespoon each. Once frozen, transfer to small ziplock bags to store in the freezer until needed.

Tri-Color Vegetable Stir-Fry

8 ounces zucchini
4 teaspoons olive oil
1/2 cup thinly sliced onion
1 cup thinly sliced carrot
1 cup sliced green and/or red bell peppers
1 cup thinly sliced red cabbage
4 teaspoons white wine vinegar
1/4 teaspoon salt
1/4 teaspoon freshly ground pepper

Cut zucchini into halves lengthwise; slice thinly crosswise. Heat wok or 10-inch nonstick skillet over medium heat. Add olive oil. Stir in onion. Add carrot, peppers and zucchini. Stir-fry for 5 minutes or until vegetables are barely tender-crisp. Add cabbage, vinegar, salt and pepper. Stir-fry for 3 to 5 minutes. Serve on white serving plates. Yield: 4 servings.

Approx Per Serving: Cal 71; Prot 1 g; Carbo 7 g; Fiber 2 g; T Fat 5 g; 56% Calories from Fat; Chol 0 mg; Sod 145 mg.

Make extra pesto, then freeze it (without cheese or nuts) in ice cube trays or small containers to enjoy throughout the winter.

Vegetable Medley

3/4 cup chopped celery
3/4 cup chopped onions
1 large clove of garlic, minced
1/4 cup olive oil
1 pound zucchini, sliced 1/4 inch thick
2 ripe tomatoes, sliced 1/8 inch thick
1 cup julienned green bell pepper
3/4 cup cut green beans
3/4 cup sliced carrot
1 8-ounce can tomato sauce
1 tablespoon prepared mustard
1/2 teaspoon each dried basil and salt
1/4 teaspoon pepper
Hot pepper sauce to taste

Sauté celery, onions and garlic in olive oil in large skillet until tender. Add zucchini, tomatoes, green pepper, beans and carrot. Simmer for 10 minutes or until tender. Add tomato sauce, mustard, basil, salt, pepper and hot sauce; mix well. Cook over low heat for 5 minutes, stirring occasionally. Serve hot or cold. Yield: 6 servings.

Approx Per Serving: Cal 133; Prot 3 g; Carbo 12 g; Fiber 3 g; T Fat 10 g; 60% Calories from Fat; Chol 0 mg; Sod 462 mg.

Michigan Baked Noodles

1 6-ounce package egg noodles, cooked
1 cup small curd cottage cheese
1 cup sour cream   1 small onion, finely chopped
1 clove of garlic, minced
1 tablespoon Worcestershire sauce   1/2 teaspoon salt
Cayenne pepper and ground black pepper to taste
Paprika to taste

Mix cooked noodles with next 8 ingredients in large bowl. Spoon into 1 1/2-quart baking dish; sprinkle with paprika. Bake at 350 degrees for 25 to 30 minutes or until browned. Yield: 8 servings.

Approx Per Serving: Cal 178; Prot 7 g; Carbo 18 g; Fiber <1 g; T Fat 8 g; 42% Calories from Fat; Chol 54 mg; Sod 277 mg.

Brandied Cranberry Relish

1 orange   4 cups cranberries
2 cups sugar   1 cup chopped pecans
3/4 cup chopped candied ginger   1/2 cup brandy

Grate rind of orange; grind orange in food grinder, discarding seed. Mix with remaining ingredients in glass bowl. Chill, covered, for 2 days before serving. Yield: 8 servings.

Approx Per Serving: Cal 429; Prot 2 g; Carbo 84 g; Fiber 3 g; T Fat 10 g; 21% Calories from Fat; Chol 0 mg; Sod 2 mg.

Orange-Cranberry Relish

4 cups frozen cranberries
1 navel orange, finely chopped
3/4 cup honey   1 cup chopped black walnuts
1 cup golden raisins

Slice frozen cranberries into halves. Combine with orange in bowl. Stir in honey, walnuts and raisins. Let stand overnight before serving. Freezes well. Yield: 12 servings.

Approx Per Serving: Cal 209; Prot 3 g; Carbo 41 g; Fiber 3 g; T Fat 6 g; 23% Calories from Fat; Chol 0 mg; Sod 4 mg.

Chinese-Style Fried Rice

4 ounces pepperoni, finely chopped
1 tablespoon oil   4 cups cooked rice
1 cup cooked mixed vegetables
1 tablespoon soy sauce   2 teaspoons minced garlic
4 eggs   1 teaspoon butter

Sauté pepperoni in oil in skillet for several minutes. Stir in rice and vegetables. Mix soy sauce, garlic and 2 eggs in small bowl; pour into rice mixture. Cook until egg mixture is absorbed into rice. Beat 2 eggs in small bowl. Scramble in butter in small skillet. Stir into rice mixture. Yield: 8 servings.

Approx Per Serving: Cal 257; Prot 9 g; Carbo 29 g; Fiber 1 g; T Fat 11 g; 40% Calories from Fat; Chol 113 mg; Sod 465 mg.

Ceci alla Nonna

2 tablespoons extra-virgin olive oil
1 large clove of garlic, sliced
1   19-ounce can ceci (chick-peas), drained
1 sprig of fresh rosemary   Juice of ½ large lemon
Salt and freshly ground pepper to taste

Pour mixture of olive oil and garlic over ceci in bowl. Add remaining ingredients; mix well. Yield: 4 servings.

Approx Per Serving: Cal 553; Prot 26 g; Carbo 82 g; Fiber 26 g; T Fat 15 g; 24% Calories from Fat; Chol 0 mg; Sod 33 mg.

Lemon Rice

1 cup thinly sliced celery   1 small onion, finely chopped
2 cups sliced mushrooms   ½ cup butter
1½ teaspoons salt   ⅛ teaspoon white pepper
¼ teaspoon dried thyme   1½ cups water
Grated rind of 1 lemon   ½ cup lemon juice
1 cup uncooked long grain white rice

Sauté vegetables in butter in skillet. Stir in salt, white pepper and thyme; remove from heat. Bring water, lemon rind and lemon juice to a boil in 2-quart saucepan. Add sautéed vegetables and rice. Simmer, covered, for 20 minutes, stirring occasionally. Yield: 8 servings.

Approx Per Serving: Cal 201; Prot 2 g; Carbo 23 g; Fiber 1 g; T Fat 12 g; 52% Calories from Fat; Chol 31 mg; Sod 512 mg.

Risotto alla Piedmontese

4 ounces lean ground beef
1 chicken liver, finely chopped
1 small onion, finely chopped
1 small clove of garlic, minced
2 tablespoons butter
Salt and pepper to taste
¼ cup dry white or red wine
1¼ cups sliced mushrooms
3 cups uncooked long grain rice
3 tablespoons tomato paste
5 to 6 cups chicken broth
¼ to ½ cup grated Parmesan cheese

Cook ground beef, chicken liver, onion and garlic in butter in 4-quart saucepan, stirring until ground beef is crumbly. Add salt, pepper and wine. Cook until liquid evaporates. Add mushrooms and rice. Cook for 2 to 3 minutes, stirring frequently. Combine tomato paste and chicken broth in small saucepan. Simmer until heated through. Add to rice mixture ½ cup at a time, stirring constantly. Cook over low heat until rice is tender. Spoon into serving bowl; top with Parmesan cheese. This recipe came from the Piedmont region of Italy and is over 100 years old. Yield: 10 servings.

Approx Per Serving: Cal 304; Prot 12 g; Carbo 48 g; Fiber 1 g; T Fat 7 g; 20% Calories from Fat; Chol 30 mg; Sod 574 mg.

Never-Fail Wild Rice

¹/₂ cup butter   1 clove of garlic, minced
2 tablespoons chopped chives   1 cup uncooked wild rice
¹/₂ cup blanched slivered almonds
8 ounces mushrooms, sliced   2 cups chicken broth
1 cup water   Salt and pepper to taste

Melt butter in skillet. Add garlic, chives, rice, almonds and mushrooms. Cook for 5 to 10 minutes or until rice begins to turn yellow. Stir in chicken broth, water, salt and pepper. Spoon into buttered 2-quart baking dish. Bake, covered, at 325 degrees for 1 to 2 hours or until rice is fluffy and tender and liquid is absorbed. Yield: 8 servings.

Approx Per Serving: Cal 240; Prot 7 g; Carbo 19 g; Fiber 2 g; T Fat 17 g; 60% Calories from Fat; Chol 31 mg; Sod 294 mg.

Cajun Remoulade

3 ounces mayonnaise   2 ounces sour cream
2 ounces gherkins, chopped
¹/₂ teaspoon Cajun seasoning
¹/₂ teaspoon fresh lemon juice
¹/₂ teaspoon freshly chopped chives

Mix all ingredients in bowl. Chill until serving time. Excellent with Salmon Rouladen. Yield: 7 (1-ounce) servings.

Approx Per Serving: Cal 115; Prot <1 g; Carbo 4 g; Fiber <1 g; T Fat 11 g; 86% Calories from Fat; Chol 11 mg; Sod 131 mg.

Morel Sauce

2 ounces dried morels, stems removed
¹/₂ cup milk
3 tablespoons butter
5 tablespoons flour
4 cups cream
¹/₃ cup dry white wine
All-purpose seasoning and pepper to taste

Soak morels in ¹/₂ cup milk and enough warm water to cover in glass bowl for 3 hours. Pour liquid from mushrooms through paper towel-lined sieve; reserve. Cook reserved liquid in saucepan until reduced to ¹/₃ cup. Slice morels into halves lengthwise; rinse several times under cold water and set aside. Melt butter in saucepan over medium heat. Blend in flour slowly. Add cream a small amount at a time. Cook over low heat until thickened, stirring constantly. Add ¹/₃ cup mushroom liquid, wine, seasonings and morels. Simmer until heated through. Yield: 8 servings.

Approx Per Serving: Cal 484; Prot 4 g; Carbo 8 g; Fiber <1 g; T Fat 49 g; 90% Calories from Fat; Chol 177 mg; Sod 88 mg.

Make *Chicken-Noodle Rice* by sautéing 1 cup rice in ¹/₄ cup butter and adding 1 envelope chicken-noodle soup mix and 4 cups hot water. Simmer for 30 minutes.

Green Information and Inspiration

Through The Pennsylvania Horticultural Society, members find year-round inspiration. They attend lectures and demonstrations that range from bulb forcing and Ikebana to pruning and compost management. The Society arranges visits to unparalleled public and private gardens in Pennsylvania, Delaware, New Jersey, New York and New England. Field trips and tours bring experts and interested novices together for excursions to famous arboreta and nurseries throughout the United States and to major activities in other countries, from flower shows in London, Nairobi and Amsterdam to Australian gardens down under.

Locally, Horticultural Hotline volunteers answer calls from the desperate and the curious. For those who want to know more, The Pennsylvania Horticultural Society's vast library stocks the latest in gardening books and horticultural videos in addition to its tremendous collection of resource and historical reference volumes. Best of all, members may borrow and return material by mail. One of the most popular activities of the year occurs each fall, when the library holds a book sale in conjunction with the members' plant giveaway. The Plant Dividend distributes perennials, shrubs and trees, some of which have received the prestigious Pennsylvania Horticultural Society Gold Medal Plant Award for woody ornamentals of exceptional garden merit that grow well in the Delaware Valley. The Hotline number is (215) 988-8777 and is open Monday through Friday, 9:30 a.m. to 12:00 a.m., January through November.

Green Scene, the full color magazine published by The Pennsylvania Horticultural Society, carries gardening excitement well beyond the Delaware Valley. In addition to Society members who receive the magazine free, horticultural organizations and individuals across the country subscribe to the bimonthly publication full of informative articles and photographs by award winning authors and photographers.

Pennsylvania Horticultural Society members visit tiny gardens down the street, famous gardens around the world, and see unusual home landscaping such as this in New Zealand. – Photography by Betsy Gullan

Philadelphia Green Garden Brunch

Herb Toast *(page 185)*

The World's Best Bloody (or Virgin) Mary *(page 30)*   or   Salty Dogs
Champagne   Sangria *(page 32)*

Eggs Supreme *(page 158)*   Mandarin Roll-Ups *(page 161)*
Tomatoes with Basil and Garlic *(page 145)*   or   Sliced Watermelon
(arranged on one platter)

Sam's White Bread *(page 181)*   or   Molasses Oatmeal Bread *(page 175)*

Danish Puff *(page 170)*   Fresh Fruit

*Make a casual bouquet of flowers, grasses and greens found in your garden,
or fill a basket with beautiful edible fruit for the last course.*

Asparagus Pie

25 fresh asparagus spears, trimmed*
1/3 cup butter
5 tablespoons flour
2 cups milk
2 teaspoons lemon juice
3/4 teaspoon curry powder
1/2 teaspoon celery salt
1/8 teaspoon pepper
4 hard-boiled eggs, sliced
1 baked 9-inch pie shell
1/2 cup shredded sharp Cheddar cheese
Paprika to taste

Cut asparagus spears into 1 1/2-inch lengths. Place in skillet with enough water to cover. Cook, covered, for 2 to 3 minutes or until tender-crisp; drain and set aside. Melt butter in medium saucepan. Blend in flour. Cook over low heat until mixture bubbles; do not brown. Add milk. Cook until thickened, stirring constantly. Stir in lemon juice, curry powder, celery salt and pepper. Cook over low heat for 2 to 3 minutes, stirring constantly; remove from heat. Alternate layers of asparagus and eggs in pie shell. Pour sauce over layers. Top with cheese; sprinkle with paprika. Bake at 350 degrees for 40 to 45 minutes or until bubbly and golden brown. Let stand for 10 minutes before slicing. *May substitute one 10-ounce package frozen asparagus for fresh asparagus. Yield: 6 servings.

Approx Per Serving: Cal 419; Prot 14 g; Carbo 25 g; Fiber 2 g; T Fat 30 g; 64% Calories from Fat; Chol 191 mg; Sod 531 mg.

Cheese Enchiladas

1 large Spanish onion, chopped
2 envelopes instant chicken bouillon
1   4-ounce can chopped green chilies, drained
1   2-ounce can chopped black olives, drained
16 ounces Monterey Jack cheese, shredded
8 ounces Cheddar cheese, shredded
16 flour tortillas
1 cup light cream

Combine onion, 1 envelope bouillon and a small amount of water in glass bowl. Microwave on High until onion is tender; drain. Combine with chilies, olives, half the Monterey Jack cheese and Cheddar cheese in bowl; mix well. Spread evenly in center of each tortilla; roll up. Place in 8x8-inch baking pan sprayed with nonstick cooking spray. Combine cream, remaining Monterey Jack cheese and remaining envelope bouillon in small bowl; mix well. Pour over tortillas. Bake at 350 degrees for 25 to 30 minutes or until lightly browned. Yield: 8 servings.

Approx Per Serving: Cal 599; Prot 28 g; Carbo 43 g; Fiber 3 g; T Fat 37 g; 54% Calories from Fat; Chol 93 mg; Sod 1202 mg.

 For a zestier taste use Monterey Jack cheese with jalapeño peppers in egg and cheese dishes.

Eggs Florentine

12 hard-boiled eggs
1 teaspoon prepared mustard
3 to 4 tablespoons mayonnaise
Salt and pepper to taste
4 10-ounce packages frozen chopped spinach
1 onion, grated   1/2 cup plus 6 tablespoons butter
1/4 cup plus 6 tablespoons flour
1 10-ounce can beef broth   Nutmeg to taste
3 1/2 to 4 cups half and half
3/4 cup shredded Cheddar cheese
2 tablespoons brandy
2 tablespoons sherry
Worcestershire sauce and Tabasco sauce to taste
2 envelopes instant chicken bouillon
Paprika to taste

Slice eggs into halves lengthwise; remove yolks. Mash yolks with mustard, mayonnaise, salt and pepper in bowl. Fill egg whites with mixture; set aside. Cook spinach using package directions; drain well. Sauté onion in 1/4 cup butter in medium saucepan until tender. Stir in 1/4 cup flour until blended. Add spinach, beef broth, salt, pepper and nutmeg. Cook for several minutes until thickened, stirring constantly; remove from heat. Spoon spinach mixture into 9x13-inch baking dish. Top with eggs. Melt 6 tablespoons butter in saucepan. Whisk in remaining 6 tablespoons flour. Add half and half. Stir in cheese, brandy, sherry, Worcestershire sauce, Tabasco sauce, chicken bouillon, salt and pepper. Cook until sauce is thickened, stirring constantly. Heat remaining 1/4 cup butter in small saucepan until browned. Whisk into sauce. Pour over eggs and spinach, covering completely. Sprinkle with paprika. Bake at 325 degrees for 45 minutes or until bubbly. Yield: 12 servings.

Approx Per Serving: Cal 431; Prot 15 g; Carbo 16 g; Fiber 3 g; T Fat 35 g; 72% Calories from Fat; Chol 289 mg; Sod 637 mg.

Egg Casserole

6 to 8 slices bread
2 teaspoons butter, softened
1 to 2 teaspoons minced onion flakes
1 tablespoon bacon bits
1/2 cup shredded Cheddar cheese
6 to 7 eggs
1 1/2 cups milk

Spread bread with butter. Place in buttered 9x13-inch baking pan. Sprinkle with onion, bacon bits and cheese. Chill overnight. Beat eggs with milk in bowl; pour over bread. Chill overnight. Bake at 350 degrees for 30 minutes or until lightly browned. Yield: 7 servings.

Approx Per Serving: Cal 244; Prot 13 g; Carbo 19 g; Fiber 1 g; T Fat 13 g; 47% Calories from Fat; Chol 232 mg; Sod 333 mg.

Cheese Soufflé

6 tablespoons butter
6 tablespoons flour
Salt and pepper to taste
1 cup milk
Nutmeg to taste
6 ounces Gruyère cheese, shredded
6 eggs, separated

Preheat oven to 425 degrees. Melt 4 tablespoons butter over low heat in saucepan; whisk in flour, salt and pepper. Add milk. Cook until thickened, whisking constantly; remove from heat. Whisk in nutmeg, remaining 2 tablespoons butter and cheese. Add egg yolks 1 at a time, beating well after each addition. Beat egg whites in mixer bowl until stiff peaks form. Fold into cheese mixture. Pour into greased 2-quart soufflé dish. Reduce oven temperature to 400 degrees. Bake for 30 to 35 minutes or until soufflé is puffed and browned. Yield: 4 servings.

Approx Per Serving: Cal 526; Prot 25 g; Carbo 13 g; Fiber <1 g; T Fat 41 g; 71% Calories from Fat; Chol 421 mg; Sod 400 mg.

 A dab of cottage cheese and a pinch of rosemary spruce up your scrambled eggs.

Easy Cheese Soufflé

1 cup milk, scalded   1 cup soft bread crumbs
4 ounces Swiss cheese, cubed
1 tablespoon butter   1/2 teaspoon salt
3 eggs, separated

Combine milk, bread crumbs, cheese, butter and salt in bowl; mix well. Add beaten egg yolks. Beat egg whites in mixer bowl until stiff peaks form. Fold into cheese mixture. Pour into buttered 8-inch soufflé dish. Set dish in pan of water. Bake at 375 degrees for 45 minutes or until puffed and browned. Yield: 4 servings.

Approx Per Serving: Cal 259; Prot 16 g; Carbo 10 g; Fiber <1 g; T Fat 17 g; 61% Calories from Fat; Chol 202 mg; Sod 491 mg.

Deviled Eggs

6 hard-boiled eggs   1 1/2 tablespoons catsup
1/2 teaspoon prepared mustard
3 tablespoons mayonnaise

Slice eggs into halves lengthwise; remove yolks. Mash yolks in bowl. Add catsup, mustard and mayonnaise; mix well. Fill egg whites with mixture. Chill until serving time. Yield: 6 servings.

Approx Per Serving: Cal 133; Prot 6 g; Carbo 2 g; Fiber <1 g; T Fat 11 g; 75% Calories from Fat; Chol 217 mg; Sod 154 mg.

Eggs Supreme

4 teaspoons sugar
1 teaspoon salt
1 cup milk
6 eggs
1 teaspoon baking powder
1/2 cup flour
3 ounces cream cheese, cubed
8 ounces cottage cheese
3 tablespoons melted margarine
8 ounces Muenster cheese, cubed

Beat sugar, salt, milk and eggs in bowl. Stir in baking powder and flour. Fold in cream cheese, cottage cheese, melted margarine and Muenster cheese. Pour into greased 9x9-inch glass baking dish. Bake at 325 degrees for 40 minutes. Yield: 6 servings.

Approx Per Serving: Cal 431; Prot 23 g; Carbo 15 g; Fiber <1 g; T Fat 31 g; 64% Calories from Fat; Chol 275 mg; Sod 995 mg.

If you cook hard-boiled eggs with the papery outer skin of onions, the skins will turn the eggshells a light brown and you will never again have to guess which eggs are hard-boiled!

Mucho Nacho Omelette

1/2 cup cooked ground beef
1 cup refried beans
1   4-ounce can chopped green chilies, drained
1/2 cup sour cream
3 cups shredded Cheddar cheese
1 teaspoon Tabasco sauce
1 teaspoon chili powder
1/2 teaspoon cumin
1 teaspoon chopped garlic
18 eggs
1 cup chopped tomatoes
1/2 cup sliced black olives
1/4 cup sliced scallions

Combine ground beef, beans, chilies, sour cream, half the Cheddar cheese, Tabasco sauce, chili powder, cumin and garlic in bowl; mix well. Beat 3 eggs in bowl. Pour into omelette pan; sprinkle with 1/6 of the ground beef filling. Cook until omelette is done to taste. Remove to ovenproof plate. Repeat with remaining eggs and filling. Combine remaining cheese, tomatoes, olives and scallions in small bowl. Sprinkle equal portion of topping on each omelette. Broil for 11/2 to 2 minutes or until heated through and cheese is melted. Garnish with guacamole sauce and taco chips. Yield: 6 servings.

Approx Per Serving: Cal 609; Prot 38 g; Carbo 15 g; Fiber 5 g; T Fat 45 g; 66% Calories from Fat; Chol 714 mg; Sod 1000 mg.

Omelette aux Fines Herbes

2 eggs
2 tablespoons water
1/2 teaspoon prepared Dijon mustard
Salt and pepper to taste
1 tablespoon each minced fresh chervil and dillweed
1 teaspoon unsalted butter

Whisk eggs, water, mustard, salt, pepper, chervil and dillweed in bowl. Heat omelette pan over medium heat for 1 minute. Add butter, swirling to coat pan. Pour in egg mixture. Let stand for 10 seconds. Lift edges of omelette with spatula, letting uncooked eggs run under cooked portion. Fold over when partially set; transfer to warmed plate. Yield: 1 serving.

Approx Per Serving: Cal 196; Prot 12 g; Carbo 1 g; Fiber 0 g; T Fat 15 g; 72% Calories from Fat; Chol 436 mg; Sod 205 mg.

Fines Herbes refers to a delicate blend of fresh herbs especially suitable for savory egg dishes. Although dried versions are available, their real charm lies in their fresh quality.

Zucchini Frittata

2 cups grated zucchini
1 tablespoon salt
4 eggs, beaten
1/2 cup milk
1/4 cup grated Parmesan cheese
2 teaspoons chopped parsley
1 teaspoon oregano
2 tablespoons melted butter

Mix zucchini and salt in bowl. Place in colander; drain for 1 hour. Squeeze with paper towels to remove remaining moisture. Mix eggs, milk, cheese, parsley and oregano in bowl. Stir in zucchini. Coat 2-quart baking dish with melted butter. Pour in zucchini mixture. Bake at 375 degrees for 45 minutes. Yield: 6 servings.

Approx Per Serving: Cal 127; Prot 7 g; Carbo 4 g; Fiber 1 g; T Fat 9 g; 65% Calories from Fat; Chol 158 mg; Sod 1218 mg.

A frittata is usually an Italian version of an omelet and usually has the filling mixed into the eggs before they are cooked.

Gnocchi Southern-Style

4 cups milk
3/4 cup butter
1 cup quick-cooking hominy grits
1 teaspoon salt
1/8 teaspoon pepper
1 cup grated Gruyère cheese
1/3 cup grated Parmesan cheese
Paprika to taste

Bring milk to a boil in 3-quart saucepan. Add 1/2 cup butter; stir in grits. Cook over low heat for 3 to 5 minutes, stirring occasionally; remove from heat. Stir in salt and pepper. Beat with electric mixer for 5 minutes or until creamy. Pour into buttered 9x13-inch baking dish. Chill for 1 hour or until set. Slice into 1 1/2x2-inch rectangles. Arrange overlapping rectangles in 9x13-inch baking dish. Pour remaining 1/4 cup melted butter over gnocchi; sprinkle with cheeses and paprika. Bake at 400 degrees for 25 to 30 minutes. May prepare in advance and chill until time to bake. Yield: 8 servings.

Approx Per Serving: Cal 390; Prot 12 g; Carbo 21 g; Fiber 2 g; T Fat 29 g; 66% Calories from Fat; Chol 86 mg; Sod 589 mg.

Italian gnocchi are typically made with flour, farina or even potatoes and are served in place of potatoes.

Grits Soufflé

2 cups water
1 teaspoon salt
3/4 cup quick-cooking grits
6 tablespoons butter
3 eggs
3/4 cup milk
1/2 cup shredded Cheddar cheese

Bring water and salt to a boil in saucepan. Add grits gradually, stirring constantly. Bring to a boil; reduce heat. Simmer over low heat for 2 to 5 minutes or until thickened, stirring constantly. Stir in butter; set aside. Beat eggs in mixer bowl at high speed until thick and lemon-colored. Stir milk and half the cheese into grits. Fold in eggs. Spoon into greased 1 1/2-quart soufflé dish. Bake at 350 degrees for 40 to 45 minutes or until knife inserted near center comes out clean. Sprinkle with remaining cheese. Let stand for 5 minutes before serving. Yield: 6 servings.

Approx Per Serving: Cal 270; Prot 8 g; Carbo 17 g; Fiber 2 g; T Fat 19 g; 62% Calories from Fat; Chol 152 mg; Sod 558 mg.

Try garlic-seasoned cheese or add chopped green chilies to add zip to a grits casserole.

Mandarin Roll-Ups

1   11-ounce can mandarin oranges, drained
1½ cups cooked long grain rice
⅓ cup mayonnaise
1 tablespoon grated onion
3 tablespoons chopped pecans
2 tablespoons chopped parsley
8 thin slices ham
¼ cup orange marmalade
1 tablespoon lemon juice
¼ teaspoon ginger

Reserve 8 orange sections; chop remaining orange sections. Combine chopped oranges with rice, mayonnaise, onion, pecans and parsley in bowl. Spoon equal portions of mixture onto ham slices; roll up to enclose filling. Place seam side down in 6x10-inch baking dish. Combine marmalade, lemon juice and ginger in small bowl. Brush over ham roll-ups. Bake at 350 degrees for 25 to 30 minutes, basting occasionally with orange sauce. Yield: 8 servings.

Approx Per Serving: Cal 211; Prot 8 g; Carbo 22 g; Fiber <1 g; T Fat 11 g; 45% Calories from Fat; Chol 21 mg; Sod 433 mg.

Herb Honey may be made from your favorite herb leaves. Warm the honey and the herb leaves together. Seal in a jar and allow it to "age" for at least 2 weeks. You may use almost any herbs, singly or in combination—it's all a matter of taste.

Spinach and Ham Soufflé Roll

4 shallots, finely chopped   6 tablespoons butter
4 medium mushrooms, chopped
1 cup chopped cooked spinach
1 cup chopped cooked ham   1 tablespoon mustard
¼ teaspoon nutmeg   6 ounces cream cheese, softened
Salt and black pepper to taste
½ cup flour   ½ teaspoon salt
⅛ teaspoon white pepper   2 cups milk
5 egg, separated

Sauté shallots in 2 tablespoons butter in skillet until tender. Add mushrooms. Cook for 3 minutes. Add spinach, ham, mustard and nutmeg; mix well. Stir in cream cheese, salt and black pepper to taste; set aside. Grease 10x15-inch jelly roll pan; line with waxed paper. Grease waxed paper; dust with flour. Melt remaining 4 tablespoons butter in saucepan. Blend in flour, ½ teaspoon salt and white pepper. Stir in milk gradually. Bring to a boil. Cook for 1 minute, stirring constantly. Stir a small amount of hot sauce into beaten egg yolks; stir egg yolks into sauce. Cook over medium heat for 1 minute, stirring constantly; remove from heat and cool. Beat egg whites in mixer bowl until stiff peaks form. Fold into cooled sauce. Spread in prepared pan. Bake for 25 to 30 minutes or until puffed and browned. Invert immediately onto clean towel. Spread with spinach filling. Roll up as for jelly roll. Place seam side down on serving platter. Yield: 6 servings.

Approx Per Serving: Cal 440; Prot 20 g; Carbo 24 g; Fiber 2 g; T Fat 30 g; 61% Calories from Fat; Chol 263 mg; Sod 810 mg.

Quiche Primavera

1 unbaked 11-inch tart shell
1/4 cup sliced black olives
1 cup minced scallions
1/2 cup chopped mushrooms
4 plum tomatoes, peeled, sliced 1/2 inch thick
1/4 cup flour
Salt and pepper to taste
3 tablespoons olive oil
1 cup shredded Cheddar cheese
2 eggs, slightly beaten
1 cup heavy cream
2 tablespoons minced fresh basil
2 tablespoons minced fresh parsley
4 1/4-inch slices Provolone cheese

Bake tart shell at 425 degrees for 8 minutes; cool. Reduce oven temperature to 375 degrees. Sprinkle olives, scallions and mushrooms evenly over tart shell. Coat tomato slices with mixture of flour, salt and pepper. Sauté in olive oil in heavy skillet until lightly browned. Layer over olives and scallions; sprinkle with Cheddar cheese. Beat eggs and cream in bowl. Pour over tomatoes. Sprinkle with basil and parsley; top with Provolone cheese. Bake for 40 to 50 minutes or until knife inserted near center comes out clean. Let stand for 5 minutes before slicing.
Yield: 8 servings.

Approx Per Serving: Cal 451; Prot 12 g; Carbo 20 g; Fiber 2 g; T Fat 36 g; 72% Calories from Fat; Chol 119 mg; Sod 454 mg.

Rum Dum Diddy

1 small yellow onion, chopped
1 tablespoon butter   2 tablespoons water
1   10-ounce can tomato soup
8 ounces Cheddar cheese, shredded
1 tablespoon Worcestershire sauce
Hot pepper sauce to taste

Sauté onion in butter in saucepan until tender. Add water and soup. Simmer for several minutes. Add cheese, stirring until melted. Add remaining ingredients. Serve over French bread slices, English muffins, or toasted bread. Yield: 4 servings.

Approx Per Serving: Cal 315; Prot 16 g; Carbo 13 g; Fiber 1 g; T Fat 23 g; 64% Calories from Fat; Chol 68 mg; Sod 906 mg.

Breakfast Sandwiches

2 eggs   1 tablespoon water
2 tablespoons Boursin cheese
4 slices white bread, toasted

Beat eggs and water in bowl with wire whisk until fluffy. Cook in nonstick skillet until slightly dry. Spread Boursin cheese on 2 slices toast. Top each with half the egg mixture and remaining toast. Cut into diamond shape; garnish with watercress. Yield: 2 servings.

Approx Per Serving: Cal 281; Prot 12 g; Carbo 28 g; Fiber 1 g; T Fat 13 g; 42% Calories from Fat; Chol 229 mg; Sod 401 mg.

Breakfast Beauty

1 pound bulk sausage   1 cup cubed Cheddar cheese
6 eggs, beaten   2 cups low-fat milk
6 slices bread, cubed   1/4 cup chopped scallion tops
1/8 cup chopped red bell pepper   1 teaspoon salt

Brown sausage in skillet, stirring until crumbly; drain and cool. Stir in cheese. Beat eggs and milk in bowl. Stir in sausage mixture, bread cubes, scallions, red pepper and salt. Pour into greased 6x10-inch baking casserole. Bake at 350 degrees for 45 minutes. May make ahead and chill overnight. Yield: 6 servings.

Approx Per Serving: Cal 385; Prot 22 g; Carbo 19 g; Fiber 1 g; T Fat 24 g; 57% Calories from Fat; Chol 264 mg; Sod 1157 mg.

Egg and Sausage Casserole

1 pound sausage   16 ounces Cheddar cheese, shredded
12 eggs   1 cup heavy cream

Brown sausage in skillet, stirring until crumbly; drain. Place half the cheese in greased 9x11-inch baking dish. Break eggs in 3 rows of 4 eggs each over cheese; break yolks with knife. Top with sausage and remaining cheese. Pour cream over top. Bake at 350 degrees for 30 minutes. Let stand for 5 minutes before slicing. Yield: 8 servings.

Approx Per Serving: Cal 548; Prot 29 g; Carbo 3 g; Fiber 0 g; T Fat 47 g; 77% Calories from Fat; Chol 442 mg; Sod 811 mg.

Sausage Puff Casserole

4 slices bread, crusts trimmed
1 pound pork sausage
2 teaspoons prepared mustard
1 cup shredded Swiss cheese
4 to 5 scallions, chopped
3 eggs
2 cups half and half
Nutmeg, salt and pepper to taste

Arrange bread in 9x13-inch baking dish. Brown sausage in skillet, stirring until crumbly; drain. Stir in mustard. Spoon over bread. Sprinkle with cheese and scallions. Beat eggs, half and half, nutmeg, salt and pepper in bowl. Pour over layers. Chill, covered, overnight. Bake at 350 degrees for 45 minutes. Yield: 8 servings.

Approx Per Serving: Cal 290; Prot 14 g; Carbo 9 g; Fiber <1 g; T Fat 22 g; 68% Calories from Fat; Chol 137 mg; Sod 499 mg.

Most recipes call for only the white part of scallions or green onions. Save the green tops to add to the skillet before sautéing fish for a flavor variation.

Mock Souberag

5 to 6 tablespoons chopped fresh parsley
8 ounces Muenster cheese, shredded
8 ounces sharp Cheddar cheese, shredded
12 sheets phyllo dough   1/2 cup melted butter
1 tablespoon paprika
1 teaspoon each salt and pepper
2 eggs   1 1/3 cups milk

Combine parsley, Muenster cheese and Cheddar cheese in bowl; set aside. Butter 9x13-inch baking pan. Cut 12 sheets of phyllo to fit pan. Layer 3 sheets of phyllo in pan; brush top sheet with butter. Layer with 3 more sheets of phyllo; brush with butter. Spread with half the cheese mixture. Repeat with remaining phyllo, buttering every third sheet, ending with remaining cheese mixture. Cut into squares. Chill, covered, for 1 hour or longer. May freeze at this point and bake without thawing following procedure below. Combine paprika, salt, pepper, eggs and milk in bowl; beat well. Pour over layers. Bake at 400 degrees for 30 to 45 minutes or until lightly browned. Let stand for 5 minutes. This is an adaptation of an ethnic recipe and is delicious served with tossed salad for lunch. Yield: 15 servings.

Approx Per Serving: Cal 245; Prot 11 g; Carbo 13 g; Fiber 1 g; T Fat 17 g; 62% Calories from Fat; Chol 78 mg; Sod 462 mg.

Tomato Tart

1 3/4 cups flour
1 teaspoon instant dry milk
1/4 teaspoon salt
13 tablespoons cold unsalted butter
1 egg, beaten
1/4 cup Dijon mustard
4 ounces Gruyère cheese, shredded
3 large ripe tomatoes, peeled, sliced 1/3 inch thick
2 tablespoons minced fresh parsley
1 tablespoon minced fresh oregano or thyme
1 teaspoon minced garlic
1/4 cup extra-virgin olive oil

Combine flour, milk powder and salt in bowl. Cut in butter until mixture is crumbly. Add egg, stirring until stiff dough forms. Press into 11-inch tart pan with removable side. Chill for 30 minutes. Spread with mustard; sprinkle with cheese. Arrange overlapping slices of tomato over cheese. Bake at 400 degrees for 40 minutes. Top with mixture of parsley, oregano, garlic and olive oil. Delicious hot or cold. Yield: 8 servings.

Approx Per Serving: Cal 416; Prot 9 g; Carbo 24 g; Fiber 1 g; T Fat 32 g; 69% Calories from Fat; Chol 93 mg; Sod 331 mg.

Apples Caraway

6 Winesap or Granny Smith apples, peeled, sliced
1 cup sugar
1 tablespoon caraway seed   1/2 cup golden raisins
1/4 cup chopped walnuts

Combine apples, sugar and caraway seed in saucepan. Simmer for 20 to 30 minutes or until apples are tender; cool. Stir in raisins and walnuts. Serve hot or cold; garnish with whipped cream. Yield: 6 servings.

Approx Per Serving: Cal 278; Prot 2 g; Carbo 65 g; Fiber 4 g; T Fat 4 g; 11% Calories from Fat; Chol 0 mg; Sod 3 mg.

Rosy Baked Apples

3 large Rome Beauty apples
1/2 cup red hot cinnamon candies
1 cup boiling water

Core apples; remove 1 inch of peel from top of each apple. Place in 8x8-inch baking dish. Fill center of apples with candies. Pour boiling water over apples. Bake, covered, at 400 degrees for 15 minutes. Baste with pan drippings. Bake for 12 minutes longer; baste again. Cover and let stand until cool. Serve chilled with pan juices as sauce. Yield: 3 servings.

Approx Per Serving: Cal 290; Prot <1 g; Carbo 73 g; Fiber 5 g; T Fat 1 g; 2% Calories from Fat; Chol 0 mg; Sod 9 mg.

Mapled Applesauce

5 pounds Winesap, MacIntosh, Granny Smith and/or yellow Delicious apples
1/2 cup cider
1/4 to 1/2 cup maple syrup
Grated rind of 1/2 lemon
1/2 teaspoon cinnamon
1/8 teaspoon nutmeg
Salt to taste

Cut apples into quarters. Combine with cider in heavy stainless steel saucepan; cover. Bring to a boil, stirring often; reduce heat. Simmer, covered, for 30 minutes or until apples are tender. Increase heat to medium. Cook, uncovered, for 15 minutes longer or until liquid is reduced, stirring frequently; remove from heat. Put apples through food grinder, discarding peeling and seed. Combine with syrup, lemon rind, cinnamon, nutmeg and salt in large bowl; stir with wire whisk. Spoon into 5 hot sterilized 1-pint jars leaving 1/2 inch headspace; seal with 2-piece lids. Process in hot water bath for 10 minutes. Yield: 20 (4-ounce) servings.

Approx Per Serving: Cal 89; Prot <1 g; Carbo 23 g; Fiber 3 g; T Fat <1 g; 4% Calories from Fat; Chol 0 mg; Sod 2 mg.

Rose Hip Jam tastes like fresh apples and contains high amounts of Vitamin C. It has the texture of apple butter. Gather the rose hips in the winter. Follow basic jam directions.

Baked Bananas

4 cups whole cranberry sauce
1 cup water
$1/2$ cup honey
$1/2$ cup packed light brown sugar
6 large bananas, peeled, sliced into halves lengthwise

Combine cranberries and water in heavy saucepan. Bring to a boil. Cook for several minutes. Stir in honey and brown sugar. Place bananas in shallow baking dish. Pour cranberry mixture over top. Bake at 325 degrees for 20 minutes. Serve hot; garnish with sour cream.
Yield: 12 servings.

Approx Per Serving: Cal 153; Prot 1 g; Carbo 40 g; Fiber 2 g; T Fat <1 g; 2% Calories from Fat; Chol 0 mg; Sod 7 mg.

The banana plant is actually an herb. For a *Quick Dessert*, add a pat of butter, a tablespoon of brown sugar and a dash of cinnamon and nutmeg to a sliced banana. Wrap in foil; bake at 350 degrees for 15 minutes. Serve from the foil.

Fruit Compote

1 29-ounce can pitted black cherries
1 29-ounce can sliced peaches, drained
1 box dried apricots
Juice and grated rind of 1 orange
Juice and grated rind of 1 lemon
$1/2$ cup packed brown sugar

Combine cherries and juice, peaches, apricots, orange juice and rind and lemon juice and rind in large bowl; mix well. Spoon into baking dish. Sprinkle with brown sugar. Bake at 350 degrees for $1/2$ hours. Serve hot or cold; garnish with sour cream or whipped cream.
Yield: 12 servings.

Approx Per Serving: Cal 176; Prot 1 g; Carbo 46 g; Fiber 3 g; T Fat <1 g; 1% Calories from Fat; Chol 0 mg; Sod 12 mg.

Let 1 pint of pure clover honey stand in a warm room; pour it into a small bowl. Add 1 tablespoon of whole poppy seed. Blend well and let it stand for 2 days. The honey will develop a piquant flavor.

Blintz Soufflé

8 frozen blintzes
1/2 cup melted butter
6 eggs, beaten
2 cups sour cream
2 teaspoons vanilla extract
1/4 cup orange juice
1/4 cup sugar
2 teaspoons salt

Place frozen blintzes in single layer in 2-quart baking dish. Pour butter over blintzes. Combine eggs, sour cream, vanilla, orange juice, sugar and salt in bowl; mix well. Spread over blintzes. Bake at 350 degrees for 1 hour. May serve with additional sour cream, blueberries or strawberries. Yield: 8 servings.

Approx Per Serving: Cal 468; Prot 17 g; Carbo 34 g; Fiber <1 g; T Fat 33 g; 59% Calories from Fat; Chol 224 mg; Sod 862 mg.

Pineapples stop ripening as soon as they are picked so choose the best one your market offers. Any softening you detect at home indicates it is older, not riper.

Extra-Light Corn Fritters

4 ears of sweet corn
1/4 teaspoon salt
4 slices whole wheat bread, crusts trimmed, torn into pieces
2 egg yolks, beaten
2 egg whites
1/4 teaspoon cream of tartar
3 tablespoons butter

Pierce corn kernels by running tip of knife through center of each row. Scrape corn pulp into bowl with tablespoon. Add salt, bread and egg yolks; mix well. Beat egg whites and cream of tartar in bowl until stiff peaks form. Fold into corn mixture. Drop by tablespoonfuls into buttered skillet. Bake until bubbles appear on surface and underside is golden brown. Turn fritter over. Bake until brown. Serve immediately. Yield: 8 servings.

Approx Per Serving: Cal 124; Prot 4 g; Carbo 14 g; Fiber 2 g; T Fat 7 g; 45% Calories from Fat; Chol 65 mg; Sod 187 mg.

Crushed eggshells add calcium to your garden soil and discourage slugs.

Oatmeal Pancakes

2 eggs   4 ounces cottage cheese
1/4 cup plus 2 tablespoons uncooked oats
1/8 teaspoon salt   1 tablespoon oil

Combine eggs, cottage cheese, oats, salt and oil in blender container. Process for 5 to 6 seconds or until blended. Drop by tablespoonfuls onto hot lightly greased griddle. Bake until bubbles appear on surface and underside is golden brown. Turn pancake over. Bake for 1 minute or until golden brown. Yield: 4 servings.

Approx Per Serving: Cal 128; Prot 8 g; Carbo 6 g; Fiber 1 g; T Fat 8 g; 56% Calories from Fat; Chol 111 mg; Sod 216 mg.

Puff Pancake

1/4 cup butter   1/2 cup flour   1/2 cup milk
2 eggs, beaten   Nutmeg to taste   1 teaspoon sugar
2 tablespoons confectioners' sugar   Juice of 1/2 lemon

Melt butter in 12-inch cast-iron skillet in preheated 425-degree oven. Combine flour, milk, eggs, nutmeg and sugar in bowl; mix well. Pour into prepared skillet. Bake for 15 to 20 minutes or until brown. Sprinkle with confectioners' sugar and lemon juice. Serve immediately. Garnish with fruit, whipped cream or yogurt. Yield: 4 servings.

Approx Per Serving: Cal 237; Prot 6 g; Carbo 19 g; Fiber <1 g: T Fat 16 g; 59% Calories from Fat; Chol 142 mg; Sod 144 mg.

Apple-Walnut Coffee Cake

1 cup chopped walnuts
2/3 cup plus 21/2 cups flour
1/4 cup packed brown sugar
1 teaspoon cinnamon   11/4 cups butter, softened
11/2 cups plus 2 tablespoons sugar
2 cups sour cream
1 tablespoon baking powder
2 teaspoons baking soda
2 teaspoons vanilla extract   4 eggs
3 to 4 medium Delicious apples, peeled, thinly sliced
Nutmeg to taste

Combine walnuts, 2/3 cup flour, brown sugar and cinnamon in bowl; mix well. Cut in 1/4 cup butter until crumbly. Cream remaining 1 cup butter and 11/2 cups sugar in mixer bowl until light. Add sour cream, remaining 21/2 cups flour, baking powder, baking soda, vanilla and eggs, beating at low speed until blended. Beat at medium speed for 1 minute. Spread batter in greased 10x14-inch baking pan. Top with mixture of apples, remaining 2 tablespoons sugar and nutmeg. Sprinkle with walnut mixture. Bake at 350 degrees for 45 to 50 minutes or until coffee cake pulls from sides of pan. Remove to wire rack to cool completely. Yield: 18 servings.

Approx Per Serving: Cal 409; Prot 6 g; Carbo 45 g; Fiber 2 g; T Fat 24 g; 51% Calories from Fat; Chol 93 mg; Sod 286 mg.

Chocolate Chip Coffee Cake

2 cups flour
1½ teaspoons baking powder
1 teaspoon baking soda
½ cup margarine, softened
1½ cups sugar
2 eggs
1 cup sour cream
1 teaspoon vanilla extract
1 teaspoon cinnamon
1 cup chocolate chips
½ cup chopped pecans

Sift flour, baking powder and baking soda together. Cream margarine, 1 cup sugar and eggs in mixer bowl until light and fluffy. Add dry ingredients alternately with sour cream and vanilla, mixing well after each addition. Spread ⅓ of the batter into greased 9x13-inch baking pan. Combine remaining ½ cup sugar, cinnamon, chocolate chips and pecans in bowl; mix well. Layer half the chocolate chip mixture, remaining batter and remaining chocolate chip mixture in prepared pan. Bake at 350 degrees for 30 minutes or until coffee cake tests done. Yield: 24 servings.

Approx Per Serving: Cal 200; Prot 2 g; Carbo 25 g; Fiber 1 g; T Fat 11 g; 46% Calories from Fat; Chol 22 mg; Sod 112 mg.

Christmas Coffee Cakes

2 envelopes fast-rising yeast
¾ cup lukewarm water
2 cups lukewarm milk
½ cup sugar   2 teaspoons salt
2 eggs, slightly beaten
¾ cup melted butter
7½ to 8 cups flour
¼ cup sliced Brazil nuts
4 cups confectioners' sugar

Dissolve yeast in ½ cup lukewarm water. Let stand until foamy. Combine lukewarm milk, sugar and salt in bowl; mix well. Stir in yeast. Add eggs, ½ cup butter and enough flour to make an easily handled dough. Knead on lightly floured surface. Place in greased bowl, turning to coat surface. Let rise, covered, in a warm place until doubled in bulk. Punch dough down. Divide into 4 portions. Shape to fit round baking pans. Place in 4 greased pans. Brush with remaining ¼ cup butter. Let rise until doubled in bulk. Push Brazil nuts into tops of dough. Bake at 350 degrees for 25 to 30 minutes or until coffee cakes test done; cool. Combine confectioners' sugar and enough remaining ¼ cup water to make of desired consistency in bowl. Spread over coffee cake. Yield: 24 servings.

Approx Per Serving: Cal 335; Prot 6 g; Carbo 57 g; Fiber 2 g; T Fat 9 g; 25% Calories from Fat; Chol 36 mg; Sod 242 mg.

Mama's Coffee Cake

3 ounces pecan pieces
5 teaspoons plus 2 cups sugar
2 teaspoons cinnamon
1 cup butter, softened
2 eggs
1 cup sour cream
1 teaspoon vanilla extract
2 cups flour
1 teaspoon baking powder
1/4 teaspoon salt
2 tablespoons confectioners' sugar

Combine pecans, 5 teaspoons sugar and cinnamon in bowl; mix well. Cream butter and remaining 2 cups sugar in mixer bowl until light and fluffy. Add eggs 1 at a time, beating well after each addition. Fold in sour cream and vanilla. Stir in sifted mixture of flour, baking powder and salt. Spoon 1/3 of the batter into greased and floured bundt pan. Sprinkle with 3/4 of the pecan mixture. Layer remaining batter and pecan mixture over top. Bake at 350 degrees for 1 hour. Sprinkle with confectioners' sugar.
Yield: 12 servings.

Approx Per Serving: Cal 453; Prot 5 g; Carbo 54 g; Fiber 1 g; T Fat 25 g; 49% Calories from Fat; Chol 85 mg; Sod 224 mg.

Danish Puff

2 cups flour   11/4 cups butter, softened
1/8 teaspoon salt
2 tablespoons plus 1 cup water
1 teaspoon almond extract   1 cup flour
3 eggs, at room temperature
2 cups confectioners' sugar
1 teaspoon vanilla extract
3 tablespoons milk   1/2 cup chopped pecans

Combine 1 cup flour, 1/2 cup butter and salt in food processor container. Process until crumbly. Add 2 tablespoons water. Process until mixture forms ball. Divide dough into 2 portions. Roll into two 2x14-inch strips on ungreased baking sheet. Bring 1/2 cup butter, almond extract and remaining 1 cup water to a boil in saucepan; mix well. Remove from heat. Stir in remaining 1 cup flour. Add eggs 1 at a time, mixing well after each addition. Spread over dough strips. Bake at 350 degrees for 1 hour. Remove to wire rack to cool. Beat confectioners' sugar, remaining 1/4 cup butter, vanilla and milk in mixer bowl until of spreading consistency. Spread over baked layer; sprinkle with pecans. Cut into 1-inch slices.
Yield: 24 servings.

Approx Per Serving: Cal 189; Prot 2 g; Carbo 19 g; Fiber <1 g; T Fat 12 g; 57% Calories from Fat; Chol 53 mg; Sod 101 mg.

Moravian Sugar Cakes

**1 envelope dry yeast
1 cup lukewarm potato water
1 cup mashed potatoes
1 cup sugar
2/3 cup plus 1/2 cup butter
1 teaspoon salt
2 eggs, slightly beaten
4 to 4 1/2 cups flour
1 cup packed brown sugar**

Dissolve yeast in lukewarm potato water. Mix potatoes and sugar in bowl. Stir in yeast mixture, 2/3 cup melted butter, salt and eggs. Add flour; mix well. Let rise until doubled in bulk. Divide into 4 portions. Place in 4 greased 8x8-inch baking pans. Let rise for 1 hour. Punch 9 evenly spaced holes in dough in each pan. Fill each hole with slice of remaining 1/2 cup butter; sprinkle with brown sugar. Bake at 375 degrees for 15 to 20 minutes or until light brown. Yield: 36 servings.

Approx Per Serving: Cal 169; Prot 2 g; Carbo 26 g; Fiber 1 g; T Fat 6 g; 34% Calories from Fat; Chol 28 mg; Sod 135 mg.

Prune grape vines before the sap begins to flow, then dry the cuttings and add them to your grill or fireplace for great aroma.

Maple-Buttered Apple Muffins

**1 1/2 cups flour
1/2 cup sugar
2 teaspoons baking powder
1/2 teaspoon salt
1/4 teaspoon cinnamon
1/4 teaspoon nutmeg
1/4 cup oil   1 egg, beaten
1/2 cup skim milk
1 apple, peeled, chopped
2 tablespoons maple syrup
2 tablespoons butter, softened
1 tablespoon heavy cream**

Mix flour, sugar, baking powder, salt and spices in bowl. Add oil, egg, milk and apple, stirring just until moistened. Fill greased muffin cups 2/3 full. Bake at 400 degrees for 20 to 25 minutes or until muffins test done. Remove to wire rack to cool. Combine maple syrup, butter and cream in bowl; mix well. Spread over split apple muffins. Yield: 12 servings.

Approx Per Serving: Cal 176; Prot 3 g; Carbo 25 g; Fiber 1 g; T Fat 8 g; 39% Calories from Fat; Chol 25 mg; Sod 172 mg.

For the quickest recovery, transplant on gray days or in the evening, then keep the newcomers well watered.

Apple-Walnut Muffins

2 cups flour
3/4 cup sugar
1 tablespoon baking powder
1 1/2 teaspoons cinnamon
1/2 teaspoon salt
3/4 cup milk
2 eggs
1/4 cup melted margarine, cooled
1 1/2 cups coarsely grated apple
1/2 cup chopped walnuts

Mix flour, 1/2 cup sugar, baking powder, 1 teaspoon cinnamon and salt in bowl. Whisk milk, eggs and margarine in bowl until blended. Pour over dry ingredients, stirring just until moistened. Fold in apple. Fill greased muffin cups 2/3 full. Sprinkle with mixture of walnuts, remaining 1/4 cup sugar and remaining 1/2 teaspoon cinnamon. Bake at 375 degrees for 15 minutes or until muffins test done. Cool in pan for 5 minutes. Remove to wire rack to cool completely. Yield: 12 servings.

Approx Per Serving: Cal 230; Prot 5 g; Carbo 34 g; Fiber 1 g; T Fat 9 g; 33% Calories from Fat; Chol 38 mg; Sod 235 mg.

 Blueberries grow best in acid soil with a pH of 4.5 to 5.0.

Blueberry Muffins

1/2 cup plus 1/3 cup sugar
1/2 teaspoon allspice
2 2/3 cups flour
1/4 cup butter, softened
1/4 cup butter, softened
1 egg
4 teaspoons baking powder
1/2 teaspoon salt
1 cup milk
1 teaspoon vanilla extract
1 1/2 cups fresh blueberries

Mix 1/2 cup sugar, allspice, 1/3 cup flour and 1/4 cup butter in bowl until crumbly. Set aside. Cream remaining 1/3 cup sugar and 1/4 cup butter in mixer bowl until light and fluffy. Add egg; mix well. Stir in mixture of sifted 2 1/3 cups flour, baking powder and salt alternately with milk, beginning and ending with flour mixture. Add vanilla; mix well. Fold in blueberries. Fill greased muffin cups 2/3 full. Top with crumb mixture. Bake at 375 degrees for 20 to 25 minutes or until golden brown. Serve warm. Yield: 12 servings.

Approx Per Serving: Cal 246; Prot 4 g; Carbo 37 g; Fiber 1 g; T Fat 9 g; 33% Calories from Fat; Chol 41 mg; Sod 279 mg.

Eventful Muffins

1/2 cup sugar
2 1/4 cups flour
1 tablespoon cinnamon
2 teaspoons baking soda
1/2 cup shredded unsweetened coconut
1/2 cup golden raisins
2 cups grated carrots
1 Granny Smith apple, shredded
1   8-ounce can crushed pineapple, drained
1/2 cup chopped walnuts
3 eggs
1/2 cup oil
1/2 cup orange juice
1 teaspoon vanilla extract

Sift sugar, flour, cinnamon and baking soda into bowl. Stir in coconut, raisins, carrots, apple, pineapple and walnuts. Beat eggs, oil, orange juice and vanilla in bowl until blended. Add to flour mixture; mix well. Fill greased or paper-lined muffin cups 3/4 full. Bake at 350 degrees for 30 minutes or until muffins test done. Cool in pan for 10 minutes. Remove to wire rack to cool completely. May substitute juice drained from pineapple for part of orange juice. Freezes very well. Yield: 22 servings.

Approx Per Serving: Cal 171; Prot 3 g; Carbo 22 g; Fiber 2 g; T Fat 8 g; 42% Calories from Fat; Chol 29 mg; Sod 89 mg.

Harvest Muffins

1 cup whole wheat flour
2 tablespoons wheat germ
2 tablespoons bran   1/4 teaspoon salt
1/2 teaspoon baking soda
1/2 teaspoon baking powder
1 teaspoon cinnamon
1/4 teaspoon ground cloves
1/2 teaspoon nutmeg
1/2 teaspoon ginger
2 eggs, beaten   1/2 cup oil
1/2 cup honey
1 teaspoon vanilla extract
1/2 cup shredded apple
1/2 cup shredded carrot
3 tablespoons shredded coconut
1/2 cup (scant) raisins

Combine whole wheat flour, wheat germ, bran, salt, baking soda, baking powder and spices in bowl; mix well. Mix eggs, oil, honey and vanilla in bowl until blended. Add to flour mixture; mix well. Stir in apple, carrot, coconut and raisins. Spoon into paper-lined muffin cups. Bake at 350 degrees for 25 minutes. Remove to wire rack to cool. Yield: 11 servings.

Approx Per Serving: Cal 226; Prot 3 g; Carbo 30 g; Fiber 3 g; T Fat 12 g; 45% Calories from Fat; Chol 39 mg; Sod 117 mg.

Lemon-Orange Muffins

2¹/2 cups sugar
¹/4 cup margarine, softened
2 cups sifted flour
2 teaspoons baking powder
1 egg
1 teaspoon vanilla extract
³/4 cup milk
Juice and grated rind of 1 orange
Juice and grated rind of 1 lemon

Combine 1 cup sugar, margarine, flour, baking powder, egg, vanilla and milk in bowl; mix well. Fill greased miniature muffins cups ¹/2 full. Bake at 400 degrees for 10 minutes. Combine orange juice, orange rind, lemon juice, lemon rind and remaining 1¹/2 cups sugar in bowl; mix well. Dip warm muffins into mixture. Place on waxed paper to cool. Yield: 48 servings.

Approx Per Serving: Cal 72; Prot 1 g; Carbo 15 g; Fiber <1 g; T Fat 1 g; 15% Calories from Fat; Chol 5 mg; Sod 28 mg.

Make a *Simple Jam* by cooking diced fruit in a small amount of water until tender. Add a small amount of sugar and cook until thickened. Store in the refrigerator.

Butternut Squash Tea Muffins

2 cups all-purpose flour
1 cup whole wheat flour
2 teaspoons baking soda
1 teaspoon baking powder
1 teaspoon salt
¹/2 teaspoon nutmeg
¹/4 teaspoon allspice
2 teaspoons cinnamon
Grated rind of 1 orange
3 eggs
1 cup oil
1³/4 cups packed brown sugar
2 teaspoons vanilla extract
2¹/2 cups shredded butternut squash
¹/2 cup chopped walnuts

Combine flours, baking soda, baking powder, salt, spices and orange rind in bowl; mix well. Beat eggs, oil, brown sugar and vanilla in mixer bowl until blended. Stir in squash and walnuts. Stir in flour mixture just until moistened. Spoon into greased muffin cups. Bake at 375 degrees for 20 to 25 minutes or until muffins test done. Yield: 24 servings.

Approx Per Serving: Cal 254; Prot 3 g; Carbo 36 g; Fiber 2 g; T Fat 12 g; 40% Calories from Fat; Chol 27 mg; Sod 190 mg.

Oatmeal-Zucchini Muffins

2½ cups flour   1½ cups sugar
1 cup chopped pecans
½ cup raisins
½ cup quick-cooking oats
1 tablespoon baking powder
1 teaspoon salt   1 teaspoon cinnamon
4 eggs, slightly beaten
1 medium zucchini, shredded
¾ cup oil

Combine flour, sugar, pecans, raisins, oats, baking powder, salt and cinnamon in bowl; mix well. Mix eggs, zucchini and oil in bowl. Add to flour mixture, stirring just until moistened. Spoon batter into greased muffin cups. Bake at 400 degrees for 20 to 25 minutes or until muffins test done. Remove to wire rack to cool. May serve warm or at room temperature. Yield: 30 servings.

Approx Per Serving: Cal 177; Prot 3 g; Carbo 22 g; Fiber 1 g; T Fat 9 g; 45% Calories from Fat; Chol 28 mg; Sod 114 mg.

Zucchini bread and muffins are good ways to use zucchini from the garden when it is so plentiful, because they freeze very well.

Molasses Oatmeal Bread

2½ cups water
½ cup dry nonfat milk
3 tablespoons butter
2½ teaspoons salt
½ cup molasses
1 cup oats
2 envelopes rapid-rise yeast
5 cups (about) flour, sifted

Bring 2 cups water to a boil in saucepan. Stir in milk powder, butter and salt. Add molasses and oats. Let stand for several minutes. Dissolve yeast in remaining ½ cup warm water in small bowl. Add to batter with enough flour to make a slightly sticky dough. Knead on floured surface until smooth and elastic. Place in greased bowl, turning to coat surface. Let rise, covered, in warm place until doubled in bulk. Shape into 2 loaves in greased loaf pans. Let rise until doubled in bulk. Bake at 350 degrees for 35 to 45 minutes or until bread tests done. Yield: 12 servings.

Approx Per Serving: Cal 238; Prot 8 g; Carbo 53 g; Fiber 3 g; T Fat 4 g; 12% Calories from Fat; Chol 8 mg; Sod 488 mg.

 Hoe...hoe...hoe...weed...weed...weed for a perfect garden.

Almond Crunch Bread

2 tablespoons sugar
2 eggs
6 ounces cream cheese, softened
1 medium apple, peeled, chopped
1   14-ounce package cranberry quick bread mix
3/4 cup water
2 tablespoons oil
1 teaspoon almond extract
1/4 cup sliced almonds
1 to 2 tablespoons apple jelly, melted

Cream sugar,1 egg and cream cheese in mixer bowl until light and fluffy. Stir in half the apple. Combine bread mix, remaining apple, water, oil, slightly beaten remaining egg and almond extract in bowl, stirring just until moistened. Spoon half the batter into greased and floured 5x9-inch loaf pan. Spread with cream cheese mixture. Top with remaining batter. Sprinkle with almonds. Bake at 350 degrees for 65 to 75 minutes or until loaf tests done. Cool in pan for 15 minutes. Brush with apple jelly. Store in refrigerator. Yield: 12 servings.

Approx Per Serving: Cal 255; Prot 5 g; Carbo 32 g; Fiber <1 g; T Fat 12 g; 42% Calories from Fat; Chol 51 mg; Sod 220 mg.

 Garden lettuce for Christmas? Transplant small lettuce plants in cold frame in late fall.

Coriander-Banana Bread

2 cups flour
1 teaspoon baking soda
1 teaspoon baking powder
1/2 cup margarine, softened
1 cup sugar   3 eggs
3 ripe bananas, mashed
1/2 cup chopped walnuts
2 teaspoons coriander
1/4 teaspoon vanilla extract
1 teaspoon cinnamon

Mix flour, baking soda and baking powder together. Cream margarine and sugar in mixer bowl until light and fluffy. Add eggs 1 at a time, beating well after each addition. Stir in bananas. Add dry ingredients; mix well. Stir in walnuts, coriander, vanilla and cinnamon. Spoon into greased loaf pan. Bake at 350 degrees for 45 minutes or until loaf tests done. Cool in pan for 30 minutes. Remove to wire rack to cool completely. Yield: 12 servings.

Approx Per Serving: Cal 287; Prot 5 g; Carbo 40 g; Fiber 1 g; T Fat 12 g; 38% Calories from Fat; Chol 53 mg; Sod 204 mg.

Optional Icing for above

½ cup butter
1 box 10x sugar
2 tablespoons concentrated orange juice
orange rind if desired
Blend ingredients until smooth

Oatmeal Bread

2¼ cups water
1 cup oats
2 cups flour
1 envelope dry yeast
2 teaspoons salt
1 tablespoon butter
½ cup molasses*
3 cups flour

Stir 2 cups boiling water into oats in large bowl. Let stand, covered, for 1 hour. Mix 2 cups flour, yeast and salt together in small bowl. Combine butter, molasses and remaining ¼ cup water in saucepan. Heat to 130 degrees. Add to yeast mixture; mix well. Add to oats; beat at medium speed for 2 minutes. Add 1 cup flour; beat at high speed for 2 minutes. Stir in remaining 2 cups flour. Let rise until doubled in bulk. Punch dough down; divide into 2 portions. Place in 2 greased loaf pans. Let rise until doubled in bulk. Bake at 400 degrees for 30 minutes. Reduce oven temperature to 350 degrees. Bake for 15 minutes longer or until loaves test done. Remove to wire rack to cool. *May substitute dark corn syrup for molasses. Yield: 24 servings.

Approx Per Serving: Cal 127; Prot 3 g; Carbo 26 g; Fiber 1 g; T Fat 1 g; 7% Calories from Fat; Chol 1 mg; Sod 183 mg.

Pumpkin Bread

1¾ cups flour
1 teaspoon baking soda
1 teaspoon cinnamon
½ teaspoon nutmeg
¼ teaspoon each ground cloves and ginger
½ teaspoon salt
½ cup butter, softened
1 cup sugar   2 eggs
¾ cup canned pumpkin
¾ cup chocolate chips
¾ cup finely chopped walnuts

Grease bottom of 5x9-inch loaf pan or line bottom with greased waxed paper. Mix flour, baking soda, cinnamon, nutmeg, cloves, ginger and salt together. Cream butter in large mixer bowl until light. Add sugar gradually, beating at high speed until fluffy. Beat in eggs. Add dry ingredients alternately with pumpkin, beginning and ending with dry ingredients and mixing well at low speed after each addition. Stir in chocolate chips and ½ cup walnuts. Spoon into prepared loaf pan; sprinkle with remaining ¼ cup walnuts. Bake at 350 degrees for 1 hour and 5 minutes to 1¼ hours or until bread tests done. Cool in pan on wire rack for 1 hour. Remove to wire rack to cool for 6 hours longer. Yield: 12 servings.

Approx Per Serving: Cal 319; Prot 5 g; Carbo 39 g; Fiber 2 g; T Fat 17 g; 47% Calories from Fat; Chol 56 mg; Sod 237 mg.

Pleasure Bread

3 bananas, mashed   1/2 cup oil
1 cup sugar   2 eggs, beaten
2 cups flour
1/2 teaspoon baking powder
1 teaspoon baking soda
1/2 teaspoon salt
3 tablespoons milk
1/2 teaspoon vanilla extract
1/2 cup chopped walnuts

Combine bananas, oil and sugar in bowl; mix well. Stir in eggs, flour, baking powder, baking soda, salt, milk and vanilla. Fold in walnuts. Spoon into 2 greased miniature loaf pans. Bake at 350 degrees for 15 minutes or until loaves test done. Invert onto wire rack to cool. Yield: 12 servings.

Approx Per Serving: Cal 294; Prot 4 g; Carbo 40 g; Fiber 1 g; T Fat 14 g; 41% Calories from Fat; Chol 36 mg; Sod 186 mg.

Gardeners' gift suggestions: a new set of trowels, a live tree, a new garden calendar and *Great Recipes from Great Gardeners*. Make a terrarium or dish garden.

Brethren's Cheese Bread

2 cups sifted flour
2 teaspoons baking powder
1 tablespoon sugar
1/2 teaspoon salt
1/4 cup butter, softened
1 tablespoon grated onion
1 cup shredded Cheddar cheese
1 1/2 teaspoons dried dillweed
3/4 cup milk
1 egg, slightly beaten

Sift flour, baking powder, sugar and salt into bowl. Cut in butter until crumbly. Stir in onion, cheese and dillweed. Add mixture of milk and egg, stirring just until moistened. Spoon into greased 5x9-inch loaf pan. Bake at 350 degrees for 40 to 45 minutes or until loaf tests done. Invert onto wire rack to cool. Yield: 12 servings.

Approx Per Serving: Cal 163; Prot 5 g; Carbo 17 g; Fiber 1 g; T Fat 8 g; 45% Calories from Fat; Chol 40 mg; Sod 247 mg.

Feed birds regularly. Fill an empty half grapefruit with suet. Make a loaf cake for the birds...5 pounds ground suet (warm), 3 pounds sunflower seed, 2 pounds ground peanuts, 1 pound wild bird seed. Chill and cut into blocks to be hung in mesh bags. On feeders, place apple peeling for the robins and broken eggshells for the cardinals. Remember birds need water too!

Grandmother's Egg Bread

1 tablespoon margarine
1 cup milk
1 egg
1/2 cup flour
1/2 teaspoon salt
1/4 teaspoon baking powder
1/4 cup white cornmeal

Melt 1/2 tablespoon margarine in each of 2 ramekins in oven or microwave. Beat milk and egg in mixer bowl until blended. Add flour, salt and baking powder gradually; mix well. Stir in cornmeal. Spoon into prepared ramekins. Bake at 425 degrees for 15 to 20 minutes or until bread tests done. Yield: 2 servings.

Approx Per Serving: Cal 343; Prot 12 g; Carbo 44 g; Fiber 2 g; T Fat 13 g; 35% Calories from Fat; Chol 123 mg; Sod 727 mg.

Egg bread is traditionally served in the South as the foundation for creamed chicken, creamed turkey or pork barbecue.

Fruit-Nut Bread

1 1/2 cups chopped dates
1 cup currants
1/2 cup chopped cranberries
1 1/2 cups raisins
1 cup chopped apricots
1/2 cup golden raisins
1 1/2 cups chopped walnuts
1 cup pecan pieces
1/2 cup chopped almonds
1 tablespoon baking soda
3 cups boiling cider
6 egg whites
6 cups unbleached flour
1 tablespoon baking powder
1 1/2 cups sugar

Combine fruits and nuts in large bowl. Sprinkle with baking soda. Pour boiling cider over mixture; mix well and set aside. Beat egg whites in mixer bowl until frothy. Sift flour, baking powder and sugar together. Add egg whites and dry ingredients to fruit mixture; mix well. Spoon into four 5x9-inch loaf pans sprayed with nonstick cooking spray. Bake at 350 degrees for 1 hour or until loaves test done. Cool in pans. Invert onto wire rack to cool. Wrap in waxed paper and foil. Store in refrigerator or freezer. Yield: 48 servings.

Approx Per Serving: Cal 191; Prot 4 g; Carbo 35 g; Fiber 2 g; T Fat 5 g; 23% Calories from Fat; Chol 0 mg; Sod 81 mg.

Herb Bread

1 envelope dry yeast
1 cup lukewarm water
1 teaspoon salt
2 teaspoons sugar
1 tablespoon margarine, softened
1 teaspoon fresh marjoram
3/4 teaspoon fresh dillweed
3/4 teaspoon fresh thyme
1/2 teaspoon fresh rosemary
3 cups flour

Dissolve yeast in lukewarm water. Add salt, sugar, margarine and herbs; mix well. Add enough flour to make a soft dough. Knead on floured surface for 5 to 7 minutes or until smooth and elastic. Place in greased bowl, turning to coat surface. Let rise, covered, in a warm place for 1 hour or until doubled in bulk. Punch dough down. Place dough in greased 5x9-inch loaf pan. Cut 1/4-inch slashes 1 1/2 inches apart in top of loaf. Brush with water. Let rise for 1 hour. Brush with water. Bake at 375 degrees for 30 to 35 minutes or until loaf tests done. Invert onto wire rack to cool. Yield: 12 servings.

Approx Per Serving: Cal 127; Prot 4 g; Carbo 25 g; Fiber 1 g; T Fat 1 g; 9% Calories from Fat; Chol 0 mg; Sod 190 mg.

Honey-Whole Wheat Bread

2 envelopes dry yeast
3/4 cup 105 to 115-degree water
1 cup milk   3/4 cup shortening
1/2 cup plus 1 tablespoon honey
2 teaspoons salt
3 eggs, slightly beaten
4 1/2 cups all-purpose flour
1 cup whole wheat flour   1/2 cup oat flour
1 tablespoon butter, softened

Dissolve yeast in warm water in mixer bowl. Heat milk in saucepan until bubbles form. Remove from heat. Add shortening, 1/2 cup honey and salt, stirring until shortening melts. Add milk mixture and eggs to yeast; mix well. Mix flours together. Add 2/3 of the flour to batter. Beat at medium speed for 2 minutes. Stir in remaining flour by hand. Let rise, covered, for 1 hour. Punch dough down. Knead on floured surface until smooth and elastic. Place in greased 3-quart baking dish. Let rise for 40 to 50 minutes or until doubled in bulk. Cut 4-inch cross 1/2 inch deep on top of dough. Bake at 375 degrees for 45 to 50 minutes or until brown. Brush top of warm bread with mixture of butter and remaining 1 tablespoon honey. Yield: 24 servings.

Approx Per Serving: Cal 206; Prot 5 g; Carbo 29 g; Fiber 1 g; T Fat 8 g; 36% Calories from Fat; Chol 29 mg; Sod 196 mg.

Tomato-Herb Bread

1 small piece of ginger, minced
1/2 cup packed fresh basil leaves or
3 tablespoons dry basil leaves
1 medium scallion, chopped
3 medium tomatoes, seeded, cut into quarters
1 tablespoon tomato paste   1 cup sugar
3 eggs   1/2 cup butter, softened
1 1/2 cups all-purpose flour
1/2 cup oat flour   1 teaspoon baking soda
1 tablespoon baking powder
1 teaspoon salt

Place ginger, basil and scallion in food processor container. Process for 2 seconds. Add tomatoes and tomato paste. Process for 30 seconds or until tomatoes are puréed, scraping down side as necessary. Add sugar; process for 30 seconds. Add eggs; process for 1 minute. Add butter; process for 1 minute or until fluffy. Add flours, baking soda, baking powder and salt. Pulse just until flour is moistened. Spoon batter into 2 greased and floured loaf pans. Bake at 350 degrees for 40 to 50 minutes or until brown. Cool in pans for 10 minutes. Invert onto wire rack to cool completely. Yield: 24 servings.

Approx Per Serving: Cal 118; Prot 2 g; Carbo 17 g; Fiber 1 g; T Fat 5 g; 35% Calories from Fat; Chol 37 mg; Sod 207 mg.

Sam's White Bread

1 cup eggs   1/4 cup sugar
1/4 cup dry yeast
2 tablespoons salt
1 cup dry milk
1/2 cup shortening
4 cups lukewarm water
16 cups flour

Combine eggs, sugar, yeast, salt, milk powder, shortening and water in bowl; mix well. Add flour gradually, mixing well and kneading in enough to make a smooth and elastic dough. Place in large greased bowl, turning to coat surface. Let rise for 1 to 1 1/2 hours or until doubled in bulk. Divide into 4 portions. Roll each into 8x15-inch rectangle on floured surface. Roll up from narrow sides and place in greased French bread pans. Let rise until doubled in bulk. Bake at 375 degrees for 40 to 45 minutes or until golden brown. Remove to wire rack to cool. Yield: 48 servings.

Approx Per Serving: Cal 190; Prot 6 g; Carbo 34 g; Fiber 1 g; T Fat 3 g; 15% Calories from Fat; Chol 22 mg; Sod 283 mg.

 English Ivy roots well from cuttings in sand or water.

Decadent Corn Bread

1¹/4 cups flour   ³/4 cup cornmeal
¹/2 cup sugar
2 teaspoons baking powder
¹/2 teaspoon salt
1 cup skim milk
¹/4 cup oil   1 egg, beaten
1 cup creamed corn
1 teaspoon nutmeg
¹/4 cup maple syrup
¹/4 cup butter, softened
2 tablespoons heavy cream

Mix flour, cornmeal, sugar, baking powder and salt in bowl. Stir in milk, oil, egg and corn just until moistened. Spoon into greased 9x9-inch glass baking dish. Sprinkle with nutmeg. Bake at 400 degrees for 25 minutes. Serve with mixture of maple syrup, butter and cream. Yield: 27 servings.

Approx Per Serving: Cal 107; Prot 2 g; Carbo 15 g; Fiber 1 g; T Fat 5 g; 37% Calories from Fat; Chol 14 mg; Sod 114 mg.

For a sweet treat, toast bread slightly and then cut into strips. Spread 1 side with butter. Sprinkle with confectioners' sugar, shredded coconut and cinnamon. Brown lightly in oven.

Spoon Bread

¹/2 teaspoon baking soda   1¹/2 cups buttermilk
¹/2 cup yellow cornmeal
1 egg, beaten
¹/4 teaspoon salt
1 tablespoon (heaping) shortening

Dissolve baking soda in ¹/2 cup buttermilk. Mix cornmeal with remaining 1 cup buttermilk in bowl. Add egg and salt; mix well. Stir in baking soda mixture. Spoon into 1-quart baking dish. Top with shortening. Bake at 350 degrees for 30 to 40 minutes or until light brown. Serve immediately. Yield: 4 servings.

Approx Per Serving: Cal 148; Prot 6 g; Carbo 18 g; Fiber 1 g; T Fat 6 g; 35% Calories from Fat; Chol 57 mg; Sod 350 mg.

Herb Biscuits

1 cup melted butter   1 cup sour cream
2 cups self-rising flour
1 tablespoon dillweed or
any combination of dried herbs

Combine all ingredients in bowl; mix well. Spoon into greased miniature muffin cups. Bake at 375 degrees for 15 minutes or until light brown. Yield: 24 servings.

Approx Per Serving: Cal 125; Prot 1 g; Carbo 8 g; Fiber <1 g; T Fat 10 g; 70% Calories from Fat; Chol 25 mg; Sod 182 mg.

Marmalade Buns

8 teaspoons orange marmalade
1 cup chopped pecans
2 10-count cans buttermilk biscuits
1/2 cup melted butter
1 cup packed brown sugar
2 teaspoons cinnamon

Spread marmalade in bottom of 10-inch bundt pan. Sprinkle with pecans. Dip biscuits in butter. Roll in mixture of brown sugar and cinnamon. Arrange biscuits on edge in pan. Bake at 325 degrees for 30 to 35 minutes or until light brown. Serve warm or at room temperature. Yield: 16 servings.

Approx Per Serving: Cal 292; Prot 3 g; Carbo 40 g; Fiber 1 g; T Fat 15 g; 43% Calories from Fat; Chol 16 mg; Sod 394 mg.

Any type of crushed herb from thyme to rosemary to sage to parsley adds an extra dimension to biscuits. Add the herb when you are mixing the batter.

Butterhorns

1 envelope dry yeast
1/4 cup lukewarm water
3/4 cup milk, scalded
3/4 cup butter   1/2 cup sugar
1 teaspoon salt   2 eggs, beaten
4 cups flour

Dissolve yeast in lukewarm water. Combine milk, 1/2 cup butter, sugar and salt in bowl; mix well. Add eggs and yeast; mix well. Stir in flour. Chill, covered with waxed paper and damp towel, overnight. Divide dough into 4 portions. Roll each portion into a circle on lightly floured surface. Cut into 8 wedges. Brush with 1/4 cup melted butter. Roll up from wide end. Place on greased baking sheet; brush with remaining melted butter. Let rise in warm oven for 1 hour. Bake at 375 degrees for 10 minutes. Yield: 32 servings.

Approx Per Serving: Cal 116; Prot 2 g; Carbo 15 g; Fiber <1 g; T Fat 5 g; 39% Calories from Fat; Chol 26 mg; Sod 110 mg.

 To keep your garden looking good, carry pruning shears whenever you walk in the garden.

Cream Cheese Crescents

1 cup butter, softened
8 ounces whipped cream cheese
2¼ cups flour
3 tablespoons confectioners' sugar
1 cup sugar
1 tablespoon cinnamon
½ cup toasted chopped walnuts

Blend butter, cream cheese and flour in bowl. Chill until firm. Roll into 1/4-inch thick circle on surface dusted with confectioners' sugar. Cut into wedges. Sprinkle with mixture of sugar, cinnamon and walnuts. Roll up from wide end. Shape into crescents on nonstick baking sheet. Bake at 350 degrees for 20 minutes or until light brown. Yield: 24 servings.

Approx Per Serving: Cal 197; Prot 2 g; Carbo 19 g; Fiber 1 g; T Fat 13 g; 57% Calories from Fat; Chol 31 mg; Sod 94 mg.

Make *Easy Beer Bread* by mixing 3 cups self-rising flour and 3 tablespoons sugar with one 12-ounce can of beer at room temperature. Place in greased loaf pan and let rise for 30 minutes. Bake at 350 degrees for 1 hour.

Irish Scone

3 cups plus 1 tablespoon flour
¼ cup packed brown sugar
2 teaspoons baking soda
1½ teaspoons baking powder
½ teaspoon salt
¼ cup butter or margarine
1½ cups buttermilk
2 eggs, beaten
1 cup currants

Combine 3 cups flour, brown sugar, baking soda, baking powder and salt in bowl; mix well. Cut in butter until crumbly. Add mixture of buttermilk and eggs; mix well. Stir in mixture of currants and remaining 1 tablespoon flour. Spoon into greased and floured cast-iron skillet. Bake at 350 degrees for 45 to 50 minutes or until brown. Yield: 20 servings.

Approx Per Serving: Cal 139; Prot 4 g; Carbo 24 g; Fiber 1 g; T Fat 3 g; 21% Calories from Fat; Chol 28 mg; Sod 208 mg.

Walk around your garden in its prime and leave markers labeled with color, height and variety where you want to fill in next year.

Herb Toast

10 very thin bread slices
1/2 cup melted butter
Basil to taste

Cut bread into triangles. Brush one side with butter. Place on baking sheet. Sprinkle basil on both sides of bread. Bake at 300 degrees for 30 to 40 minutes or until bread is crisp. Turn off oven. Remove toast when oven is cool. Store in airtight containers. May substitute basil with thyme, coarse cracked pepper, poppy seed, sesame seed, curry powder or Parmesan cheese for basil.
Yield: 10 servings.

Approx Per Serving: Cal 136; Prot 2 g; Carbo 10 g; Fiber <1 g; T Fat 10 g; 66% Calories from Fat; Chol 25 mg; Sod 180 mg.

To substitute all-purpose flour for self-rising flour, stir in 1 1/2 teaspoons of baking powder and 1/2 teaspoon of salt for every 1 cup of all-purpose flour.

Philadelphia Soft Pretzels

2 envelopes dry yeast
1 cup warm water
2 tablespoons sugar
3 cups flour
2 teaspoons baking soda
1 egg, beaten
2 tablespoons kosher salt

Dissolve yeast in water in bowl. Stir in sugar. Add flour gradually, mixing well. Knead on floured surface for 5 minutes. Place in greased bowl, turning to grease surface. Let rise, covered, until doubled in bulk. Fill large shallow saucepan half full with water. Stir in baking soda. Bring to a slow boil. Roll dough into a 1/2-inch thick rectangle on floured surface. Cut into 3/4-inch strips with sawing motion; twist into pretzel shapes. Place dough strips 1 at a time on wide spatula. Place in boiling soda water for 5 to 10 seconds; remove to greased baking sheet. Brush with egg; sprinkle with salt. Bake at 400 degrees for 12 to 15 minutes or until golden brown. Serve warm with mustard. Serve within 8 hours. Yield: 16 servings.

Approx Per Serving: Cal 99; Prot 3 g; Carbo 20 g; Fiber 1 g; T Fat 1 g; 6% Calories from Fat; Chol 13 mg; Sod 907 mg.

Youth Education

The Pennsylvania Horticultural Society reaches out to gardeners of the future through imaginative, inspiring programs. Every year in May, the three-day Junior Flower Show attracts school groups, Scouts, 4-H members, and hundreds of youngsters who enter creative classes and win their first horticultural prizes.

Youth programs weave in and out of city community-based programs encouraging young people to take pride in their neighborhoods and understand the important role of horticulture in the urban environment. Children work with their elders tending a tree nursery for a city park or a neighborhood vegetable garden. More than one community has dedicated a plot "For Children Only," giving the kids a tremendous sense of achievement as they watch their very own marigolds, corn and other delicious edibles thrive in the middle of the city.

Beyond their neighborhoods, The Pennsylvania Horticultural Society gives children opportunities that range from trips to area arboreta to outings at pick-your-own strawberry farms. Popular outreach programs include a rousing edition of "Environmental Jeopardy," based on the well-known TV game show. The Society's Heritage Garden project gives children a glimpse of the past and hope for the future.

From the youngest toddlers earnestly painting pumpkins at the Harvest Show, to the hardworking teens at the Philadelphia Flower Show, the Pennsylvania Horticultural Society includes children in just about every activity.

Expressions of pride and accomplishment on the faces of children in Pennsylvania Horticultural Society Youth programs leave little doubt about the next generation of gardeners. – Photography by Ira Beckoff

Junior Flower Show Judges' Window Box Lunch

Summer Borscht *(page 37)*

Marmalade Buns *(page 183)*

Chicken Salad Deluxe *(page 59)*

A piece of fresh fruit or container of mixed fruit

Dirt Cake *(page 210)*

Present the lunch in a small window box.

Stencil a logo or design to the side of a 12- to 14-inch plastic window box amply lined with large sheets of grass-green tissue or plastic. Arrange fresh flowers, greens or herbs in water picks around edibles in individual sealed containers.

Cheesy Seashell Pasta

4 to 8 ounces bacon, chopped
8 to 10 ounces peas or snow peas
1   16-ounce package seashell pasta, cooked
8 ounces ricotta cheese
3/4 cup freshly grated Parmesan cheese
Cayenne pepper to taste

Cook bacon in skillet until crisp; drain. Add peas. Cook over low heat until peas are heated through. Mix with pasta and remaining ingredients in large bowl. May add tiny shrimp, scallops or Cheddar cheese. Yield: 8 servings.

Approx Per Serving: Cal 370; Prot 18 g; Carbo 49 g; Fiber 4 g; T Fat 11 g; 27% Calories from Fat; Chol 27 mg; Sod 458 mg.

Cheese Tetrazzini

1   16-ounce package spaghettini, broken, cooked
16 ounces extra-sharp Cheddar cheese, shredded
1 to 1 1/2 cups milk   Salt, pepper and paprika to taste
1 1/2 tablespoons butter

Alternate layers of cooked pasta and cheese in greased 9x13-inch baking dish. Mix milk, salt and pepper; pour over layers. Sprinkle with paprika; dot with butter. Bake at 350 degrees for 1 hour. Yield: 6 servings.

Approx Per Serving: Cal 646; Prot 30 g; Carbo 61 g; Fiber 3 g; T Fat 31 g; 43% Calories from Fat; Chol 96 mg; Sod 520 mg.

Chicken Tetrazzini

1/4 cup chopped green bell pepper
1/2 small onion, chopped
2 teaspoons margarine
1 1/4 cups broken uncooked spaghetti, cooked
1 1/2 cups chopped cooked chicken
1/4 cup chopped pimento
1/2 cup chicken broth
1/2 teaspoon salt
1   10-ounce can cream of chicken soup
1/3 teaspoon pepper
8 ounces sharp Cheddar cheese, shredded

Sauté green pepper and onion in margarine in skillet until tender. Combine with cooked pasta, chicken, pimento, chicken broth, salt, soup, pepper and half the cheese in large bowl; mix well. Pour into greased 1-quart casserole. Top with remaining cheese. Bake at 350 degrees for 45 minutes. May freeze baked or unbaked. Yield: 4 servings.

Approx Per Serving: Cal 491; Prot 35 g; Carbo 22 g; Fiber 2 g; T Fat 29 g; 54% Calories from Fat; Chol 112 mg; Sod 1341 mg.

 Add 1 tablespoon olive oil to water when cooking pasta to keep it from sticking together.

Chicken and Shells with Peppers

1 pound chicken breast filets, skinned, cubed
Salt and pepper to taste
2 teaspoons butter
8 ounces fresh mushrooms
3 green onions, sliced
1 10-ounce can cream of mushroom soup
1/4 cup milk
1 7-ounce jar roasted sweet peppers, drained
1 cup frozen peas, thawed
4 ounces shell pasta, cooked

Rinse chicken and pat dry; sprinkle with salt and pepper. Sauté in butter in skillet until lightly browned; set aside. Sauté mushrooms and green onions in skillet until tender. Combine with chicken, soup, milk, peppers, peas and pasta in large bowl, tossing to mix. Pour into 8x12-inch greased casserole. Bake at 350 degrees for 45 minutes. Yield: 6 servings.

Approx Per Serving: Cal 265; Prot 24 g; Carbo 25 g; Fiber 3 g; T Fat 8 g; 27% Calories from Fat; Chol 54 mg; Sod 921 mg.

 When planting tomatoes, choose a site that had no tomatoes, eggplant or potatoes the previous year.

Sausage and Tomato Fettucini

8 ounces sweet Italian sausage, crumbled
2 cloves of garlic, minced
2 tablespoons olive oil
1/2 cup butter
2 tablespoons fresh summer savory leaves
1 tablespoon chopped fresh basil
8 sun-dried tomatoes, chopped
1/2 cup chicken stock
1 16-ounce package fettucini, cooked
Salt and pepper to taste
2 ounces feta cheese, crumbled
1/2 cup chopped fresh parsley

Sauté crumbled sausage and garlic in olive oil in skillet until browned. Add butter, savory, basil, tomatoes and chicken stock. Simmer over very low heat, stirring occasionally. Pour over cooked fettucini, mixing well. Place on ovenproof platter; sprinkle with salt, pepper and feta cheese. Broil until cheese is melted. Top with parsley. May substitute mozzarella cheese for feta cheese. Yield: 4 servings.

Approx Per Serving: Cal 1052; Prot 25 g; Carbo 98 g; Fiber 9 g; T Fat 64 g; 54% Calories from Fat; Chol 95 mg; Sod 720 mg.

Fettucini with Vegetables

8 cups water   6 ounces uncooked fettucini
2 cups diagonally sliced carrots
2 cups broccoli flowerets
1/3 cup unsalted butter   2 tablespoons flour
1/2 teaspoon salt   1/2 teaspoon nutmeg   1 cup milk
1/4 cup freshly grated Parmesan cheese

Bring water to boil in 4-quart saucepan. Add fettucini and carrots. Cook over medium heat for 6 minutes. Add broccoli. Cook for 4 to 5 minutes longer or until vegetables are tender; drain and set aside. Melt butter in saucepan. Stir in flour, salt and nutmeg. Cook over medium heat until smooth and bubbly, stirring constantly. Stir in milk. Cook for 8 to 10 minutes or until sauce begins to boil, stirring constantly. Cook for 1 minute longer. Stir in fettucini mixture; reduce heat to low. Cook until heated through. Sprinkle with Parmesan cheese. Yield: 6 servings.

Approx Per Serving: Cal 263; Prot 8 g; Carbo 29 g; Fiber 3 g; T Fat 13 g; 44% Calories from Fat; Chol 36 mg; Sod 360 mg.

 Cut peonies will last longer if you lightly burn the stems.

Golden Gate Pasta

1 ounce red onion, cut into julienne strips
1 ounce broccoli flowerets
1 ounce mushrooms, sliced
1/2 ounce dried tomatoes, chopped
1/2 ounce green bell pepper, cut into julienne strips
1/2 ounce carrot, shredded
1/8 teaspoon minced shallot
2 tablespoons pure olive oil
2 tablespoons butter
1/2 ounce each lemon juice and white wine
11/2 ounces chicken stock
Salt and pepper to taste
4 ounces pasta, cooked

Sauté onion, broccoli, mushrooms, tomatoes, bell pepper, carrot and shallot in mixture of olive oil and butter in skillet until tender-crisp. Add lemon juice, wine, chicken stock, salt and pepper; mix well. Add cooked pasta, tossing to coat. Serve immediately. Yield: 1 serving.

Approx Per Serving: Cal 927; Prot 18 g; Carbo 95 g; Fiber 8 g; T Fat 53 g; 52% Calories from Fat; Chol 62 mg; Sod 348 mg.

Ham and Pasta Casserole

1 cup chopped onion
1/4 cup butter
1/4 cup flour
2 chicken bouillon cubes
2 cups milk
Pepper to taste
4 cups cooked multi-colored pasta
2 cups chopped cooked ham
1 1/2 cups shredded Cheddar cheese
4 hard-boiled eggs, chopped
1/2 cup buttered bread crumbs

Sauté onion in butter in saucepan until tender. Stir in flour. Add bouillon cubes, milk and pepper. Cook over low heat until smooth, stirring constantly. Alternate layers of pasta, ham, cheese, eggs and sauce in 2-quart casserole until all ingredients are used. Top with bread crumbs. Bake at 350 degrees for 30 to 45 minutes or until bubbly. Yield: 8 servings.

Approx Per Serving: Cal 393; Prot 23 g; Carbo 29 g; Fiber 2 g; T Fat 20 g; 47% Calories from Fat; Chol 172 mg; Sod 1038 mg.

 Cold eggs are easier to separate because the fat in the yolk is firmer.

Lemon-Pepper Pasta

4 red bell peppers
1 cup minced onion
1 cup chopped carrot
1/2 cup chopped celery
1 tablespoon olive oil
3 cups unsalted chicken broth
1 bay leaf
1   4-ounce can tomato paste
1/2 tablespoon red wine vinegar
2 tablespoons lemon juice
Salt and pepper to taste
1 cup heavy cream
16 ounces fresh lemon-pepper pasta, cooked
1/4 cup finely chopped fresh parsley, chives or dill

Broil red peppers until skin is charred; remove to large bowl of ice water. Remove skins; set aside to dry. Sauté onion, carrot and celery in oil in skillet over medium-high heat for 10 minutes. Add chicken broth, bay leaf and tomato paste. Simmer, covered, for 30 minutes or until thickened, stirring occasionally. Remove from heat; discard bay leaf. Cut red peppers into halves, discarding seed. Process in food processor until puréed. Add to sauce. Stir in vinegar, lemon juice, salt and pepper. Simmer gently. Add cream gradually, stirring constantly. Serve over cooked pasta; top with fresh herbs.
Yield: 6 servings.

Approx Per Serving: Cal 448; Prot 15 g; Carbo 53 g; Fiber 3 g; T Fat 21 g; 41% Calories from Fat; Chol 122 mg; Sod 99 mg.

Linguine with Broccoli Rape

1¹/₂ pounds broccoli rape, trimmed
3 cloves of garlic, minced
3 to 4 tablespoons extra-virgin olive oil
Salt to taste
¹/₄ teaspoon crushed red pepper
1   16-ounce package linguine, cooked

Cut broccoli rape into 1¹/₂-inch pieces, separating stems, leaves and flowers. Sauté stems and garlic in hot oil in skillet until tender-crisp. Add leaves, flowers, salt and red pepper. Cook until leaves are tender. Pour over cooked linguine, tossing to coat. Yield: 6 servings.

Approx Per Serving: Cal 392; Prot 13 g; Carbo 63 g; Fiber 7 g; T Fat 10 g; 23% Calories from Fat; Chol 0 mg; Sod 33 mg.

Use cooked vermicelli or spaghetti as a substitute for a regular pie shell when making a meat or vegetable pie.

Pasta Cornucopia

2 tablespoons minced garlic
¹/₂ cup olive oil
1 long thin eggplant, cut into ¹/₄-inch cubes
2 cups coarsely chopped mushrooms
2 zucchini, cut into ¹/₄-inch slices
2 yellow squash, cut into ¹/₄-inch slices
¹/₄ cup red wine
2 tablespoons chopped fresh basil
1 tablespoon chopped fresh thyme
6 Italian plum tomatoes, chopped
1   16-ounce package linguine, cooked
2 tablespoons grated Parmesan cheese

Heat garlic in half the olive oil in skillet until hot; add eggplant. Sauté until browned; drain and set aside. Add remaining olive oil. Sauté mushrooms for 1 minute; add zucchini. Sauté for 1 minute; add yellow squash. Sauté for 1 minute; add red wine. Cook for 3 minutes to reduce liquid; add basil, thyme and tomatoes. Sauté for 2 minutes; add eggplant cubes. Cook for 5 minutes; remove from heat and cover. Place equal portions of pasta in 6 serving bowls; top each with vegetable mixture and sprinkle with 1 teaspoon Parmesan cheese. Garnish with sprig of fresh basil. May substitute one 28-ounce can plum tomatoes for fresh tomatoes. Yield: 6 servings.

Approx Per Serving: Cal 536; Prot 15 g; Carbo 75 g; Fiber 10 g; T Fat 20 g; 34% Calories from Fat; Chol 1 mg; Sod 52 mg.

Pesto Genovese

1/4 cup pine nuts   4 cloves of garlic
1 teaspoon salt   1/2 teaspoon pepper
3 to 4 cups fresh basil
3/4 cup grated Parmesan cheese   2 cups olive oil

Combine pine nuts, garlic, salt, pepper, basil, Parmesan cheese and olive oil in food processor. Process until coarsely chopped. Toss with freshly cooked pasta or gnocchi. Do not cook pesto! Freezes well. Yield: 6 servings.

Approx Per Serving: Cal 757; Prot 7 g; Carbo 12 g; Fiber 3 g; T Fat 79 g; 90% Calories from Fat; Chol 8 mg; Sod 555 mg.

Pasta with Lemon Cream

Grated zest of 1 lemon   1 cup half and half
1/4 cup vodka   Juice of 1/2 lemon
Freshly grated nutmeg to taste
14 ounces pasta, cooked

Cook lemon zest and half and half over very low heat in large skillet for 5 minutes. Stir in vodka, lemon juice and nutmeg. Add cooked pasta. Cook over medium heat until pasta absorbs most of the liquid and sauce thickens. May add grated lemon rind. Yield: 4 servings.

Approx Per Serving: Cal 479; Prot 14 g; Carbo 78 g; Fiber 4 g; T Fat 8 g; 15% Calories from Fat; Chol 22 mg; Sod 27 mg.

Pasta with Mushroom Sauce

1/4 cup unsalted butter
1 medium onion, minced
12 ounces fresh mushrooms
1/2 teaspoon salt
3 tablespoons dry Marsala wine
1/2 cup light cream
Freshly ground pepper to taste
14 ounces fettucini, cooked
2 tablespoons minced Italian parsley
1/4 cup grated Parmesan cheese
Parsley to taste

Melt butter over low heat in saucepan; add onion. Cook until tender; add mushrooms. Cook 4 to 5 minutes; add salt and wine. Cook over medium-high heat until liquid evaporates, stirring frequently; reduce heat. Stir in cream and pepper. Pour over cooked fettucini, tossing to coat. Sprinkle with Parmesan cheese and parsley. Yield: 4 servings.

Approx Per Serving: Cal 583; Prot 18 g; Carbo 84 g; Fiber 7 g; T Fat 18 g; 29% Calories from Fat; Chol 46 mg; Sod 382 mg.

Make a quick *Chicken Sauce for Pasta* by heating 1 can cream of chicken soup, 1 small can evaporated skim milk, 1 can chunk chicken, 1/2 cup grated Parmesan cheese and basil to taste.

Pasta with Peas and Squash

1 cup trimmed sugar snap peas
1 zucchini, sliced
1 yellow squash, sliced
¼ cup olive oil
2 cloves of garlic, minced
Fresh parsley, basil and chives to taste
½ cup chicken stock
8 ounces pasta, cooked
½ cup grated Parmesan cheese

Sauté peas and squash in oil in skillet until tender. Add garlic, herbs and chicken stock. Simmer until heated through. Pour over cooked pasta in bowl, tossing to mix. Top with Parmesan cheese. Yield: 4 servings.

Approx Per Serving: Cal 434; Prot 16 g; Carbo 54 g; Fiber 6 g; T Fat 18 g; 37% Calories from Fat; Chol 8 mg; Sod 292 mg.

For a quick pasta dish, pick up chopped fresh vegetables at the salad bar in your local market. Stir-fry them just until tender-crisp and toss them with your favorite pasta.

Pasta-in-a-Pot

1 pound ground chuck
1 clove of garlic, minced
2 tablespoons minced parsley
1 teaspoon each basil and salt
½ teaspoon each pepper and oregano
2 15-ounce cans tomato sauce
16 ounces cottage cheese
3 cups cooked pasta shells
½ cup shredded mozzarella cheese

Brown ground chuck in skillet, stirring until crumbly; drain. Add garlic, parsley, basil, salt, pepper, oregano and tomato sauce. Simmer for several minutes, stirring occasionally. Stir in cottage cheese. Combine with cooked pasta shells in bowl, tossing to coat. Pour into baking dish; top with mozzarella cheese. Bake, covered, at 350 degrees for 20 minutes. Bake, uncovered, for 10 minutes longer. Yield: 5 servings.

Approx Per Serving: Cal 455; Prot 36 g; Carbo 34 g; Fiber 4 g; T Fat 20 g; 39% Calories from Fat; Chol 81 mg; Sod 1918 mg.

Homegrown catnip is not only a treat for your feline, but its crushed leaves on their trails will also repel kitchen ants.

Pasta Primavera

4 asparagus spears, cut up
2 cups broccoli flowerets
1 small zucchini, cut up   1 clove of garlic, minced
1 small shallot, minced
6 cherry tomatoes, cut into halves
2 tablespoons extra-virgin olive oil
1/3 cup white wine   2 tablespoons butter
1/2 cup light cream
1/4 cup chopped fresh basil
1 tablespoon fresh chopped parsley
1/2 cup freshly grated Parmesan cheese
8 ounces linguine, cooked

Blanch asparagus, broccoli and zucchini in boiling water in medium saucepan for 1 minute; drain and set aside. Sauté garlic, shallot and cherry tomatoes in olive oil in large skillet for 1 to 2 minutes. Add wine. Cook to reduce liquid slightly; remove from heat. Add blanched vegetables; cover to keep warm. Melt butter in large saucepan. Add cream, basil, parsley and cheese; mix well. Stir in vegetable mixture and cooked linguine. Serve hot. Yield: 2 servings.

Approx Per Serving: Cal 1021; Prot 31 g; Carbo 107 g; Fiber 11 g; T Fat 52 g; 46% Calories from Fat; Chol 113 mg; Sod 535 mg.

Pasta with Grave Lox

2 Vidalia onions, thinly sliced
6 tablespoons butter
9 scallions, thinly sliced
1 clove of garlic, minced
1/2 cup white wine
1/2 cup chicken stock
1/4 cup heavy cream
Salt and pepper to taste
12 ounces fresh pasta, cooked
2 ounces smoked salmon,
cut into thin strips
2 tablespoons salmon roe

Sauté onions in 4 tablespoons butter in large skillet over low heat for 6 minutes; add scallions and garlic. Sauté for 1 to 2 minutes. Stir in wine and chicken stock. Cook over medium-high heat for 1 to 2 minutes to reduce liquid; reduce heat. Stir in cream, salt and pepper. Toss pasta, remaining 2 tablespoons melted butter, sauce and salmon in large bowl. Serve on warm plates. Sprinkle with salmon roe. Garnish with chives. Yield: 4 servings.

Approx Per Serving: Cal 564; Prot 19 g; Carbo 54 g; Fiber 2 g; T Fat 28 g; 46% Calories from Fat; Chol 193 mg; Sod 513 mg.

Tortellini con Salmone

¹/₄ cup butter   1 cup frozen peas, thawed
1 cup chopped smoked salmon   2 cups whipping cream
1 cup grated Parmesan cheese   Ground pepper to taste
24 ounces cheese tortellini, cooked

Melt butter in skillet; add peas and salmon. Sauté for several minutes. Stir in cream and cheese. Cook over medium heat until thickened, stirring frequently; add pepper. Toss with tortellini in serving bowl. Yield: 4 servings.

Approx Per Serving: Cal 1217; Prot 48 g; Carbo 88 g; Fiber 2 g; T Fat 76 g; 56% Calories from Fat; Chol 303 mg; Sod 1578 mg.

Creamed Pasta with Scallops

2 cloves of garlic, minced   4 tablespoons unsalted butter
2 cups heavy cream   Nutmeg to taste
1 pound scallops   2 tablespoons chopped smoked salmon
16 ounces linguine, cooked

Sauté garlic in 2 tablespoons butter until tender; add cream and nutmeg. Simmer until reduced by ¹/₃; add scallops and salmon. Heat until cooked through. Toss pasta with 2 tablespoons butter in bowl. Place on 6 heated serving plates; top with sauce. Garnish with chopped parsley. Yield: 6 servings.

Approx Per Serving: Cal 695; Prot 26 g; Carbo 61 g; Fiber 3 g; T Fat 39 g; 50% Calories from Fat; Chol 157 mg; Sod 248 mg.

Smoked Scallop Sauce for Pasta

¹/₄ cup chopped shallots
2 tablespoons chopped gingerroot
2 tablespoons lemon zest
3 tablespoons unsalted butter
¹/₄ cup lemon juice
1 cup white wine
2 cups heavy cream
¹/₂ cup half and half
¹/₂ cup grated Parmesan cheese
1 pound smoked scallops
Salt and pepper to taste

Sauté shallots, gingerroot and lemon zest in butter in saucepan until tender. Add lemon juice and wine. Cook until liquid is reduced to one third. Add cream and half and half. Cook until reduced to half the amount and sauce is thickened; strain sauce. Combine with Parmesan cheese, scallops, salt and pepper in large saucepan. Cook over very low heat until heated through. Serve over pasta. Yield: 8 servings.

Approx Per Serving: Cal 366; Prot 14 g; Carbo 6 g; Fiber <1 g; T Fat 30 g; 77% Calories from Fat; Chol 123 mg; Sod 215 mg.

Hard seeds, such as corn, peas, and parsley, will sprout better if they're soaked in water overnight before planting.

Radiatore à la Greque

12 ounces medium shrimp, cooked, peeled
8 ounces feta cheese, crumbled
6 scallions, chopped   1¹/₂ teaspoons dried oregano
1   16-ounce can crushed tomatoes
Salt and pepper to taste
16 ounces radiatore pasta, cooked

Combine first 7 ingredients in large bowl. Let stand at room temperature for 2 hours. Stir cooked pasta into sauce, tossing to coat. Serve immediately. Yield: 6 servings.

Approx Per Serving: Cal 442; Prot 26 g; Carbo 62 g; Fiber 4 g; T Fat 10 g; 20% Calories from Fat; Chol 122 mg; Sod 647 mg.

Shrimp Scampi Spaghetti

2 cloves of garlic, minced
¹/₄ cup canola oil   2 tablespoons low-fat margarine
2 tablespoons cream sherry
2 pounds shrimp, peeled, deveined
16 ounces spaghetti, cooked

Sauté garlic in oil and margarine in skillet until tender. Add sherry and shrimp. Cook for 2 minutes on each side or until shrimp are pink. Serve over cooked spaghetti. Garnish with parsley and lemon slice. Yield: 4 servings.

Approx Per Serving: Cal 776; Prot 52 g; Carbo 89 g; Fiber 5 g; T Fat 20 g; 24% Calories from Fat; Chol 354 mg; Sod 478 mg.

Linguine with Shrimp

2¹/₂ tablespoons margarine
2¹/₂ tablespoons flour
1¹/₄ cups milk
Seasoned salt to taste
Freshly ground green peppercorns to taste
2 tablespoons chopped fresh dill
2 tomatoes, peeled, seeded, chopped
8 scallions, cut into 1-inch pieces
1 pound shrimp, peeled
2 tablespoons butter
1 tablespoon oil
9 ounces linguine, cooked
2 tablespoons chopped parsley

Melt 2¹/₂ tablespoons margarine in skillet. Stir in flour until blended. Cook over low heat for 3 minutes; add milk gradually. Whisk over low heat for 3 to 4 minutes. Add salt, pepper, dill and tomatoes. Simmer for several minutes, stirring frequently. Sauté scallions and shrimp in butter and oil in skillet for 5 minutes. Add to sauce. Serve over cooked linguine. Top with parsley.
Yield: 4 servings.

Approx Per Serving: Cal 555; Prot 31 g; Carbo 60 g; Fiber 5 g; T Fat 21 g; 34% Calories from Fat; Chol 203 mg; Sod 376 mg.

Tortellini alla d'Oro

8 ounces tiny shrimp
2 tablespoons minced garlic
3/4 cup olive oil
1 large tomato, chopped
1 12-ounce can artichoke hearts, drained,
cut into fourths
3 pounds cheese tortellini, cooked
1 teaspoon salt
2 tablespoons chopped basil
1/2 cup grated Parmesan cheese

Blanch shrimp in boiling water for 2 minutes; drain and rinse. Sauté shrimp and garlic in olive oil in skillet for 1 minute. Stir in tomato and artichoke hearts. Pour over cooked tortellini; sprinkle with salt, basil and Parmesan cheese. Yield: 8 servings.

Approx Per Serving: Cal 774; Prot 34 g; Carbo 83 g; Fiber <1 g; T Fat 35 g; 40% Calories from Fat; Chol 129 mg; Sod 1148 mg.

There are 3 major types of wheat used today. Soft wheat is low in gluten and is used for cakes and pastries. Hard wheat is high in gluten and is best for breads. Durum is the hardest, and durum flour is used in the making of pastas.

Spaghetti Carbonara

1 clove of garlic, minced
1 teaspoon chopped onion
2 ounces prosciutto, chopped
3 ounces smoked bacon, cut into thin slices
2 teaspoons butter
1/2 ounce white wine
3 ounces heavy cream
2 eggs, beaten
1 tablespoon grated Parmesan cheese
1 leaf fresh sage
1 leaf fresh rosemary
Salt and pepper to taste
6 ounces spaghetti, cooked

Sauté garlic, onion, prosciutto and bacon in butter in large skillet until lightly browned. Stir in wine. Simmer to reduce liquid. Beat cream, eggs, cheese, sage, rosemary, salt and pepper in bowl. Add spaghetti to prosciutto mixture. Simmer for 1 to 2 minutes. Add cream mixture, tossing to coat. Garnish with chopped parsley. Yield: 1 serving.

Approx Per Serving: Cal 1420; Prot 60 g; Carbo 133 g; Fiber 7 g; T Fat 70 g; 45% Calories from Fat; Chol 620 mg; Sod 1493 mg.

Spinach and Artichoke Lasagna

1 red bell pepper, seeded, chopped
1/2 cup chopped onion
7 tablespoons butter
2 10-ounce packages frozen chopped spinach,
thawed, drained
3/4 cup ricotta cheese   1 egg, beaten
3/4 cup grated Parmesan cheese
1 10-ounce package frozen artichokes,
thawed, cut into halves
2 1/4 cups shredded mozzarella cheese
1/4 cup flour
Salt and pepper to taste
2 cups milk   8 lasagna noodles
1/4 cup grated Parmesan cheese

Sauté red pepper and onion in 3 tablespoons butter in skillet until tender. Combine with next 5 ingredients and 2 cups mozzarella cheese in bowl; mix well. Blend remaining 4 tablespoons melted butter, flour, salt and pepper in saucepan; stir in milk. Bring to a boil. Cook until thickened, stirring constantly. Spread half the white sauce in 9x13-inch baking dish. Layer with 1/3 of the spinach mixture, half the noodles, remaining spinach mixture, remaining noodles and remaining white sauce. Top with 1/4 cup Parmesan cheese and remaining 1/4 cup mozzarella cheese. Bake at 375 degrees for 45 to 50 minutes. Yield: 10 servings.

Approx Per Serving: Cal 379; Prot 19 g; Carbo 30 g; Fiber 4 g; T Fat 21 g; 49% Calories from Fat; Chol 85 mg; Sod 422 mg.

Spinach Italiano

6 10-ounce packages frozen chopped spinach,
thawed, drained
4 eggs, beaten   2 1/2 cups cooked orzo
3 pounds ricotta cheese
1/2 cup grated Parmesan cheese   Salt and pepper to taste

Mix all ingredients in bowl. Spread in lightly greased 9x13-inch baking dish. Bake at 350 degrees for 30 to 40 minutes; cool. Cut into squares. Yield: 15 servings.

Approx Per Serving: Cal 249; Prot 17 g; Carbo 14 g; Fiber 3 g; T Fat 14 g; 50% Calories from Fat; Chol 105 mg; Sod 243 mg.

Vodka-Tomato Spinach Pasta

2 cloves of garlic, minced   1 dried chili pepper, chopped
3 tablespoons olive oil   3 cups chopped tomatoes
1 bay leaf   1/4 to 1/3 cup vodka   1/3 cup cream
1/4 cup chopped parsley   Salt to taste
8 ounces spinach pasta, cooked

Sauté garlic and pepper in olive oil in skillet for 1 minute. Stir in undrained tomatoes, bay leaf and vodka; boil. Simmer for 1 minute, stirring frequently. Add cream, parsley and salt. Simmer over low heat until heated through. Remove bay leaf. Serve over spinach pasta. Yield: 4 servings.

Approx Per Serving: Cal 447; Prot 13 g; Carbo 47 g; Fiber 2 g; T Fat 19 g; 38% Calories from Fat; Chol 27 mg; Sod 31 mg.

Tomato and Basil Fettucini

8 sun-dried tomatoes
1/2 cup boiling water
1/2 cup olive oil
1/4 cup butter
4 cloves of garlic, minced
1/4 cup prepared basil pesto
Salt and pepper to taste
8 ounces fettucini, cooked

Soak tomatoes in boiling water for 20 to 30 minutes or until tender. Drain, reserving liquid. Chop tomatoes and set aside. Heat oil in saucepan over medium-high heat; add butter. Sauté garlic in butter and oil for 2 minutes; add pesto, salt, pepper and reserved tomato liquid. Simmer until heated through. Pour over cooked fettucini; add tomatoes. Toss to coat. Serve with Parmesan cheese. Yield: 6 servings.

Approx Per Serving: Cal 591; Prot 8 g; Carbo 38 g; Fiber 5 g; T Fat 47 g; 69% Calories from Fat; Chol 23 mg; Sod 143 mg.

Make a tangy sauce for pasta—*Anchovy Pesto.* Crush 1 anchovy filet with 2 tablespoons grated Parmesan cheese. Mix with equal parts softened butter.

Tomato-Cheese-Basil Concoction

2 pounds ripe firm tomatoes, sliced 1/3 inch thick
1/2 teaspoon salt   1 cup packed freshly chopped basil
3/4 cup low-fat ricotta cheese
3 ounces mozzarella cheese, shredded
8 ounces pasta, cooked

Combine tomatoes, salt, basil, ricotta cheese and mozzarella cheese in bowl; mix well. Pour over pasta, tossing to coat. Yield: 6 servings.

Approx Per Serving: Cal 264; Prot 13 g; Carbo 40 g; Fiber 5 g; T Fat 6 g; 21% Calories from Fat; Chol 21 mg; Sod 284 mg.

Tomato-Mozzarella Pasta

6 to 8 tomatoes   8 ounces mozzarella cheese, shredded
1/4 cup freshly minced basil   5 tablespoons olive oil
2 cloves of garlic, minced   1 tablespoon minced parsley
Salt and freshly ground pepper to taste
16 ounces pasta, cooked

Peel, seed and coarsely chop tomatoes, reserving liquid. Mix tomatoes, reserved liquid, mozzarella cheese, basil, oil, garlic, parsley, salt and pepper in bowl; mix well. Let stand at room temperature for 1 hour. Pour over cooked pasta, tossing to coat. Yield: 4 servings.

Approx Per Serving: Cal 782; Prot 28 g; Carbo 99 g; Fiber 9 g; T Fat 30 g; 35% Calories from Fat; Chol 44 mg; Sod 235 mg.

Tomato Sauce de Corniglio

1/4 cup dried porcini mushrooms
3 cups water   1 onion, minced
3 tablespoons olive oil
1/2 carrot, minced
1/4 stalk celery, minced
2 cloves of garlic, minced
1/8 teaspoon crushed rosemary
1   8-ounce can tomato paste
1 tablespoon unsalted butter
1   28-ounce can whole tomatoes
1 bay leaf
1/8 teaspoon dried basil
Salt and pepper to taste

Soak mushrooms in 1 cup water for 1 hour; drain and set aside, reserving liquid. Sauté onion in oil in skillet over low heat until tender. Add carrot, celery and garlic. Cook until tender. Add mushrooms, rosemary, tomato paste and butter; mix well. Bring to a boil. Add remaining 2 cups water, stirring vigorously for 2 minutes; reduce heat to low. Add whole tomatoes, bay leaf, basil, salt and pepper. Simmer, partially covered, for 2 hours and 40 minutes. Stir in reserved mushroom liquid. Cook for 20 minutes longer. Remove bay leaf. Serve over tortellini, pasta or polenta. Corniglio is a mountain village near Parma, Italy, famous for the local chestnut forests where porcini mushrooms grow in abundance. Yield: 10 servings.

Approx Per Serving: Cal 94; Prot 2 g; Carbo 11 g; Fiber 3 g; T Fat 6 g; 50% Calories from Fat; Chol 3 mg; Sod 147 mg.

Tortelli di Toscana

6 eggs, less 1 yolk
2 cups flour
1/2 teaspoon salt
1/2 teaspoon olive oil
1 tablespoon warm water
1/2 to 1 cup instant potato flakes
16 ounces ricotta cheese
8 ounces cream cheese, softened
3 tablespoons grated Parmesan cheese
1 cup finely chopped Swiss chard
1/4 teaspoon nutmeg
1/4 teaspoon ground allspice
Salt and pepper to taste

Combine 4 beaten eggs less 1 yolk, flour, 1/2 teaspoon salt, olive oil and water in bowl; mix well. Stir in enough potato flakes to make crumbly dough. Roll out thinly on floured surface. Cut into squares; set aside. Combine ricotta, cream cheese, Parmesan cheese, remaining 2 eggs, chard, nutmeg, allspice, salt to taste and pepper in large bowl; mix well. Spoon small amount of filling onto half the pasta squares. Top with remaining squares; seal edges. Drop into boiling salted water. Cook until done to taste. Tortelli is the northern Italian term for ravioli. This recipe is popular in Reggio-Emilia and Tuscany. Yield: 6 servings.

Approx Per Serving: Cal 620; Prot 25 g; Carbo 64 g; Fiber 3 g; T Fat 29 g; 43% Calories from Fat; Chol 259 mg; Sod 526 mg.

Vodka Rigatoni

1 tablespoon minced garlic
1/4 cup margarine
3 cups cream
1/2 cup grated Parmesan cheese
2 tablespoons freshly chopped parsley
3 ounces vodka
1/2 cup tomato sauce
16 ounces rigatoni, cooked

Sauté garlic in margarine in saucepan for 1 minute; reduce heat to low. Add cream, Parmesan cheese, parsley, vodka and tomato sauce; mix well. Simmer for 20 minutes, stirring frequently. Pour over cooked rigatoni, tossing to coat. Yield: 8 servings.

Approx Per Serving: Cal 623; Prot 11 g; Carbo 47 g; Fiber 3 g; T Fat 41 g; 61% Calories from Fat; Chol 126 mg; Sod 289 mg.

For outdoor table cloths, select shower curtains from the clearance table. Turn under edge with hole with tape or cut to fit table. Place 2 picnic tables the same size side by side to form a large square table with benches on all 4 sides.

Vegetables with Bow Ties

4 carrots, cut into julienne strips
2 zucchini, cut into julienne strips
1 green bell pepper, cut into julienne strips
1 clove of garlic, minced
3 tablespoons butter
8 ounces process cheese spread
1/4 cup half and half
1 teaspoon crushed dried basil
3 cups bow tie pasta, cooked

Sauté carrots, zucchini, green pepper and garlic in butter in large skillet until tender-crisp; reduce heat to low. Add cheese, half and half and basil. Cook until cheese is melted, stirring constantly. Add cooked pasta, tossing to coat. Cook until heated through. Yield: 8 servings.

Approx Per Serving: Cal 236; Prot 9 g; Carbo 25 g; Fiber 3 g; T Fat 12 g; 43% Calories from Fat; Chol 30 mg; Sod 434 mg.

Know your tomatoes: determinate bush varieties are usually small, need no staking and are best for containers or small gardens. Indeterminate varieties grow tall, need to be staked or caged, like to be pruned, and will provide fruit over a longer period of time.

The Harvest Show

While the fall's cool, crisp air brings out the finest in late summer crops, the Pennsylvania Horticultural Society's Harvest Show brings out the best in the area's gardeners. Old and young come from city plots, suburban yards and country fields to show and share their treasures at The Pennsylvania Horticultural Society's annual Harvest Show.

Scarecrows peek from behind big bales of hay while kids scramble between the Autumn Games (anyone for the Ten Meter Pumpkin Push?) and the calmer events under the Children's Activity Tent, including painting pumpkins and making leaf masks or collages with seeds.

Adults attend free lectures about growing, cooking, drying or preserving their harvest bounty, then join their children to watch demonstrations from bee keepers, weavers, and a variety of crafts people.

During the course of the Harvest Show weekend, visitors see just about everything a Pennsylvania garden can produce, from tobacco and peanuts grown in a community garden to an eye scorching arrangement of three dozen different cultivars of glitzy celosia flowers.

Throughout the competitive classes, enthusiastic growers make new friends and talk about *next year's* garden (better and more pest-free than ever) while they share secrets and solutions to common problems. The gardening spirit shines brightest when a visitor admires a blue ribbon tomato and the proud prize winner reaches into her pocket to share a few heirloom seeds.

A summer of vegetable gardening rewards us with treats for the eye as well as for the taste buds. – Photography by Walter Chandoha

Harvest Show Schedule-Writing Luncheon

Cucumber Canapés
(mayonnaise-spread party rye with lemon-pepper sprinkled cucumbers)

Harvest Muffins *(page 173)*

Yum-Yum Chinese Salad *(page 60)*   or   Wild Rice-Smoked Turkey Salad *(page 73)*

Vegetable Aspic *(page 71)*

Fudge Pie *(page 236)*
(served with heavy cream and strawberries)

Cut a watermelon either in half or in the shape of a basket with a handle.
Cut fruit and vegetables, using flower-shaped cookie cutters; secure on long wooden picks. Add
greens, herbs, or edible flowers to the fruits and vegetables in the watermelon container.

Acini-de-Pepe Dessert

8 ounces uncooked acini-de-pepe
1   20-ounce can crushed pineapple
1   11-ounce can mandarin oranges
1 egg
1/2 cup sugar
2 tablespoons flour
1/2 teaspoon salt
9 ounces whipped topping

Cook pasta using package directions; drain. Drain pineapple and mandarin oranges, reserving juice. Beat egg with sugar, flour and salt in double boiler. Stir in reserved juice. Cook until thickened, stirring constantly. Add pasta. Cool slightly. Fold in fruit and whipped topping. Chill until serving time. May add maraschino cherries if desired. Yield: 8 servings.

Approx Per Serving: Cal 351; Prot 5 g; Carbo 63 g; Fiber 3 g; T Fat 9 g; 23% Calories from Fat; Chol 27 mg; Sod 154 mg.

When narcissus are past their prime, remove the dead flower heads, then let the leaves die naturally to return strength to the plant. Avoid tying, braiding or anything else that constricts the natural flow.

Grapefruit Alaska

2 pink grapefruits
3 egg whites, at room temperature
1/2 cup (or more) sugar
2 cups vanilla ice cream

Cut grapefruit into halves. Cut around sections with serrated knife, leaving sections in place. Chill in refrigerator. Beat egg whites with salt and cream of tartar in mixer bowl until soft peaks form. Add sugar gradually, beating constantly until stiff peaks form. Scoop 1/2 cup ice cream onto each grapefruit half; place on baking sheet. Cover top of grapefruit and ice cream completely with meringue. Broil on center oven rack until light brown or bake at 450 degrees for 3 to 5 minutes. Serve immediately. Yield: 4 servings.

Approx Per Serving: Cal 280; Prot 6 g; Carbo 51 g; Fiber 2 g; T Fat 7 g; 23% Calories from Fat; Chol 30 mg; Sod 96 mg.

If your garden has a nematode problem, dip the roots of your tomato plants in a solution of 0.25 percent corn oil mixed in a gallon of water, before planting them in the ground.

Flaming Baked Alaska

1 quart strawberry ripple ice cream, softened
2 cups biscuit mix
3 tablespoons sugar
1/2 cup milk
1 egg
3 tablespoons melted butter
4 egg whites, at room temperature
1/2 teaspoon cream of tartar
1/2 teaspoon vanilla extract
1/2 cup sugar
1 pint fresh strawberries, sliced
4 sugar cubes
1 tablespoon (or more) rum

Spoon ice cream into foil-lined 8-inch pan. Freeze until firm. Combine biscuit mix, 3 tablespoons sugar, milk, egg and butter in mixer bowl; mix until smooth. Spoon into greased 9-inch cake pan. Bake at 425 degrees for 15 minutes. Remove to wire rack to cool. Place on serving plate. Beat egg whites with cream of tartar and vanilla in mixer bowl until soft peaks form. Add 1/2 cup sugar gradually, beating constantly until stiff peaks form. Place ice cream on cake; remove foil. Spoon strawberries onto ice cream. Cover completely with meringue. Bake at 500 degrees for 3 to 5 minutes or until light brown. Soak sugar cubes in rum; place in meringue. Ignite sugar cubes and serve immediately. May vary ice cream and fruit to suit tastes. Yield: 8 servings.

Approx Per Serving: Cal 421; Prot 8 g; Carbo 59 g; Fiber 1 g; T Fat 17 g; 37% Calories from Fat; Chol 70 mg; Sod 532 mg.

Banana Split Dessert

1 1/2 cups melted margarine
2 cups graham cracker crumbs
2 eggs
2 cups confectioners' sugar
4 to 5 bananas, sliced
1 20-ounce can crushed pineapple
12 ounces whipped topping

Mix 1/2 cup melted margarine and graham cracker crumbs in 9x13-inch dish; press evenly over bottom. Combine eggs, confectioners' sugar and 1 cup softened margarine in mixer bowl; beat for 15 minutes. Spoon into prepared dish. Layer with bananas, pineapple and whipped topping. Chill, covered, overnight. Garnish with cherries and walnuts. Yield: 12 servings.

Approx Per Serving: Cal 551; Prot 4 g; Carbo 63 g; Fiber 2 g; T Fat 33 g; 53% Calories from Fat; Chol 36 mg; Sod 410 mg.

Make *Easy Fruit Dessert* by combining fresh fruit with a liqueur: Curaçao with oranges or pineapple; Grand Marnier with grapefruit or strawberries; Kirsch with bananas, peaches or melon; Champagne with strawberries or peaches; and Ruby Port with pears or figs.

Almond-Apple Cheesecake

1¼ cups flour
½ cup butter, softened
⅓ cup plus ¾ cup sugar
¾ cup almonds
¾ teaspoon vanilla extract
8 ounces cream cheese, softened
2 eggs
½ teaspoon vanilla extract
3 to 4 cups sliced peeled apples
½ teaspoon cinnamon

Combine 1¼ cups flour, ½ cup butter, ⅓ cup sugar, ½ cup chopped almonds and ¼ teaspoon vanilla in bowl; mix well. Press over bottom and side of 9-inch springform pan. Bake at 400 degrees for 5 minutes. Cool for 5 minutes. Combine cream cheese, eggs, ¼ cup sugar and remaining ½ teaspoon vanilla in mixer bowl; mix well. Spoon into crust. Toss apples with remaining ½ cup sugar and cinnamon in bowl. Arrange over cream cheese mixture; sprinkle with remaining ¼ cup sliced almonds. Bake for 25 minutes longer or until filling is firm and apples are cooked through. Cool on wire rack. Place on serving plate; remove side of pan. Yield: 12 servings.

Approx Per Serving: Cal 329; Prot 5 g; Carbo 35 g; Fiber 2 g; T Fat 19 g; 52% Calories from Fat; Chol 77 mg; Sod 134 mg.

Chocolate Eclair Dessert

1 16-ounce package graham crackers
2 4-ounce packages vanilla instant pudding mix
3 cups milk
5 tablespoons Frangelica liqueur
8 ounces whipped topping
1 16-ounce can chocolate frosting

Line 9x13-inch dish with graham crackers. Prepare pudding mix with milk in bowl; mix well. Fold in Frangelica and whipped topping. Spread half the mixture in prepared dish. Add a second layer of crackers and remaining pudding mixture. Spread frosting on remaining crackers; arrange over top of dessert. Chill overnight. Yield: 12 servings.

Approx Per Serving: Cal 511; Prot 6 g; Carbo 80 g; Fiber 1 g; T Fat 17 g; 31% Calories from Fat; Chol 8 mg; Sod 471 mg.

Instant chocolate piping can be accomplished by placing chocolate chips in a heavy-duty ziplock bag. Immerse the bag in hot water to melt the chocolate. Snip off a small corner of the bag, twist the bag and pipe the chocolate out of the hole.

Chocolate-Peppermint Delight

1 cup chocolate wafer crumbs
²/3 cup butter, softened
2 cups confectioners' sugar
3 eggs, separated
2 1-ounce squares chocolate, melted, cooled
¹/2 cup chopped pecans
Salt to taste
1 teaspoon vanilla extract
1 quart peppermint stick ice cream
¹/2 cup chocolate wafer crumbs

Spread 1 cup wafer crumbs in round pan. Cream butter and confectioners' sugar in mixer bowl until light and fluffy. Beat in egg yolks. Add chocolate, pecans, salt and vanilla; mix well. Fold in stiffly beaten egg whites. Spread evenly in prepared pan. Freeze until firm. Spread ice cream over top; sprinkle with ¹/2 cup wafer crumbs. Freeze until serving time. May substitute vanilla wafers for chocolate wafers, walnuts for pecans and coffee or mint ice cream for peppermint stick ice cream.
Yield: 12 servings.

Approx Per Serving: Cal 488; Prot 7 g; Carbo 54 g; Fiber 1 g; T Fat 30 g; 55% Calories from Fat; Chol 122 mg; Sod 265 mg.

Dirt Cake

1¹/2 pounds Oreo cookies, crushed
¹/2 cup melted butter
1 6-ounce package vanilla instant pudding mix
3¹/2 cups milk
8 ounces cream cheese, softened
10 ounces whipped topping

Mix cookie crumbs with butter in bowl. Press part of the mixture over bottom and side of 8-inch flowerpot lined with plastic wrap. Prepare pudding mix with milk in bowl. Add cream cheese and whipped topping; mix well. Alternate layers of pudding mixture and remaining cookie crumbs in prepared flowerpot, ending with crumbs. Chill until serving time. Insert silk or plastic flowers at serving time; garnish with gummy worms. Yield: 16 servings.

Approx Per Serving: Cal 436; Prot 5 g; Carbo 48 g; Fiber 1 g; T Fat 26 g; 52% Calories from Fat; Chol 38 mg; Sod 389 mg.

Make a delicious *Dessert Sauce* of 1 cup sour cream, ¹/2 cup packed brown sugar and ¹/2 teaspoon vanilla extract.

Eggnog Bavarian

2 envelopes unflavored gelatin
½ cup cold water
1 quart eggnog
½ cup (or less) bourbon
⅔ cup egg whites, stiffly beaten
2 cups heavy cream, whipped
2 3-ounce packages ladyfingers
Nutmeg to taste

Soften gelatin in cold water for 5 minutes. Heat ¾ cup eggnog in saucepan over medium heat. Add gelatin, stirring to dissolve completely. Combine with remaining eggnog and bourbon in large bowl; mix well. Chill until thickened. Beat eggnog mixture until frothy. Fold in egg whites and whipped cream. Line large glass bowl with ladyfingers. Spoon eggnog mixture into bowl; sprinkle with nutmeg. Chill, covered, until serving time.
Yield: 10 servings.

Approx Per Serving: Cal 399; Prot 9 g; Carbo 26 g; Fiber <1 g;
T Fat 27 g; 63% Calories from Fat; Chol 125 mg; Sod 106 mg.

Special-Request Flan

1 cup sugar
2 8-ounce cans evaporated milk
1 14-ounce can sweetened condensed milk
4 eggs
1 teaspoon vanilla extract
1 teaspoon cinnamon

Sprinkle sugar in deep 9-inch baking pan. Place on burner over very low heat. Heat until sugar melts and turns light brown, tilting pan to coat evenly. Combine evaporated milk, condensed milk, egg, vanilla and cinnamon in mixer bowl; beat until smooth. Spoon into prepared pan; place in larger pan of hot water. Bake at 375 to 400 degrees for 45 to 60 minutes or until knife inserted in center comes out clean. Cool in pan on wire rack for 1 to 2 hours. Invert onto serving plate. Yield: 12 servings.

Approx Per Serving: Cal 248; Prot 7 g; Carbo 39 g; Fiber 0 g;
T Fat 8 g; 27% Calories from Fat; Chol 93 mg; Sod 106 mg.

 Shrubs planted too close together get poor air circulation and grow unevenly.

Flan

1³/4 cups sugar
3 eggs
5 egg yolks
2   13-ounce cans evaporated skim milk
2 teaspoons vanilla extract
6 tablespoons Cognac

Sprinkle ³/4 cup sugar in heatproof glass dish. Place on burner over low heat. Heat until sugar melts and turns golden brown, stirring constantly and tilting dish to coat evenly. Cool slightly. Beat eggs and egg yolks in mixer bowl. Add remaining 1 cup sugar, evaporated milk, vanilla and Cognac; mix well. Spoon into prepared dish; place in larger pan of water. Bake at 350 degrees for 1 hour or until knife inserted in center comes out clean. Cool slightly. Invert onto serving plate. May substitute rum for Cognac. Yield: 8 servings.

Approx Per Serving: Cal 335; Prot 11 g; Carbo 58 g; Fiber 0 g; T Fat 6 g; 16% Calories from Fat; Chol 217 mg; Sod 138 mg.

To soften hardened brown sugar, add several drops of water to the package of brown sugar and microwave for about 15 seconds.

Ladyfinger Dessert

1 cup chocolate chips   Instant coffee powder to taste
2 cups heavy cream, whipped
2   3-ounce packages ladyfingers

Melt chocolate chips in double boiler. Stir in coffee. Cool slightly. Fold in whipped cream. Layer ladyfingers and chocolate mixture 1/4 at a time on large plate; spread chocolate mixture to frost side. Chill until serving time. Yield: 8 servings.

Approx Per Serving: Cal 389; Prot 4 g; Carbo 28 g; Fiber 1 g; T Fat 31 g; 69% Calories from Fat; Chol 82 mg; Sod 40 mg.

Lemon Custard Puffs

2 tablespoons melted butter
5 tablespoons lemon juice   Grated rind of 1 lemon
3 eggs, separated   1¹/2 cups milk   1 cup sugar
1/4 cup flour   1/2 teaspoon salt

Mix first 4 ingredients and beaten egg yolks in bowl. Mix in sugar, flour and salt. Fold in stiffly beaten egg whites. Spoon into 7 greased custard cups; place in pan of hot water. Bake at 350 degrees for 35 minutes or until golden brown. Garnish with nutmeg or whipped cream and fruit. Yield: 7 servings.

Approx Per Serving: Cal 224; Prot 5 g; Carbo 36 g; Fiber <1 g; T Fat 8 g; 29% Calories from Fat; Chol 107 mg; Sod 228 mg.

Lemon Snow

1 envelope unflavored gelatin
1¼ cups cold water
1 cup sugar
¼ cup fresh lemon juice
1 teaspoon grated lemon rind
3 egg whites
¼ teaspoon salt
4 egg yolks
2 cups milk, scalded
⅛ teaspoon salt
1 teaspoon vanilla extract

Soften gelatin in ¼ cup cold water in bowl for 5 minutes. Stir in 1 cup boiling water until dissolved. Add ¾ cup sugar, lemon juice and lemon rind. Chill for 2 hours or until partially set. Beat egg whites in mixer bowl until stiff peaks form. Add gelatin mixture and ¼ teaspoon salt gradually, beating constantly. Spoon into serving bowl. Chill, covered, until serving time. Beat egg yolks in double boiler. Add warm milk very gradually, beating constantly. Add ⅛ teaspoon salt and remaining ¼ cup sugar. Cook until thickened, stirring constantly. Stir in vanilla. Chill until serving time. Serve custard with lemon mixture. May serve with raspberries if desired. Yield: 6 servings.

Approx Per Serving: Cal 235; Prot 7 g; Carbo 38 g; Fiber <1 g; T Fat 6 g; 24% Calories from Fat; Chol 153 mg; Sod 199 mg.

Chocolate Mousse

½ cup semisweet chocolate chips, melted
3 eggs, separated
½ teaspoon vanilla extract
2 tablespoons (about) rum
1 cup heavy cream, whipped

Combine melted chocolate, egg yolks, vanilla and rum in bowl; mix well. Fold into stiffly beaten egg whites. Chill in refrigerator. Top servings with whipped cream. Garnish with chocolate curls or crystallized flowers. Make several recipes of this instead of increasing recipe. Yield: 6 servings.

Approx Per Serving: Cal 259; Prot 4 g; Carbo 9 g; Fiber <1 g; T Fat 23 g; 79% Calories from Fat; Chol 161 mg; Sod 46 mg.

To store extra egg whites or yolks, cover yolks with cold water and store in the refrigerator; leftover whites can be frozen or stored in a jar in the refrigerator.

Lemon Mousse

1¹/₂ envelopes unflavored gelatin
¹/₄ cup cold water
1 cup sugar
3 eggs, separated
Juice and grated rind of 2 lemons
1 teaspoon vanilla extract
2 cups heavy cream

Soften gelatin in cold water in double boiler. Heat over boiling water until dissolved. Combine sugar, egg yolks, lemon juice, lemon rind and vanilla in mixer bowl; mix well. Beat in gelatin. Fold in stiffly beaten egg whites. Whip ²/₃ of the cream in mixer bowl until soft peaks form. Fold into mousse. Spoon into mold. Chill overnight. Unmold onto serving plate. Whip remaining cream in mixer bowl until soft peaks form. Spread over mousse. Garnish with additional grated lemon rind or fresh flowers. Yield: 10 servings.

Approx Per Serving: Cal 271; Prot 4 g; Carbo 22 g; Fiber <1 g; T Fat 19 g; 62% Calories from Fat; Chol 129 mg; Sod 37 mg.

 Shred oak leaves for mulching rhododendrons and azaleas.

Amber Pudding

2 cups sugar
6¹/₂ tablespoons butter
5 ounces almonds with skins
1 quart vanilla ice cream, softened
1 quart coffee ice cream, softened
1   16-ounce can buttercream frosting

Combine sugar, butter and almonds in saucepan. Cook for 8 to 10 minutes. Pour onto oiled baking sheet with sides; let stand until cool and firm. Break into crumbs. Line buttered 2-quart melon mold with vanilla ice cream. Freeze until firm. Fill center with coffee ice cream. Freeze until firm. Unmold onto serving plate. Spread with frosting; sprinkle with almond crunch mixture. Freeze, wrapped with plastic wrap, until serving time. Serve with a mixture of light custard and whipped cream flavored with rum. May substitute hazelnuts for almonds. Yield: 12 servings.

Approx Per Serving: Cal 587; Prot 6 g; Carbo 80 g; Fiber 1 g; T Fat 28 g; 42% Calories from Fat; Chol 56 mg; Sod 213 mg. Nutritional information does not include custard sauce.

Make a *Custard Sauce* by combining 3 or 4 egg yolks with ¹/₄ cup sugar in double boiler. Add 2 cups scalded milk and cook over hot water until thickened, stirring constantly. Chill until serving time.

Yankee Blueberry Pudding

10 thin slices firm bread
1/2 cup (or less) butter, softened
1 quart blueberries
1 1/2 cups sugar
1 teaspoon cinnamon
3/4 cup water
1 1/2 tablespoons unflavored gelatin

Trim crusts from bread and spread with butter. Cut each slice into 3 strips. Line melon mold with part of the strips, reserving remaining strips for top. Combine blueberries, sugar, cinnamon and 1/2 cup water in saucepan. Cook for 10 minutes. Soften gelatin in remaining 1/4 cup cold water in bowl. Stir into blueberry mixture until dissolved. Spoon into prepared mold. Top with reserved bread strips. Chill overnight. Unmold onto serving plate. Garnish servings with whipping cream. Yield: 8 servings.

Approx Per Serving: Cal 358; Prot 4 g; Carbo 60 g; Fiber 3 g; T Fat 13 g; 31% Calories from Fat; Chol 31 mg; Sod 230 mg.

 Make a collar of tin, tarpaper or wire to protect small fruit trees from rodents.

Bride's Pudding

2 envelopes unflavored gelatin
1/2 cup cold water
1/3 cup boiling water
6 egg whites
3/4 cup sugar
1 teaspoon vanilla extract
2 cups heavy cream, whipped
1   14-ounce can coconut

Soften gelatin in cold water in bowl. Stir in boiling water until dissolved; cool to room temperature. Beat egg whites in mixer bowl until frothy. Add sugar gradually, beating constantly until soft peaks form. Beat in gelatin and vanilla. Fold in whipped cream. Spread half the coconut evenly in springform pan. Spoon pudding into pan; top with remaining coconut. Chill until serving time. May serve with puréed fruit or fresh berries. Yield: 8 servings.

Approx Per Serving: Cal 515; Prot 7 g; Carbo 41 g; Fiber 6 g; T Fat 38 g; 64% Calories from Fat; Chol 82 mg; Sod 71 mg.

 Try a plastic bag over an ailing houseplant for a week to increase humidity.

Steamed Persimmon Pudding

1 cup flour
1 cup sugar
2 teaspoons baking soda
1 teaspoon cinnamon
1/2 teaspoon salt
1 cup persimmon purée
1/3 cup plus 2 tablespoons melted butter
2 eggs
1/2 teaspoon vanilla extract
1/2 cup milk
2 cups confectioners' sugar, sifted
1/4 cup dry sherry
1 cup heavy cream, whipped

Mix flour, sugar, baking soda, cinnamon and salt in bowl. Add persimmon purée, 1/3 cup melted butter, 1 egg, vanilla and milk; mix well. Spoon into greased pudding mold or 1-pound coffee can. Steam for 2 hours. Combine remaining egg, 2 tablespoons softened butter, confectioners' sugar and sherry in bowl; mix well. Fold in whipped cream. Serve pudding hot with sherry sauce. Yield: 8 servings.

Approx Per Serving: Cal 524; Prot 5 g; Carbo 74 g; Fiber 1 g; T Fat 24 g; 40% Calories from Fat; Chol 125 mg; Sod 464 mg.

Pineapple-Buttermilk Sherbet

Grated rind of 1 lemon
Juice of 2 lemons   1 quart buttermilk
1 1/2 cups sugar
1 6-ounce can crushed juice-pack pineapple

Combine lemon rind, lemon juice, buttermilk, sugar and pineapple in order listed in bowl, mixing well after each addition. Spoon into freezer container. Freeze until firm. Beat until smooth. Return to freezer container. Freeze until firm. Yield: 6 servings.

Approx Per Serving: Cal 280; Prot 6 g; Carbo 64 g; Fiber <1 g; T Fat 2 g; 5% Calories from Fat; Chol 6 mg; Sod 173 mg.

Strawberry-Basil Parfait

10 fresh basil leaves   3 cups fresh strawberries
1 cup vanilla ice cream, softened
6 basil leaves

Purée 10 basil leaves with 1 cup strawberries in food processor or blender. Spoon into 6 parfait glasses or champagne flutes. Fill glasses halfway with strawberries. Spoon ice cream over strawberries. Top each with remaining strawberries and 1 fresh basil leaf. Yield: 6 servings.

Approx Per Serving: Cal 75; Prot 1 g; Carbo 12 g; Fiber 4 g; T Fat 3 g; 31% Calories from Fat; Chol 10 mg; Sod 19 mg.

Monte Bello Tiramisu

3 egg yolks
1/4 cup sugar
1 1/4 cups mascarpone cheese
2 egg whites, stiffly beaten
1/2 cup espresso
3 tablespoons Amaretto
16 ladyfingers
3 1/2 ounces bittersweet chocolate, grated

Beat egg yolks and sugar in mixer bowl until thick and lemon-colored. Fold in cheese 1 tablespoon at a time. Fold in egg whites. Blend coffee and liqueur in bowl; drizzle over ladyfingers. Alternate layers of ladyfingers and filling in 8x8-inch dish; sprinkle with chocolate. Chill overnight. May substitute baking cocoa for chocolate. Yield: 8 servings.

Approx Per Serving: Cal 360; Prot 8 g; Carbo 32 g; Fiber <1 g; T Fat 23 g; 56% Calories from Fat; Chol 174 mg; Sod 145 mg.

Bittersweet and semisweet mean pretty much the same thing—slightly sweetened and without milk or cream. Domestic brands are usually called semisweet, while imported brands often use the term bittersweet.

Blitz Cake

1/2 cup butter, softened   1 1/2 cups sugar
4 eggs, separated   2 tablespoons milk
1 cup flour, sifted
1 teaspoon baking powder
1/4 teaspoon salt   1/2 cup chopped pecans
1 cup heavy cream, whipped

Combine butter, 1/2 cup sugar, slightly beaten egg yolks, milk, flour, baking powder and salt in bowl; mix well. Pour into two floured or waxed paper-lined 9-inch round cake pans. Beat egg whites with remaining 1 cup sugar. Spread over batter. Sprinkle with pecans. Bake at 350 degrees for 30 minutes. Cool in pans for several minutes. Remove to wire rack to cool completely. Spread whipped cream between layers. Yield: 10 servings.

Approx Per Serving: Cal 398; Prot 5 g; Carbo 42 g; Fiber 1 g T Fat 25 g; 54% Calories from Fat; Chol 143 mg; Sod 198 mg.

In the fall place cuttings from impatiens, fuchsias, geraniums, and begonias in sandy soil to be potted up later for winter bloom.

Daffodil Cake

6 eggs, separated
1 teaspoon cream of tartar
1/4 teaspoon salt
1 1/4 cups sugar
1 cup flour
2 tablespoons cold water
1 teaspoon baking powder
2 teaspoons vanilla extract
1/2 cup butter, softened
1   1-pound package confectioners' sugar
5 tablespoons milk

Beat egg whites with cream of tartar in mixer bowl until stiff. Mix salt, 3/4 cup sugar and 1/2 cup flour in bowl. Stir into egg whites. Spoon into 10-inch tube pan. Beat egg yolks in bowl. Add water, remaining 1/2 cup sugar, remaining 1/2 cup flour, baking powder and 1 teaspoon vanilla; mix well. Place dollops of yolk mixture over egg white mixture. Cut through with knife to marbleize. Bake at 350 degrees for 45 to 50 minutes or until lightly browned. Cool in pan for several minutes. Invert onto serving plate. Mix butter, confectioners' sugar and milk in bowl until of spreading consistency. Beat in remaining 1 teaspoon vanilla. Spread over top and side of cooled cake. Yield: 12 servings.

Approx Per Serving: Cal 405; Prot 4 g; Carbo 74 g; Fiber <1 g; T Fat 11 g; 24% Calories from Fat; Chol 128 mg; Sod 169 mg.

Chocolate Cake

2 ounces unsweetened chocolate, melted
1/2 cup butter
1 cup boiling water
2 cups sugar
2 eggs, separated
2 cups flour
1 teaspoon baking soda
1 teaspoon vanilla extract
1/2 cup sour cream

Mix chocolate, butter and boiling water in bowl. Beat sugar and egg yolks in mixer bowl until sugar is dissolved. Add flour, baking soda, vanilla, sour cream and chocolate mixture. Beat at medium speed until blended. Fold in stiffly beaten egg whites. Pour into nonstick 9x9-inch cake pan. Bake at 300 degrees for 45 minutes or until cake tests done. Yield: 16 servings.

Approx Per Serving: Cal 247; Prot 3 g; Carbo 38 g; Fiber 1 g; T Fat 10 g; 35% Calories from Fat; Chol 45 mg; Sod 112 mg.

Line greased cake pans with fresh rose geranium leaves before filling them with white cake batter. The flavor is subtle but delightful. Remove the leaves while the cake is still warm.

Gooey Chocolate Cake

2 cups sugar
2 cups flour
1¹/2 teaspoons baking soda
¹/2 teaspoon salt
1 cup water
4 ounces semisweet chocolate
1 cup margarine
1 cup sour cream*
2 eggs
2 teaspoons vanilla extract

Sift sugar, flour, baking soda and salt together. Combine water, chocolate and margarine in saucepan. Cook until chocolate and margarine are melted. Stir into flour mixture. Add sour cream, eggs and vanilla; mix well. Pour into greased 9x12-inch cake pan. Bake at 325 degrees for 30 to 40 minutes or until cake tests done. *May substitute sour milk or sour eggnog for sour cream. May dust baked cake with nutmeg to taste. Yield: 15 servings.

Approx Per Serving: Cal 352; Prot 4 g; Carbo 45 g; Fiber <1 g; T Fat 19 g; 47% Calories from Fat; Chol 35 mg; Sod 315 mg.

Decorate the top of an unfrosted cake by sifting confectioners' sugar over a doily and removing doily to leave design.

Seven-Layer Chocolate Cake

3¹/2 cups cake flour
3¹/2 teaspoons baking powder
¹/2 teaspoon plus ¹/8 teaspoon salt   1 cup milk
2 teaspoons vanilla extract
1 teaspoon almond extract
1¹/2 cups butter, softened
2 cups sugar   4 eggs
4 ounces unsweetened chocolate
1   1-pound package confectioners' sugar, sifted
¹/2 to ²/3 cup evaporated milk

Sift flour, baking powder and ¹/2 teaspoon salt together. Mix milk, 1 teaspoon vanilla and almond extract in bowl. Cream 1 cup butter in mixer bowl. Add sugar; beat until light and fluffy. Beat in eggs 1 at a time. Add flour mixture and milk mixture alternately to creamed mixture, beating well after each addition. Pour 1 cup batter into each of seven 8-inch round greased and floured cake pans. Bake at 350 degrees for 10 minutes; layers will be thin. Cool in pans for several minutes. Remove to wire rack to cool completely. Melt chocolate and remaining ¹/2 cup butter in double boiler over hot water. Sift confectioners' sugar and remaining ¹/8 teaspoon salt together. Stir into chocolate mixture. Beat in remaining 1 teaspoon vanilla. Add enough evaporated milk to make of spreading consistency. Spread between layers and over top and side of cake. Yield: 16 servings.

Approx Per Serving: Cal 525; Prot 6 g; Carbo 76 g; Fiber 2 g; T Fat 24 g; 40% Calories from Fat; Chol 105 mg; Sod 337 mg.

Chunky Fruitcake

1¹/2 cups unsweetened orange juice
1 cup rolled oats
1/4 cup butter, softened
2 eggs
2¹/2 cups unbleached flour
1 teaspoon baking soda
2 teaspoons baking powder
1 cup chopped fresh cranberries
1 cup chopped dried apricots
1 cup chopped dates
1 cup raisins
1 cup chopped walnuts
1 cup heavy cream
1/2 teaspoon orange extract

Combine orange juice, oats, butter and eggs in bowl; beat well. Add flour, baking soda and baking powder; mix well. Stir in fruits and walnuts. Spoon into oiled and floured bundt pan. Bake at 350 degrees for 35 to 40 minutes or until cake is browned and tests done. Cool in pan for several minutes. Remove to wire rack to cool completely. Beat cream with orange extract. Spread over cooled cake. May freeze. Yield: 12 servings.

Approx Per Serving: Cal 446; Prot 8 g; Carbo 65 g; Fiber 6 g; T Fat 20 g; 37% Calories from Fat; Chol 73 mg; Sod 180 mg.

Farmers' Fruitcake

1 cup chopped dried apples
1¹/4 cups water
1 cup molasses
1 cup sugar
1/2 cup butter, softened
1 teaspoon baking soda
3/4 cup sour milk
2 teaspoons cinnamon
1/2 teaspoon cloves
1 egg, lightly beaten
2 cups flour
1 teaspoon baking powder

Soak apples in 1 cup cold water in refrigerator overnight. Combine with molasses in saucepan. Simmer for 1 hour. Cool completely. Beat sugar and butter in bowl. Dissolve baking soda in 1/4 cup hot water. Stir into sugar mixture. Add sour milk, spices and egg. Stir in flour and baking powder; mix well. Stir in molasses mixture. Pour into nonstick 9x9-inch cake pan. Bake at 350 degrees for 40 to 50 minutes or until cake tests done. May freeze. Yield: 12 servings.

Approx Per Serving: Cal 248; Prot 3 g; Carbo 52 g; Fiber 1 g; T Fat 9 g; 26% Calories from Fat; Chol 41 mg; Sod 183 mg.

Irish Boiled Fruitcake

2 cups (or more) flour
1 teaspoon baking soda
1 teaspoon cinnamon
1 teaspoon cloves
8 ounces raisins
1/2 cup butter
1 cup sugar
1 cup Guinness stout beer
2 eggs, slightly beaten

Sift flour, baking soda, cinnamon and cloves together. Combine raisins, butter, sugar and stout in saucepan. Bring to a boil. Remove from heat and cool to room temperature. Stir in flour mixture. Add eggs; mix well. Pour into buttered cake pan or loaf pan. Bake at 350 degrees for 1 hour or until cake tests done. Yield: 12 servings.

Approx Per Serving: Cal 286; Prot 4 g; Carbo 48 g; Fiber 2 g; T Fat 9 g; 28% Calories from Fat; Chol 56 mg; Sod 149 mg.

Dust raisins and nuts with flour before adding them to cake batter to prevent their sinking to the bottom of the pan.

Rose Geranium Cake

24 rose geranium leaves
2 sticks butter
1³/4 cups sugar
3 egg whites
2 eggs
3 cups sifted flour
4 teaspoons baking powder
1/2 teaspoon salt
1/2 cup water
1 teaspoon vanilla extract
3/4 cup milk

Wrap 6 rose geranium leaves around each stick of butter. Let stand in refrigerator overnight. Discard leaves. Line 2 waxed paper-lined cake pans with remaining rose geranium leaves. Cream softened butter and sugar in mixer bowl until light and fluffy. Beat in egg whites and eggs. Add remaining dry ingredients and liquid ingredients alternately to creamed mixture, beating well after each addition. Pour into prepared pans. Bake at 350 degrees for 30 to 35 minutes or until layers test done. Cool in pans for several minutes. Invert onto wire rack. Remove leaves from layers with toothpicks; frosting will cover resulting roughness. Frost as desired. Yield: 12 servings.

Approx Per Serving: Cal 381; Prot 6 g; Carbo 52 g; Fiber 1 g; T Fat 17 g; 40% Calories from Fat; Chol 79 mg; Sod 359 mg.

Plum Torte

1 cup sugar
1/2 cup unsalted butter
1 cup unbleached flour, sifted
1 teaspoon baking powder
1/8 teaspoon salt
2 eggs, beaten
12 pitted plums, cut into halves
Sugar and lemon juice to taste
1 teaspoon cinnamon

Cream 1 cup sugar and butter in mixer bowl until light and fluffy. Add flour, baking powder, salt and eggs; beat well. Spoon into 8-inch springform pan. Place plum halves skin side up on top of batter. Sprinkle with additional sugar, lemon juice and cinnamon. Bake at 350 degrees for 1 hour; cool. Serve with vanilla ice cream or whipped cream. Yield: 8 servings.

Approx Per Serving: Cal 322; Prot 4 g; Carbo 48 g; Fiber 2 g
T Fat 14 g; 37% Calories from Fat; Chol 84 mg; Sod 95 mg.

Save your fireplace wood ashes to put on the garden in spring. Slugs won't crawl across them and your plants will benefit.

Cream Cheese Pound Cake

1 cup butter, softened
8 ounces cream cheese, softened
9 eggs   2 cups sugar
8 ounces orange juice
1 tablespoon vanilla extract   3 cups flour
1 tablespoon baking powder

Cream butter and cream cheese in mixer bowl until light and fluffy. Add eggs 1 at a time, beating well after each addition. Add sugar gradually, beating constantly. Stir in orange juice and vanilla. Combine flour and baking powder; stir into batter gradually. Pour into greased and floured 9-inch tube pan. Bake at 325 degrees for 1 1/2 hours or until cake tests done. Cool in pan for several minutes. Remove to wire rack to cool completely.
Yield: 12 servings.

Approx Per Serving: Cal 516; Prot 10 g; Carbo 61 g; Fiber 1 g
T Fat 27 g; 46% Calories from Fat; Chol 222 mg; Sod 321 mg.

Use wood ashes on your delphiniums, iris, peonies, lilacs, roses, clematis and pansies. Ashes will also repel cutworms.

Pecan-Brown Sugar Pound Cake

1 cup butter, softened
1 cup shortening
3¹/₄ cups packed light brown sugar
5 eggs
2¹/₄ cups flour
¹/₂ teaspoon baking powder
1 cup milk
1¹/₂ teaspoons vanilla extract
1¹/₄ cups ground toasted pecans

Cream butter and shortening in mixer bowl until light and fluffy. Add brown sugar, beating constantly. Add eggs 1 at a time, beating well after each addition. Sift flour and baking powder together. Add to batter alternately with mixture of milk and vanilla and ground pecans, mixing well. Pour into greased and floured 9-inch tube pan. Bake at 300 degrees for 1³/₄ hours. Cool in pan for several minutes. Remove to wire rack to cool completely. Yield: 12 servings.

Approx Per Serving: Cal 809; Prot 8 g; Carbo 82 g; Fiber 2 g T Fat 52 g; 57% Calories from Fat; Chol 133 mg; Sod 207 mg.

For a quick and delicious frosting for your cake or cookies, add maple syrup to confectioners' sugar. Stir until smooth and creamy. Spread over cake or cookies.

Rabbit Run Pound Cake

1¹/₂ cups butter, softened
3 cups plus 1 tablespoon sugar
6 eggs, at room temperature
8 ounces cream cheese, softened
3 cups flour
1 tablespoon almond extract
5 tablespoons Cointreau
Juice of ¹/₂ lemon
¹/₄ cup strawberry jelly
2 tablespoons light rum

Cream butter and 3 cups sugar in mixer bowl until light and fluffy. Add eggs 1 at a time, beating well after each addition. Beat in cream cheese. Add flour and almond extract gradually, beating well. Pour into 10-inch greased and floured tube pan. Bake at 325 degrees for 1¹/₄ hours. Combine Cointreau, lemon juice, remaining 1 tablespoon sugar, jelly and rum in saucepan; mix well. Cook over low heat until jelly melts. Pour over warm cake. Let stand in pan until cooled. Remove to serving plate; do not invert. Yield: 12 servings.

Approx Per Serving: Cal 655; Prot 8 g; Carbo 82 g; Fiber 1 g T Fat 33 g; 45% Calories from Fat; Chol 189 mg; Sod 287 mg.

Prince of Wales Cakes

1 cup raisins
1/2 cup butter, softened
1 cup sugar
3 eggs
3 tablespoons dark molasses
1/2 cup milk
1 teaspoon baking soda
2 cups plus 1 tablespoon flour
1/2 teaspoon nutmeg
1 teaspoon each ground cloves, cinnamon and salt

Cook raisins in water to cover in saucepan for 10 minutes; drain and set aside. Cream butter in mixer bowl until light and fluffy. Add sugar, eggs, molasses and mixture of milk and baking powder; beat well. Sift flour, spices and salt together. Stir into batter gradually. Dust raisins with remaining 1 tablespoon flour; stir into batter. Pour into 2 greased and floured 9-inch round pans. Bake at 350 degrees for 30 to 40 minutes or until cakes test done. Cool in pans for several minutes; remove to wire rack to cool completely. Dust with confectioners' sugar or frost with butter frosting. Yield: 16 servings.

Approx Per Serving: Cal 216; Prot 3 g; Carbo 35 g; Fiber 1 g
T Fat 7 g; 30% Calories from Fat; Chol 57 mg; Sod 121 mg.

Sweet Potato Cake

1 large sweet potato, peeled, grated
3 cups sugar
4 cups sifted flour
1 tablespoon baking powder
1/4 teaspoon salt
1/2 teaspoon allspice
1 cup butter, softened
6 eggs
1 teaspoon each vanilla and lemon extract
1 1/2 cups milk
1 cup chopped pecans

Combine sweet potato with 1/2 cup sugar in small bowl. Mix well and set aside. Sift flour, baking powder, salt and allspice in bowl twice. Cream butter and remaining 2 1/2 cups sugar in mixer bowl until light and fluffy. Beat in eggs, vanilla and lemon extracts. Add sifted dry ingredients alternately with milk, beating well after each addition. Add sweet potato mixture and pecans, beating at low speed. Pour into greased and floured 9-inch tube pan. Bake at 350 degrees for 1 1/2 hours. Cool in pan for several minutes. Remove to wire rack to cool completely. Serve with favorite icing or sauce. Yield: 12 servings.

Approx Per Serving: Cal 607; Prot 9 g; Carbo 86 g; Fiber 2 g
T Fat 26 g; 38% Calories from Fat; Chol 152 mg; Sod 307 mg.

Tiramisu

16 ounces mascarpone cheese
1/2 cup plus 2 tablespoons sifted confectioners' sugar
3 tablespoons plus 1/3 cup Kahlua liqueur
3 ounces semisweet chocolate, coarsely grated
1 1/2 teaspoons vanilla extract   1/2 teaspoon salt
2 cups heavy cream, whipped
2 tablespoons water
2 teaspoons instant espresso coffee granules
2   4-ounce packages ladyfingers

Mix cheese, 1/2 cup confectioners' sugar, 3 tablespoons liqueur, 2 ounces chocolate, 1 teaspoon vanilla and salt in large bowl with wire whisk. Fold in 1 cup whipped cream; set aside. Mix remaining 1/3 cup Kahlua, water, espresso granules and 1/2 teaspoon vanilla in small bowl. Separate ladyfingers into halves lengthwise. Line 10-cup glass bowl with 1/4 of the ladyfingers; brush with 2 tablespoons espresso mixture. Spoon 1/3 of the mascarpone mixture over ladyfingers. Repeat layers twice. Top with remaining ladyfingers. Brush with remaining espresso mixture. Sprinkle with remaining 1 ounce grated chocolate, reserving 1 tablespoon. Add remaining 2 tablespoons confectioners' sugar to remaining 1 cup whipped cream. Pipe rosettes over top of dessert. Sprinkle with reserved grated chocolate. Chill, covered, for 6 hours.
Yield: 10 servings.

Approx Per Serving: Cal 477; Prot 6 g; Carbo 35 g; Fiber <1 g
T Fat 34 g; 65% Calories from Fat; Chol 98 mg; Sod 271 mg.

Transformations Cake

1/2 cup canola oil
1/2 cup honey
1 tablespoon sugar
3 tablespoons molasses
1 egg
1 cup whole wheat flour
2/3 cup soybean flour
1/3 cup rice polish
1 teaspoon cinnamon
1/2 teaspoon each ground cloves, allspice, nutmeg and cardamom
2 teaspoons baking soda
1 1/2 cups cubed homemade zucchini pineapple
3/4 cup toasted sesame seed
3/4 cup currants

Beat oil, honey, sugar and molasses in mixer bowl until light and fluffy. Add egg, beating well. Sift flours, rice polish, spices and baking soda together. Add to molasses mixture alternately with zucchini pineapple. Stir in sesame seed and currants. Pour into buttered and floured 9x9-inch glass cake pan. Bake at 350 degrees for 45 to 50 minutes or until cake tests done. Cool in pan for several minutes. Remove to wire rack to cool completely.
Yield: 8 servings.

Approx Per Serving: Cal 586; Prot 10 g; Carbo 92 g; Fiber 5 g
T Fat 24 g; 35% Calories from Fat; Chol 27 mg; Sod 230 mg.

Apricot Squares

1 cup margarine, softened
1/2 cup sugar
2 cups sifted flour
4 eggs, separated
2   12-ounce cans apricot filling
1 cup sugar
1 teaspoon vanilla extract
1/2 cup chopped pecans

Cream margarine and 1/2 cup sugar in mixer bowl until light and fluffy. Add 1 cup flour; mix well. Add egg yolks and remaining flour; mix well. Pat into nonstick 11x17-inch baking pan. Bake at 300 degrees for 10 minutes. Cool on wire rack. Spread apricot filling over baked layer. Combine egg whites, 1 cup sugar and vanilla in mixer bowl. Beat until stiff. Spread over apricot layer. Top with pecans. Bake on top oven rack for 20 minutes. Remove to wire rack to cool. Cut into 1 1/2-inch squares.
Yield: 77 servings.

Approx Per Serving: Cal 65; Prot 1 g; Carbo 9 g; Fiber <1 g
T Fat 3 g; 44% Calories from Fat; Chol 11 mg; Sod 34 mg.

Even a small garden can have fruit trees. Dwarf apple trees bred for your section of the country can produce up to 3 bushels of regular-size apples in a season.

Best Apple Bars

2 cups sifted flour
2 teaspoons baking powder
1/2 teaspoon salt
1/2 teaspoon cinnamon
1/2 cup melted margarine
1 cup packed brown sugar
1 cup sugar
2 eggs
2 teaspoons vanilla extract
1 cup raisins
1 cup chopped peeled apple
1 cup coarsely chopped walnuts

Sift flour, baking powder, salt and cinnamon together. Combine margarine, brown sugar, sugar, eggs and vanilla in mixer bowl; mix until smooth. Stir in dry ingredients, raisins, apple and walnuts. Spread in nonstick 9x13-inch baking pan. Bake at 350 degrees for 30 to 35 minutes or until edges pull from sides of pan. Cut into bars when cool. Serve with whipped topping or ice cream.
Yield: 24 servings.

Approx Per Serving: Cal 206; Prot 3 g; Carbo 34 g; Fiber 1 g;
T Fat 7 g; 32% Calories from Fat; Chol 18 mg; Sod 129 mg.

Butterscotch Brownies

2 cups sifted flour   2 teaspoons baking powder
1 teaspoon salt
2 cups butterscotch chips
1 cup butter   4 eggs, beaten
2 cups packed brown sugar
1 to 2 cups chopped pecans
1½ teaspoons vanilla extract
½ teaspoon almond extract

Sift flour, baking powder and salt together. Melt butterscotch chips and butter in saucepan over low heat; mix well. Cool for 5 minutes. Mix eggs, brown sugar and dry ingredients in bowl. Fold in butterscotch mixture, pecans and flavorings. Spread in buttered and floured 9x13-inch baking pan. Bake at 300 degrees on top oven rack for 40 to 60 minutes or until brownies test done.
Yield: 32 servings.

Approx Per Serving: Cal 238; Prot 3 g; Carbo 28 g; Fiber 1 g; T Fat 14 g; 50% Calories from Fat; Chol 42 mg; Sod 160 mg.

If you have a juniper tree growing nearby, harvest the berries and dry them. The dried berries are a great addition to sauerkraut, pork or lamb dishes, stuffed cabbage rolls or in stuffings. Store them in a glass screw-top jar; they will keep for months.

Chocolate Bars

2 ounces unsweetened chocolate
½ cup butter
2 eggs   1 cup sugar
½ teaspoon vanilla extract
½ cup sifted flour
½ cup chopped walnuts

Melt chocolate and butter in saucepan over low heat; mix well. Beat eggs in mixer bowl until frothy. Add sugar and vanilla. Beat until thick. Add chocolate mixture; mix well. Stir in flour. Spread in waxed paper-lined 8x8-inch baking pan. Sprinkle with walnuts. Bake at 325 degrees for 30 minutes. Cut into bars while warm. Remove to wire rack to cool completely. Yield: 24 servings.

Approx Per Serving: Cal 109; Prot 1 g; Carbo 11 g; Fiber 1 g; T Fat 7 g; 56% Calories from Fat; Chol 28 mg; Sod 39 mg.

To mail cookies, use unbuttered, unsalted popcorn in the bottom of the shipping box to protect them from being crushed.

Cookies Fit for a Gardener

1/2 cup flour
1 cup sugar
Salt to taste
2 ounces unsweetened chocolate
1/2 cup butter
2 eggs, beaten
1 teaspoon vanilla extract
1 cup finely chopped walnuts

Sift flour, sugar and salt together. Melt chocolate and butter in double boiler over boiling water; mix well. Add flour mixture, beating with wire whisk until blended. Stir in eggs and vanilla. Spread onto nonstick 10x15-inch baking pan. Sprinkle with walnuts. Bake at 400 degrees for 8 minutes. Cut into squares while warm.
Yield: 24 servings.

Approx Per Serving: Cal 126; Prot 2 g; Carbo 12 g; Fiber 1 g; T Fat 9 g; 59% Calories from Fat; Chol 28 mg; Sod 39 mg.

For a fragrant kitchen and good cooking, keep parsley, chives, rosemary, small basils and other favorite herbs growing on a sunny windowsill all winter.

Hermits

2 1/4 cups flour   2 teaspoons baking soda
3/4 teaspoon ginger
1 teaspoon cinnamon
3/4 teaspoon ground cloves
1/4 cup oil   1/2 cup butter, softened
1 1/4 cups sugar
1 egg   1/4 cup molasses
1 cup raisins

Sift flour, baking soda, ginger, cinnamon and cloves together. Cream oil, butter and 1 cup sugar in mixer bowl until light and fluffy. Add egg and molasses; mix well. Stir in dry ingredients. Fold in raisins. Spread in ungreased 12x17-inch baking pan. Sprinkle with remaining 1/4 cup sugar. Bake at 375 degrees for 10 minutes. Cool slightly; cut into squares. Yield: 48 servings.

Approx Per Serving: Cal 84; Prot 1 g; Carbo 13 g; Fiber <1 g; T Fat 3 g; 34% Calories from Fat; Chol 10 mg; Sod 53 mg.

To combat whiteflies, make your own insecticidal soap spray by mixing 2 tablespoons of a mild liquid soap in a gallon of water.

Holly Leaves

1/2 cup butter   30 large marshmallows
1 1/4 teaspoons green food coloring
3 cups cornflakes   100 red hot cinnamon candies

Melt butter and marshmallows in saucepan; mix well. Add green food coloring; mix well. Stir in cornflakes. Shape into holly leaves. Place on waxed paper-lined dish. Top with cinnamon candies. Yield: 100 servings.

Approx Per Serving: Cal 18; Prot <1 g; Carbo 3 g; Fiber <1 g; T Fat 1 g; 44% Calories from Fat; Chol 2 mg; Sod 18 mg.

Lemon Bars

1 cup melted butter   2 cups plus 6 tablespoons flour
1/2 cup plus 3 tablespoons confectioners' sugar   4 eggs
2 cups sugar   1 tablespoon (scant) lemon juice
Grated rind of 1 lemon

Mix butter, 2 cups flour and 1/2 cup confectioners' sugar in bowl. Pat into nonstick 9x13-inch baking pan. Bake at 350 degrees for 15 minutes. Combine eggs, sugar, 6 tablespoons flour, lemon juice and lemon rind in mixer bowl, mixing well. Pour over baked layer. Bake for 20 minutes. Cool; sprinkle with remaining 3 tablespoons confectioners' sugar. Cut into bars. Yield: 36 servings.

Approx Per Serving: Cal 136; Prot 2 g; Carbo 20 g; Fiber <1 g; T Fat 6 g; 38% Calories from Fat; Chol 38 mg; Sod 51 mg.

Caramel-Oatmeal Bars

1 3/4 cups oats
1 3/4 cups flour
3/4 cup packed brown sugar
1/2 teaspoon baking soda
3/4 cup melted margarine
1 cup chocolate chips
1   12-ounce jar caramel ice cream topping

Combine oats, 1 1/2 cups flour, brown sugar and baking soda in bowl; mix well. Stir in margarine. Reserve 1 cup mixture. Press remaining mixture into greased 9x13-inch baking pan. Bake at 350 degrees for 10 to 12 minutes or until light brown. Cool for 10 minutes. Top with chocolate chips. Drizzle with mixture of caramel ice cream topping and remaining 1/4 cup flour. Top with remaining oat mixture. Bake for 18 to 22 minutes or until edges pull from sides of pan. Remove to wire rack to cool. Chill until firm. Cut into bars. Yield: 30 servings.

Approx Per Serving: Cal 175; Prot 2 g; Carbo 28 g; Fiber 1 g; T Fat 7 g; 35% Calories from Fat; Chol 0 mg; Sod 98 mg.

When greasing your cookie sheets, always use vegetable shortening. Butter or oil will cause cookies to burn. Better yet, a sheet of baker's parchment on the cookie sheet yields evenly baked cookies.

Southern Pecan Bars

1 cup plus 2 tablespoons flour
1/4 teaspoon baking powder
1/4 cup butter, softened
1/3 cup plus 1/4 cup packed brown sugar
1/4 cup finely chopped pecans
2 eggs
3/4 cup dark corn syrup
1 teaspoon vanilla extract
1/2 teaspoon salt
3/4 cup pecan halves
Juice of 1 lemon
Grated rind of 1 lemon
1 cup confectioners' sugar

Sift 1 cup flour and baking powder together. Combine butter and 1/3 cup brown sugar in mixer bowl; mix well. Add dry ingredients, mixing until crumbly. Stir in chopped pecans. Pat into greased 9x13-inch baking pan. Bake at 350 degrees for 10 minutes. Beat eggs in mixer bowl until frothy. Add corn syrup, remaining 1/4 cup brown sugar, vanilla, salt and remaining 2 tablespoons flour; mix well. Spread over baked layer. Top with pecan halves. Bake for 25 to 30 minutes or until edges pull from sides of pan. Remove to wire rack to cool. Drizzle with mixture of lemon juice, lemon rind and confectioners' sugar. Cut into bars. Yield: 30 servings.

Approx Per Serving: Cal 120; Prot 1 g; Carbo 20 g; Fiber <1 g; T Fat 4 g; 32% Calories from Fat; Chol 18 mg; Sod 64 mg.

Pecan Wafers

1/2 cup butter
1/2 cup sugar
1 egg, beaten
3/4 cup flour
1 teaspoon vanilla extract
24 pecan halves

Melt butter in saucepan. Add sugar gradually, beating constantly. Stir in egg, flour and vanilla. Drop by 1/2 teaspoonfuls 2 inches apart onto cold nonstick cookie sheet. Top each with pecan half. Bake at 300 degrees for 10 to 12 minutes or until edges turn brown. Remove to wire rack to cool. Yield: 24 servings.

Approx Per Serving: Cal 79; Prot 1 g; Carbo 7 g; Fiber <1 g; T Fat 5 g; 59% Calories from Fat; Chol 19 mg; Sod 35 mg.

Make *Easy Shortbread* by creaming 1 1/2 cups butter with 3/4 cup sugar and mix in 3 cups flour. Pat into 9x13-inch baking pan and bake at 300 degrees for 1 hour. Sprinkle generously with sugar while hot.

Raspberry-Walnut Shortbread

1¹/₄ cups plus 2 tablespoons sifted flour
¹/₂ cup sugar
¹/₂ cup unsalted butter, softened
¹/₃ cup raspberry jam
2 eggs
¹/₂ cup packed dark brown sugar
1 teaspoon vanilla extract
¹/₄ teaspoon (scant) salt
¹/₈ teaspoon baking soda
1 cup chopped walnuts

Mix 1¹/₄ cups flour and sugar in bowl. Cut in butter until crumbly. Press in lightly greased 9x9-inch baking pan. Bake at 350 degrees for 20 minutes or until edges turn light brown. Spread jam over baked layer. Combine eggs, brown sugar and vanilla in bowl; mix well. Stir in mixture of remaining 2 tablespoons flour, salt and baking soda. Add walnuts; mix well. Spoon over jam. Bake for 20-25 minutes. Cut into bars when cool. Yield: 16 servings.

Approx Per Serving: Cal 219; Prot 3 g; Carbo 28 g; Fiber 1 g; T Fat 11 g; 45% Calories from Fat; Chol 42 mg; Sod 55 mg.

Swedish Christmas Cookies

2 cups sifted flour
1¹/₂ teaspoons baking powder
¹/₂ teaspoon salt
²/₃ cup butter, softened
1 cup sugar
1 egg
1 teaspoon vanilla extract
1 cup finely chopped walnuts
¹/₂ cup colored sugar

Mix flour, baking powder and salt together. Beat butter in mixer bowl until light and fluffy. Beat in sugar gradually. Add egg and vanilla; mix well. Add ¹/₂ of the dry ingredients; mix well. Mix in remaining dry ingredients with hands until stiff dough forms. Chill for 8 hours to 10 days. Shape into log. Cut into ¹/₈-inch slices; form into heart shapes. Sprinkle with walnuts and colored sugar. Place on nonstick cookie sheet. Bake at 350 degrees for 8 to 10 minutes. Cool on wire rack. Tint sugar with food coloring. Yield: 24 servings.

Approx Per Serving: Cal 164; Prot 2 g; Carbo 21 g; Fiber 1 g; T Fat 9 g; 46% Calories from Fat; Chol 23 mg; Sod 112 mg.

Chocolate-Almond Macaroons

1¹/₂ cups finely ground blanched almonds
1¹/₂ cups sifted confectioners' sugar
3 egg whites 7 tablespoons sugar
7 tablespoons water 4 egg yolks
²/₃ cup butter, softened
4 teaspoons baking cocoa
3 tablespoons plus 1 teaspoon melted shortening
10 ounces semisweet chocolate, melted

Mix almonds and confectioners' sugar in bowl. Beat egg whites in mixer bowl just until stiff peaks form. Fold in almond mixture ¹/₃ at a time. Drop by teaspoonfuls 1 inch apart onto nonstick cookie sheet. Bake at 350 degrees for 15 to 18 minutes or until light brown. Cool for 5 minutes. Remove to wire rack to cool completely. Mix sugar and water in saucepan. Cook over medium heat to 230 to 240 degrees on candy thermometer or until the syrup spins a 2-inch thread when dropped from a fork. Beat eggs yolks in mixer bowl until blended. Add the hot syrup gradually, beating until mixture is thick and lemon-colored. Let cool to room temperature. Beat in butter 1 tablespoon at a time, just until blended. Stir in baking cocoa. Chill mixture if it gets dark and runny, then rebeat. Spread over bottom of each macaroon. Chill for 15 minutes or until firm. Dip the frosted side in mixture of shortening and chocolate. Chill for 10 minutes or until chocolate is set. Store in refrigerator or freezer. Yield: 42 servings.

Approx Per Serving: Cal 127; Prot 2 g; Carbo 11 g; Fiber 1 g; T Fat 9 g; 63% Calories from Fat; Chol 28 mg; Sod 30 mg.

Candied Apple Pie

8 Granny Smith apples, peeled, cored, sliced
1¹/₂ cups flour 1¹/₂ cups packed light brown sugar
³/₄ cup butter

Mound apples in 9 or 10-inch pie plate; pack firmly. Combine flour, brown sugar and butter in bowl; mix until crumbly. Pat over apples. Bake at 350 degrees for 40 to 50 minutes or until browned and bubbly. Serve hot pie with sweetened whipped cream or vanilla ice cream; serve cold pie with cheese. Yield: 8 servings.

Approx Per Serving: Cal 502; Prot 3 g; Carbo 87 g; Fiber 3 g T Fat 18 g; 31% Calories from Fat; Chol 47 mg; Sod 168 mg.

Crunch-Top Apple Pies

6 cups sliced apples 2 unbaked 9-inch pie shells
1¹/₂ cups sugar 1¹/₂ cups graham cracker crumbs
³/₄ cup flour ³/₄ cup chopped walnuts
³/₄ teaspoon cinnamon ¹/₄ teaspoon salt
³/₄ cup melted butter

Arrange apples in pie shells. Mix next 6 ingredients in bowl. Sprinkle over apples. Drizzle with butter. Bake at 350 degrees for 1 hour. Yield: 16 servings.

Approx Per Serving: Cal 391; Prot 4 g; Carbo 49 g; Fiber 2 g; T Fat 21 g; 47% Calories from Fat; Chol 23 mg; Sod 314 mg.

Blackberry-Blueberry Pie

2½ cups flour   1 teaspoon salt
5 tablespoons plus 1 cup sugar
1 teaspoon cinnamon   ¾ cup shortening
11 tablespoons water
3 tablespoons fresh lemon juice
1 pint blackberries   1 pint blueberries
1 cup Crème de Cassis   Grated rind of 1 lemon
2 tablespoons cornstarch

Sift flour, salt, 5 tablespoons sugar and cinnamon together. Cut in shortening until crumbly. Add mixture of 3 tablespoons ice water and 1 tablespoon lemon juice 1 tablespoon at a time, mixing with fork until mixture forms ball. Roll slightly more than half the dough between 2 sheets of floured plastic wrap. Fit into pie plate. Roll remaining dough into circle; set aside. Combine berries, Crème de Cassis and lemon rind in bowl. Let stand for several hours; drain, reserving liquid. Combine reserved liquid, remaining 1 cup sugar, ½ cup water, remaining 2 tablespoons lemon juice and cornstarch in saucepan. Cook over medium heat until thickened and glossy, stirring constantly. Stir into berry mixture. Pour into pastry-lined pie plate. Top with remaining pastry, fluting edge and cutting vents. Bake at 350 degrees for 45 to 60 minutes or until golden brown. Yield: 9 servings.

Approx Per Serving: Cal 543; Prot 4 g; Carbo 79 g; Fiber 4 g;
T Fat 18 g; 29% Calories from Fat; Chol 0 mg; Sod 242 mg.

Blueberry Pie

2¾ cups flour   1 teaspoon salt
1¾ cups shortening   6 tablespoons ice water
2 teaspoons cornstarch   ⅔ cup sugar
1½ tablespoons lemon juice
5 cups fresh or frozen blueberries
1 tablespoon butter

Combine 2½ cups flour and salt in bowl. Cut in shortening until crumbly. Add water 1 tablespoon at a time, mixing with fork until mixture forms ball. Roll into 2 circles between sheets of floured waxed paper. Fit 1 pastry into pie plate. Mix remaining ¼ cup flour, cornstarch, sugar and lemon juice in bowl. Stir in blueberries. Spoon into pie shell. Dot with butter. Let stand for 15 minutes. Top with remaining pastry, fluting edge and cutting vents. Bake at 450 degrees for 10 minutes. Reduce oven temperature to 350 degrees. Bake for 30 minutes longer or until golden brown. Yield: 8 servings.

Approx Per Serving: Cal 486; Prot 5 g; Carbo 63 g; Fiber 4 g;
T Fat 25 g; 45% Calories from Fat; Chol 4 mg; Sod 286 mg.

Patch tears in pastry with a bit of pastry and a touch of water rather than rerolling it. Rerolling causes pastry to be tough.

Fresh Berry Pie

3/4 cup ground pecans
1/3 cup whole wheat flour
2 tablespoons wheat germ
2 tablespoons each oil and honey
1/8 teaspoon salt
1 teaspoon almond extract
3 1/2 cups raspberries
1 cup water
3 tablespoons cornstarch
1/2 to 3/4 cup sugar

Mix pecans, flour, wheat germ, oil, honey, salt and flavoring in bowl. Press over bottom and side of 9-inch pie plate. Bake at 350 degrees for 12 to 15 minutes or until browned. Mash 1/2 cup raspberries in 1/2 cup water in saucepan. Simmer for 5 minutes. Mix cornstarch and sugar in bowl. Add remaining 1/2 cup water gradually to make a paste. Stir into cooked berries. Cook until thickened. Let stand to cool. Stir in remaining 3 cups raspberries. Mound in cooled crust. Chill until serving time. May substitute strawberries, blueberries or peaches for raspberries. Yield: 8 servings.

Approx Per Serving: Cal 325; Prot 3 g; Carbo 40 g; Fiber 6 g; T Fat 19 g; 50% Calories from Fat; Chol 0 mg; Sod 34 mg.

Heavenly Cheese Pie

1/2 cup melted butter
1 cup flour
6 ounces cream cheese, softened
1 cup confectioners' sugar
2 cups whipped topping
1 24-ounce jar cherry pie filling

Mix butter and flour in bowl. Pat into 9-inch pie plate. Bake at 400 degrees for 15 minutes or until browned. Mix cream cheese, confectioners' sugar and whipped topping in bowl. Spoon into cooled pie crust. Top with pie filling. May substitute fresh fruit glaze or 16 ounces frozen strawberries thickened with 1 1/2 tablespoons cornstarch for cherry pie filling. Yield: 8 servings.

Approx Per Serving: Cal 431; Prot 4 g; Carbo 53 g; Fiber 2 g; T Fat 24 g; 49% Calories from Fat; Chol 54 mg; Sod 190 mg.

Make a quick *Lemon Pie* by bringing 6 ounces frozen lemonade concentrate and 3 1/2 cups whipped topping to room temperature. Combine with one 14-ounce can sweetened condensed milk, beat until smooth and pour into baked pie shell. Chill for 30 minutes.

Chocolate-Pecan Pie

2 eggs
1/8 teaspoon salt
1/2 cup packed brown sugar
2 cups semisweet chocolate chips
1 cup chopped pecans
1 unbaked 9-inch pie shell
12 pecan halves

Beat eggs and salt in bowl until thick and lemon-colored. Add brown sugar; mix well. Blend in 1 cup melted chocolate chips. Add 1 cup whole chocolate chips and pecans; mix well. Pour into pie shell. Decorate with pecan halves. Bake at 375 degrees for 20 to 25 minutes or until knife inserted near center comes out clean. Yield: 8 servings.

Approx Per Serving: Cal 528; Prot 6 g; Carbo 54 g; Fiber 3 g; T Fat 36 g; 57% Calories from Fat; Chol 53 mg; Sod 202 mg.

 Add cranberries and walnuts to your favorite apple pie recipe to turn it into a holiday treat.

Chocolate Silk Pie

3/4 cup sugar   1/4 cup butter, softened
1 1/2 ounces melted unsweetened chocolate
3 eggs   1 baked 10-inch pie shell
1 cup heavy cream, whipped

Cream sugar and butter in mixer bowl until light and fluffy. Stir in melted chocolate. Beat in eggs 1 at a time at medium speed for 5 minutes. Pour into pie shell. Chill for 3 hours or longer. Top with whipped cream. Yield: 8 servings.

Approx Per Serving: Cal 407; Prot 5 g; Carbo 32 g; Fiber 1 g; T Fat 30 g; 64% Calories from Fat; Chol 136 mg; Sod 239 mg.

Crustless Cranberry Pie

3 cups cranberries   1 1/4 cups sugar   1/2 cup walnuts
2 eggs   3/4 cup cake flour   1/2 cup melted butter
1/4 cup melted margarine

Spread cranberries in greased 10-inch deep-dish pie pan. Sprinkle with 3/4 cup sugar and walnuts. Beat eggs in bowl until light and lemon-colored. Add remaining 1/2 cup sugar, cake flour, melted butter and margarine gradually, beating until smooth. Spread over cranberries. Bake at 325 degrees for 45 minutes or until top is browned. Yield: 8 servings.

Approx Per Serving: Cal 395; Prot 4 g; Carbo 45 g; Fiber 2 g; T Fat 23 g; 52% Calories from Fat; Chol 84 mg; Sod 183 mg.

Fudge Pie

1 cup sugar
1/2 cup butter, softened
2 eggs, separated
2 ounces melted unsweetened chocolate
1/2 cup flour
1 teaspoon vanilla extract
1/8 teaspoon salt

Cream sugar and butter in mixer bowl until light and fluffy. Beat in egg yolks and chocolate. Stir in flour. Beat in vanilla. Beat egg whites with salt in mixer bowl until stiff peaks form. Fold into creamed mixture. Pour into greased pie plate. Bake at 325 degrees for 30 minutes. Yield: 8 servings.

Approx Per Serving: Cal 282; Prot 3 g; Carbo 33 g; Fiber 1 g; T Fat 17 g; 51% Calories from Fat; Chol 84 mg; Sod 146 mg.

For *Peanut Butter Pie*, blend 4 ounces cream cheese, 1/2 cup peanut butter, 1/2 cup milk, 3/4 cup confectioners' sugar and 8 ounces whipped topping. Spoon into chocolate cookie crumb pie shell, drizzle with chocolate syrup and sprinkle with 1/4 cup peanuts.

Mincemeat for Pies

1   5 to 5 1/2-pound uncooked boneless beef roast
1 pound dark raisins
1 pound golden raisins
4 ounces citron
5 oranges
4 lemons
4 ounces candied lemon rind
8 ounces candied orange rind
4 pounds Winesap apples, coarsely ground
1 pound currants
2   1-pound packages brown sugar
32 ounces dark Jamaican rum
32 ounces Canadian Whiskey
1 tablespoon each cinnamon, ground cloves,
allspice, nutmeg and salt

Grind beef, raisins, citron, oranges, lemons and candied rinds very fine. Combine with apples, currants, brown sugar, rum, whiskey and seasonings in large bowl. Store in cool place for 8 weeks. Use 2 cups mincemeat as filling for each 2-crust pie; bake pies at 375 degrees for 30 minutes or until golden brown. May freeze mincemeat in desired portions after curing. Yield: 20 pints.

Approx Per Pint: Cal 883; Prot 27 g; Carbo 134 g; Fiber 8 g; T Fat 8 g; 8% Calories from Fat; Chol 70 mg; Sod 402 mg.

Strawberry-Lemon Curd Pie

1/4 cup unsalted butter
3 egg yolks
1 egg
10 tablespoons sugar
1/2 cup lemon juice
1 tablespoon grated lemon rind
1 baked 9-inch pie shell
1 cup heavy cream
2 pints fresh strawberries, cut into halves

Melt butter in saucepan. Beat egg yolks, egg and 1/2 cup sugar in bowl. Stir in lemon juice. Add to melted butter. Cook over low heat for 5 minutes or until thickened, stirring constantly; do not boil. Stir in lemon rind. Let stand to cool. Spread thin layer of cooked lemon curd in pie shell. Chill for 30 minutes. Beat cream with remaining 2 tablespoons sugar in bowl until soft peaks form. Blend small amount of whipped cream with remaining lemon curd. Fold in remaining whipped cream. Arrange strawberries in pie shell. Cover with whipped cream mixture. Chill for 4 hours. Garnish with additional strawberry halves. Yield: 8 servings.

Approx Per Serving: Cal 386; Prot 4 g; Carbo 33 g; Fiber 2 g; T Fat 27 g; 62% Calories from Fat; Chol 163 mg; Sod 149 mg.

Barbados Sweet Potato Pies

2 cups flour   1 teaspoon salt
2 tablespoons plus 3/4 cup sugar
13 tablespoons butter   4 eggs
3 tablespoons ice water
2 or 3 drops of lemon juice
3 large sweet potatoes or yams
3/4 cup heavy cream   1/2 teaspoon salt
1/4 teaspoon nutmeg   1/4 cup Barbados rum

Sift flour, 1 teaspoon salt and 2 tablespoons sugar together. Stir in 10 tablespoons butter until crumbly. Beat 1 egg slightly with fork in bowl. Stir in ice water and lemon juice. Add to flour mixture slowly. Toss gently until soft dough forms. Divide dough into 2 sections. Chill for 10 minutes. Roll into two 12-inch circles on floured surface. Fit into ungreased 9-inch pie plates. Bake at 350 degrees for 10 minutes. Boil sweet potatoes in water in saucepan until tender. Peel and mash potatoes. Add remaining 3 tablespoons butter and cream. Whip until creamy. Add 3 egg yolks, 3/4 cup sugar, 1/2 teaspoon salt, nutmeg and rum; beat well. Fold into 3 softly beaten egg whites. Spoon into cooled shells. Trim excess crust. Bake at 350 degrees for 30 to 40 minutes or until golden brown. Serve warm. Yield: 16 servings.

Approx Per Serving: Cal 278; Prot 4 g; Carbo 30 g; Fiber 1 g; T Fat 15 g; 50% Calories from Fat; Chol 94 mg; Sod 302 mg.

Gifts from the Garden

As much as pumpkins or branches of red and golden bittersweet, the Pennsylvania Horticultural Society's Harvest Show conjures up images of homemade breads, tangy herb vinegars and treasured family recipes passed on for generations. In this final section, you'll find recipes for the creative and delicious rewards that endure long after the first frost.

A gift from the garden can be as simple as a loofah gourd dried for use as a natural sponge, or it can be as elegant as fruit from our own trees, carefully dried, diced and cooked in a flaming plum pudding. The key, as any Harvest Show exhibitor will confirm, is to plan well ahead.

The schedule for the Harvest Show's 300 competitive classes is mailed in the spring, and more than a few area gardeners plan their summer crops with an eye toward a blue ribbon in the fall. One Philadelphia resident planted his whole garden with nothing but rare and unusual peppers—and sure enough, he won several ribbons at the Show and a special award at the Pennsylvania Horticultural Society's annual City Gardens Contest Awards Ceremony.

The Harvest Show's friendly atmosphere and small scale exhibits attract entrants who have the talent but may not feel ready to enter the big Philadelphia Flower Show. Yet every year, when Flower Show winners are asked how they started, invariably a few beaming prize winners recall their first hesitant entries in the Harvest Show.

Philadelphia's finest cooks judge entries in nearly a hundred different classes for preserved products at the Harvest Show. — Photography by Ira Beckoff

Gifts from the Garden Vegetarian Dinner

Broccoli and Cauliflower *(page 11)*   or   Marinated Mushrooms *(page 137)*

Oatmeal-Zucchini Muffins *(page 175)*

Eggplant for Dinner *(page 135)*   or   Fettucini with Vegetables *(page 191)*

Snap Bean Salad *(page 56)*

Fresh Berry Pie *(page 234)*   or   Banana Split Dessert *(page 208)*

*Purchase a styrofoam cone in a craft store and cover with short pieces of boxwood.
Insert large strawberries on toothpicks and place the cone on a pretty plate
or shallow bowl. At dessert time place small containers of
confectioners' sugar around the centerpiece for guests to dip strawberries.*

Apple Relish Marguerite

2 cups sugar   1 cup vinegar   2 apples, peeled, chopped
4 medium green bell peppers, chopped
1 cup chopped celery   1 cup chopped onion
8 cups chopped tomatoes   2 tablespoons mustard seed
1 tablespoon crushed cinnamon stick
1 teaspoon whole cloves   1 tablespoon salt

Combine sugar and vinegar in 4-quart saucepan. Bring to a simmer. Add apples, green peppers, celery, onion, tomatoes and seasonings. Simmer for 45 minutes. Serve with beef, pork or lamb. Do not double recipe or process ingredients in blender. Yield: 128 (1-tablespoon) servings.

Approx Per Serving: Cal 17; Prot <1 g; Carbo 4 g; Fiber <1 g; T Fat <1 g; 4% Calories from Fat; Chol 0 mg; Sod 52 mg.

Sour Cherry Relish

1 cup orange juice   7/8 cup sugar
2 sticks cinnamon   1 pint frozen sour cherries

Boil orange juice, sugar and cinnamon in saucepan for 5 minutes, stirring occasionally; remove from heat. Add frozen cherries. Let stand for 24 hours; discard cinnamon. Serve with meat or poultry or over ice cream, frozen yogurt or cake. Yield: 32 (1-tablespoon) servings.

Approx Per Serving: Cal 29; Prot <1 g; Carbo 7 g; Fiber <1 g; T Fat <1 g; 2% Calories from Fat; Chol 0 mg; Sod <1 mg.

Dilled Green Beans

4 pounds whole green beans, stemmed
1³/₄ teaspoons crushed hot red pepper
3¹/₂ teaspoons each mustard seed and dillseed
7 cloves of garlic   5 cups light vinegar
5 cups water   ¹/₂ cup pickling salt

Trim green beans to fit seven 1-pint jars. Add hot pepper, mustard seed, dillseed and garlic to jars. Bring vinegar, water and salt to a boil in saucepan. Pour into jars, leaving ¹/₂ inch headspace; seal with 2-piece lids. Process in boiling water bath for 5 minutes. Let stand for 2 weeks before serving. Yield: 28 (¹/₂-cup) servings.

Approx Per Serving: Cal 30; Prot 1 g; Carbo 8 g; Fiber 1 g; T Fat <1 g; 8% Calories from Fat; Chol 0 mg; Sod 1831 mg.

Basil and Wine Vinegar

3 cups light vinegar   ¹/₂ cup Chablis wine
4 cups purple basil leaves

Pour vinegar and wine over basil in glass container. Let stand, covered, away from bright light for 2 weeks or until dark red in color but before brownish hue develops. Strain through fine sieve into sterilized glass container. Dilute with wine-vinegar to taste. Yield: 56 (1-tablespoon) servings.

Approx Per Serving: Cal 3; Prot <1 g; Carbo 1 g; Fiber 0 g; T Fat 0 g; 0% Calories from Fat; Chol 0 mg; Sod <1 mg.

Blueberry Sauce

1 cup blueberries   1/2 cup Crème de Cassis
1/3 cup apple juice   2 tablespoons brown sugar
1 1/2 tablespoons cornstarch

Bring blueberries and liqueur to a boil in small saucepan. Blend apple juice, brown sugar and cornstarch in small bowl. Add to blueberries. Cook until thickened, stirring constantly. Serve over ice cream or waffles. May reheat over hot water or in microwave.
Yield: 16 (1-tablespoon) servings.

Approx Per Serving: Cal 48; Prot <1 g; Carbo 8 g; Fiber <1 g; T Fat <1 g; 1% Calories from Fat; Chol 0 mg; Sod 2 mg.

American Cranberry Sauce

1 1/2 cups pure maple syrup   1 1/2 cups spring water
1 teaspoon ground or chopped ginger
4 cups cranberries

Bring syrup, water and ginger to a boil in heavy 2 to 2 1/2-quart saucepan over medium heat. Stir in cranberries. Simmer for 5 minutes or until berries begin to pop, stirring occasionally. Spoon into serving bowl. Chill until serving time. Serve with roast turkey, goose or chicken.
Yield: 16 (1/4-cup) servings.

Approx Per Serving: Cal 87; Prot <1 g; Carbo 22 g; Fiber 1 g; T Fat <1 g; 0% Calories from Fat; Chol 0 mg; Sod 5 mg.

Barbecue Sauce

1/3 cup prepared mustard
1 tablespoon dry mustard
1 cup wine vinegar
1   28-ounce bottle of catsup
1   12-ounce bottle of chili sauce
1 1/2 cups packed brown sugar
1 cup fresh lemon juice
1 cup A-1 sauce
1/4 cup Worcestershire sauce
1 tablespoon soy sauce
Garlic powder to taste

Combine prepared and dry mustards in bowl, stirring to form paste. Add remaining ingredients; mix well. May add water for desired consistency. Chill for 24 hours before using. Yield: 8 (1-cup) servings.

Approx Per Serving: Cal 404; Prot 5 g; Carbo 98 g; Fiber 3 g; T Fat 1 g; 3% Calories from Fat; Chol 0 mg; Sod 1959 mg.

Bury a whole vanilla bean inside a jar of granulated sugar. Within 2 weeks the bean will scent the sugar with its aroma. Use the flavored sugar as you would regular sugar—in cakes, cookies and desserts.

Cranberry-Peach Chutney

1¹/2 cups raisins
16 ounces dried peaches, chopped
5 16-ounce cans whole cranberry sauce
¹/2 cup Irish whiskey
Juice and rind of 1 orange 1¹/2 cups sugar
1 cup basil vinegar 1 teaspoon cinnamon
¹/2 teaspoon each ginger, allspice, nutmeg
and ground cloves

Combine raisins, peaches, cranberry sauce and whiskey in bowl. Let stand overnight. Combine with orange juice and rind, sugar, vinegar and spices in saucepan. Simmer for 20 minutes or until thickened. Spoon into 10 hot sterilized half-pint jars, leaving ¹/4 inch headspace; seal with 2-piece lids. Let stand for 3 to 4 weeks before serving. May use any plain or herbed vinegar.
Yield: 160 (1-tablespoon) servings.

Approx Per Serving: Cal 42; Prot <1 g; Carbo 11 g; Fiber 1 g;
T Fat <1 g; 1% Calories from Fat; Chol 0 mg; Sod 5 mg.

Serve soup in butternut squash bowls. Cut cleaned squash into halves. Slice a tiny piece off bottoms to help the 'bowls' sit firmly in plates. Scoop out fleshy matter and save for another meal. Fill with cold or warm soup. Garnish.

Elderberry Cordial

2 teaspoons each whole allspice and whole cloves
2 teaspoons broken cinnamon stick
4 quarts elderberries 2 quarts (about) water
4 cups (about) sugar 2 cups (about) brandy

Tie allspice, cloves and cinnamon in cheesecloth bag. Combine elderberries with water in large saucepan. Boil until elderberries are tender. Strain through cheesecloth. Measure juice. Combine with spice bag and 2 cups sugar for each quart juice in saucepan. Boil for 20 to 60 minutes or until of desired consistency. Cool and measure juice. Combine with 2 cups brandy for each quart juice in bowl. Pour into bottles; cork tightly. Age for 3 months or longer in cool dark place. This recipe is based on 18th century "receipts" and has been prepared on site at the Colonial Pennsylvania Plantation using elderberries from the kitchen garden. Yield: 48 (1-ounce) servings.

Approx Per Serving: Cal 122; Prot <1 g; Carbo 29 g; Fiber 3 g;
T Fat <1 g; 2% Calories from Fat; Chol 0 mg; Sod 1 mg.

Dress up 6-inch nursery pots of flowers or herbs by covering them with bandannas secured with a rubber band or, for a different look, take the bandannas and thoroughly wet them with a solution of straight starch, found in the supermarket detergent section. Place the wet bandannas on a smooth surface in the sun to dry, then secure them around the nursery pots.

Apricot Liqueur

1   11-ounce package apricots
1   11-ounce package rock candy
1 fifth of vodka

Combine apricots, rock candy and vodka in large jar; seal with lid. Let stand for 10 days, inverting jar each day. Easy and fun! Yield: 8 servings.

Approx Per Serving: Cal 447; Prot 1 g; Carbo 62 g; Fiber 3 g; T Fat <1 g; 0% Calories from Fat; Chol 0 mg; Sod 13 mg.

Kumquat Marmalade

2¹/₂ cups very thinly sliced kumquats
4 cups water   2 cups (about) sugar
1 tablespoon lemon juice

Soak sliced kumquats in water in bowl overnight. Place in 6-quart saucepan. Boil for 30 minutes. Measure mixture and combine with equal amount of sugar in 3-quart saucepan. Bring to a rolling boil. Boil for 3 minutes or until mixture sheets from spoon. Stir in lemon juice. Spoon into hot sterilized 1-pint jar, leaving ¹/₄ inch headspace; seal with 2-piece lid. Yield: 32 (1-tablespoon) servings.

Approx Per Serving: Cal 56; Prot <1 g; Carbo 15 g; Fiber <1 g; T Fat <1 g; 0% Calories from Fat; Chol 0 mg; Sod 1 mg.

Mango Salsa

4 cloves of garlic   Finely grated rind of 1 lime
1 jalapeño pepper, seeded, minced
¹/₃ cup olive oil   Juice of 2 limes
1 cup white wine   ¹/₄ cup chopped cilantro
Salt and pepper to taste   2 large mangos

Mash garlic with lime rind and jalapeño pepper in bowl. Stir in olive oil. Whisk in lime juice and wine. Stir in cilantro, salt and pepper. Bring mixture to a boil in saucepan. Peel mangos and cut into halves, discarding pits. Chop mangos in food processor. Add to lime mixture. Cook just until heated through. Serve hot or chilled. May use lime mixture as marinade for meat, fish or shellfish. Yield: 50 (1-tablespoon) servings.

Approx Per Serving: Cal 22; Prot <1 g; Carbo 2 g; Fiber <1 g; T Fat 1 g; 59% Calories from Fat; Chol 0 mg; Sod 1 mg.

For **Homestyle Horseradish**, dig horseradish roots from ground after hard frost but before ground is frozen, digging as deeply as possible with pitchfork. Scrub and rinse roots. Scrape roots with vegetable peeler; cut into 1-inch pieces. Process horseradish in food processor fitted with steel blade, adding enough vinegar to moisten. Season with salt. Spoon into sterilized jars; seal with 2-piece lids. Store in refrigerator. Protect eyes with clear plastic goggles and tie scarf over nose and mouth while processing horseradish roots.

Gifts from the Garden

sa

Mango and Peach Chutney

4 pounds mangos
2 pounds peaches
1 pound onions, chopped
1 pound golden raisins
5 frying peppers, chopped
1 1/2 cups cider vinegar
2 cups sugar
2 cups packed brown sugar
Chopped gingerroot to taste
2 teaspoons coriander
1 1/2 teaspoons each allspice, cinnamon,
ground cloves and nutmeg

Peel and chop mangos and peaches, discarding pits. Combine with onions, raisins, peppers, vinegar, sugar, brown sugar and spices in large saucepan. Simmer for 20 minutes. Spoon into 16 half-pint jars, leaving 1/4 inch headspace; seal with 2-piece lids.
Yield: 256 (1-tablespoon) servings.

Approx Per Serving: Cal 27; Prot <1 g; Carbo 7 g; Fiber 1 g; T Fat <1 g; 1% Calories from Fat; Chol 0 mg; Sod 1 mg.

Cranberry Chutney

1 cup sugar   1 cup water
2 cups fresh cranberries
1/2 cup seedless raisins
1/4 cup chopped or slivered almonds
2 tablespoons cider vinegar
1 tablespoon light brown sugar
1/4 teaspoon ginger   1/4 teaspoon garlic salt
1/4 teaspoon cayenne pepper

Bring sugar and water to a boil in heavy saucepan. Add cranberries, raisins, almonds, vinegar, brown sugar, ginger, garlic salt and cayenne pepper; mix well. Simmer for 10 minutes or until thickened to desired consistency. Spoon into refrigerator container; cool to room temperature. Store in refrigerator. May omit cayenne pepper.
Yield: 16 servings.

Approx Per Serving: Cal 85; Prot 1 g; Carbo 19 g; Fiber 1 g; T Fat 1 g; 11% Calories from Fat; Chol 0 mg; Sod 34 mg.

Dip your pruners and clippers in alcohol after working around the yard to prevent diseases spreading from one plant to the next.

Pear and Blueberry Conserve

3 pounds pears, peeled, chopped   3¹/₂ cups blueberries
1 each lemon and orange, cut into quarters, thinly sliced
1 cup pecan pieces

Combine fruit in 12-quart saucepan. Bring to a boil; reduce heat. Simmer for 15 to 20 minutes, stirring frequently. Add pecans. Simmer for 10 minutes longer or until thickened to desired consistency. Spoon into 7 hot sterilized wide-mouth half-pint jars, leaving ¹/₄ inch headspace; seal with 2-piece lids. Process in boiling water bath for 10 minutes. May substitute walnuts for pecans. Yield: 112 (1-tablespoon) servings.

Approx Per Serving: Cal 18; Prot <1 g; Carbo 3 g; Fiber 1 g; T Fat 1 g; 37% Calories from Fat; Chol 0 mg; Sod <1 mg.

Red Fruit Relish

1 seedless orange   1 lemon, seeded
1 quart cranberries, rinsed, stems removed
1 cup (or more) sugar   ¹/₂ cup brandy

Cut unpeeled orange and lemon into eighths. Process with cranberries in food processor until evenly chopped. Mix with sugar and brandy in bowl. Chill for several hours. Yield: 12 servings.

Approx Per Serving: Cal 109; Prot <1 g; Carbo 26 g; Fiber 2 g; T Fat <1 g; 1% Calories from Fat; Chol 0 mg; Sod 1 mg.

Red and Green Pepper Relish

12 each red and green bell peppers, finely chopped
12 small onions, finely chopped
5 cups light vinegar   2 cups sugar   Melted paraffin

Cook bell peppers in water in saucepan for 10 minutes; drain. Mix with onions, vinegar and sugar in saucepan. Boil for 10 minutes. Spoon into 24 sterilized half-pint jars; top with paraffin. Yield: 384 (1-tablespoon) servings.

Approx Per Serving: Cal 7; Prot <1 g; Carbo 2 g; Fiber <1 g; T Fat <1 g; 4% Calories from Fat; Chol 0 mg; Sod <1 mg.

Bread and Butter Pickles

3 quarts cucumbers, sliced   1 large onion, thinly sliced
4 cups light vinegar   4 cups sugar
¹/₄ teaspoon turmeric   1¹/₃ teaspoons celery salt
¹/₃ cup pickling salt

Alternate layers of cucumbers and onion in 6 sterilized 1-pint jars, packing layers firmly. Combine vinegar, sugar, turmeric, celery salt and pickling salt in bowl; mix well. Pour into jars, leaving ¹/₂ inch headspace; seal tightly. Store in refrigerator for 5 days before serving. May store in refrigerator for several months. May substitute zucchini for cucumbers. Yield: 192 (1-tablespoon) servings.

Approx Per Serving: Cal 18; Prot <1 g; Carbo 5 g; Fiber <1 g; T Fat <1 g; 1% Calories from Fat; Chol 0 mg; Sod 188 mg.

Crunchy Sweet Pickles

10 medium cucumbers
4 cups cider vinegar
8 cups sugar
2 tablespoons mixed pickling spices
5 teaspoons kosher salt

Combine cucumbers with boiling water to cover in crock or large jar; weight with plate or bowl. Let stand at room temperature for 24 hours. Drain and repeat process on next 3 days; drain. Slice cucumbers into 1/2-inch pieces, discarding slices with hollow centers. Return to crock. Bring vinegar, sugar, pickling spices and salt to a boil in saucepan. Pour over cucumbers; weight with plate. Let stand for 2 days. Place mixture in saucepan. Bring to a boil. Spoon into 7 hot sterilized 1-pint jars, leaving 1/2 inch headspace; seal with 2-piece lids. Process in boiling water bath for 5 minutes. Saladin cucumbers are good for this recipe. Yield: 224 (1-tablespoon) servings.

Approx Per Serving: Cal 30; Prot <1 g; Carbo 8 g; Fiber <1 g; T Fat <1 g; 0% Calories from Fat; Chol 0 mg; Sod 48 mg.

Add several sprigs of rosemary to currant jelly while it's cooking. The flavor it imparts is subtle but delightful.

Strawberry Sunshine

8 cups strawberries or sour cherries   8 cups sugar

Combine strawberries and sugar in saucepan. Cook over medium heat for 15 minutes. Spread mixture on large tray or platter. Place in protected place in sun; let stand for up to 2 days or until thickened to desired consistency. Spoon into 4 sterilized half-pint jars, leaving 1/4 inch headspace; seal with 2-piece lids. Yield: 64 (1-tablespoon) servings.

Approx Per Serving: Cal 102; Prot <1 g; Carbo 26 g; Fiber <1 g; T Fat <1 g; 1% Calories from Fat; Chol 0 mg; Sod 1 mg.

Tomato Preserves

4 pounds tomatoes   3 lemons, very thinly sliced
4 cups water   8 cups sugar

Blanch tomatoes in boiling water in saucepan; drain. Peel and chop tomatoes. Cook in saucepan over low heat until tender. Cook lemons in 4 cups water in small saucepan until tender. Add sugar. Cook until sugar dissolves. Add to tomatoes. Cook until of desired consistency. Spoon into 8 sterilized 1-pint jars, leaving 1/4 inch headspace; seal with 2-piece lids. Serve with meat or as preserves. Yield: 148 (1-tablespoon) servings.

Approx Per Serving: Cal 44; Prot <1 g; Carbo 11 g; Fiber <1 g; T Fat <1 g; 1% Calories from Fat; Chol 0 mg; Sod 1 mg.

Tomato Relish

16 quarts tomatoes
10 large white onions, chopped
14 large green bell peppers, chopped
1 cup packed light brown sugar
2 cups (scant) light cider vinegar
1½ tablespoons allspice
1 teaspoon ground cloves
½ cup (or more) chopped fresh basil
1½ teaspoons celery seed
1 teaspoon each ginger, cinnamon and nutmeg
¼ cup (or less) salt
1 tablespoon freshly ground pepper

Peel and chop tomatoes; drain accumulated juice several times. Combine with onions, green peppers, brown sugar, vinegar and seasonings in large saucepan. Simmer, loosely covered, for 4 to 6 hours or until thickened to desired consistency. Spoon into 12 sterilized 1-pint jars, leaving ½ inch headspace; seal with 2-piece lids. Serve with hamburgers or other meat. May omit ginger, cinnamon and/or nutmeg. Yield: 384 (1-tablespoon) servings.

Approx Per Serving: Cal 9; Prot <1 g; Carbo 2 g; Fiber <1 g; T Fat <1 g; 6% Calories from Fat; Chol 0 mg; Sod 69 mg.

The Tomato Experience

1 clove of garlic, minced
1 carrot, chopped
1 stalk celery, chopped
1 green bell pepper, chopped
3 tablespoons olive oil
8 fresh tomatoes, peeled, chopped
1   8-ounce can tomatoes, crushed
2 tablespoons tomato paste
¼ cup chopped parsley
1 cup water
2 large mushrooms, chopped
1 teaspoon sugar
1 teaspoon oregano
½ teaspoon thyme
3 or 4 fresh basil leaves
Salt and pepper to taste

Sauté garlic, carrot, celery and green pepper in olive oil in saucepan until tender. Add fresh tomatoes, canned tomatoes, tomato paste, parsley and water. Bring to a simmer. Stir in mushrooms, sugar and seasonings. Simmer for 2 hours. Cool to room temperature. Spoon into freezer containers. Freeze until needed. Serve alone or with pasta, meat loaf, veal or seafood.
Yield: 80 (1-tablespoon) servings.

Approx Per Serving: Cal 9; Prot <1 g; Carbo 1 g; Fiber <1 g; T Fat 1 g; 51% Calories from Fat; Chol 0 mg; Sod 7 mg.

Garlic Oil

5 cloves of garlic
Salt and fresh herbs to taste
1 cup virgin olive oil

Process garlic, salt and herbs in food processor until minced. Add oil. Process until smooth. Serve over hot bread, pasta or vegetables. Yield: 8 (1-ounce) servings.

Approx Per Serving: Cal 241; Prot <1 g; Carbo 1 g; Fiber <1 g; T Fat 27 g; 99% Calories from Fat; Chol 0 mg; Sod <1 mg.

Flowerpot Herbal Butter

1 cup unsalted butter, softened
1 tablespoon chopped nasturtium petals
2 teaspoons chopped lemon-thyme leaves
1/3 teaspoon lemon juice
1 small shallot, minced
1/6 teaspoon crushed dried thyme
Salt to taste

Cream butter in mixer bowl until light and fluffy. Stir in nasturtium petals, lemon-thyme, lemon juice, shallot, thyme and salt, mixing well. Serve in small flowerpot with nasturtiums inserted in butter.
Yield: 8 (1-ounce) servings.

Approx Per Serving: Cal 209; Prot <1 g; Carbo 1 g; Fiber <1 g; T Fat 23 g; 97% Calories from Fat; Chol 62 mg; Sod 4 mg.

Hot and Sweet Mustard

3 to 4 ounces dry mustard
1 tablespoon mustard seed, crushed
1 cup light vinegar
2 eggs
1 cup sugar
1 cup sour cream

Mix dry mustard, mustard seed and vinegar in double boiler. Let stand, covered, for 8 hours or longer. Add eggs and sugar; mix well. Cook over simmering water for 30 minutes, stirring occasionally. Cool to room temperature. Stir in sour cream. Spoon into 6 half-pint jars. Store in refrigerator for 3 months or longer. Serve with pretzels or on sandwiches or grilled meats. May add 2 tablespoons dill, use tarragon vinegar or omit mustard seed.
Yield: 96 (1-tablespoon) servings.

Approx Per Serving: Cal 22; Prot 1 g; Carbo 3 g; Fiber 0 g; T Fat 1 g; 41% Calories from Fat; Chol 6 mg; Sod 3 mg.

Dry mustard is the residue which remains after the oil is expressed from the seed. Ground seed varies from white, which is considered the finest, through brown, considered next best, to yellow.

Candied Pecans

1 egg white   1 tablespoon water
1 teaspoon sugar   1/2 teaspoon salt
1 teaspoon cinnamon   1/2 teaspoon nutmeg
1 pound pecans

Combine egg white, water and sugar in bowl. Whisk until frothy. Add salt, cinnamon and nutmeg; mix well. Fold in pecans. Spread on nonstick baking sheet. Bake at 300 degrees for 25 minutes. Let stand until cool; break apart. Yield: 12 servings.

Approx Per Serving: Cal 255; Prot 3 g; Carbo 7 g; Fiber 2 g; T Fat 26 g; 85% Calories from Fat; Chol 0 mg; Sod 93 mg.

Spiced Pecans

1 egg, beaten   2 tablespoons cinnamon
1 teaspoon salt   3/4 cup sugar
1 pound pecan halves

Combine egg, cinnamon, salt and sugar in bowl; mix well. Stir in pecans until coated on all sides. Spread on greased baking sheet. Bake at 300 degrees for 30 minutes, tossing with fork 2 times. Yield: 12 servings.

Approx Per Serving: Cal 310; Prot 3 g; Carbo 20 g; Fiber 2 g; T Fat 26 g; 71% Calories from Fat; Chol 18 mg; Sod 184 mg.

Chinese Fried Walnuts

6 cups water   4 cups walnut halves
1/2 cup sugar   Oil for frying   Salt to taste

Bring water to a boil in saucepan. Add walnuts. Bring to a boil. Cook for 1 minute. Rinse walnuts in sieve under running hot water; drain. Stir warm walnuts with sugar in large bowl until sugar is dissolved. Let stand for 5 minutes to dissolve sugar if necessary. Heat 1 inch oil to 350 degrees in saucepan. Add half the walnuts. Fry for 5 minutes or until golden brown, stirring often with slotted spoon. Drain in sieve; sprinkle with salt. Toss to keep walnuts from sticking together. Cool on paper towels. Repeat with remaining walnuts. Store in tightly covered container for up to 2 weeks. Yield: 16 servings.

Approx Per Serving: Cal 185; Prot 4 g; Carbo 11 g; Fiber 2 g; T Fat 16 g; 71% Calories from Fat; Chol 0 mg; Sod 3 mg. Nutritional information does not include oil for frying.

Make *Nut Puffs* by beating 1 cup softened unsalted butter and 1/2 cup confectioners' sugar in mixer bowl until light and fluffy. Add 2 cups flour, 1/2 cup finely chopped walnuts and 1/8 teaspoon salt; mix well. Shape into 1-inch balls. Place 1 inch apart on ungreased baking sheet. Bake at 300 degrees for 25 minutes or until golden brown. Roll warm nut puffs in 1 cup confectioners' sugar. Remove to wire rack to cool completely. Store in airtight container.

These recipes have been carefully edited in a style that allows approximate nutritional values to be computed. Persons with dietary or health problems or whose diets require close monitoring should not rely solely on the nutritional information provided; they should consult their physicians or a registered dietitian for specific information.

Nutritional information for these recipes is computed from information derived from many sources, including materials supplied by the United States Department of Agriculture, computer databanks, and journals in which the information is assumed to be in the public domain. Because of new products and changes in familiar products as well as the trend to supply more information on packages, we strongly urge you to read package labels.

Abbreviations for Nutritional Profile

Calories — Cal	Carbohydrates — Carbo	Total Fat — T Fat	Sodium — Sod
Protein— Prot	Dietary Fiber — Fiber	Cholesterol — Chol	Gram/Milligram — g/mg

Measurements and Ingredient Guidelines

- **Measurements**—All volume measurements are level.
- **Optional ingredients** are not included in the profiles. Ingredients without measurements that are listed in the nature of "serve withs" or garnishes i.e. corn chips with dips or parsley sprigs are not included in the profiles. If a choice of ingredients has been given, the nutritional profile reflects the first choice. If a choice of amounts has been given, the nutritional profile reflects the greater amount. Salt and other seasonings or ingredients to taste have not been included in the nutritional profiles.
- **Dairy Products**—The percentage of fat in commercial dairy products may vary across the country to accommodate regional tastes and state laws. Unless otherwise specified, the following guidelines were used for analysis: whole milk, 3.5%; low-fat, 1.0%; whipping cream, 37.6%; half and half, 11.7%; cottage cheese, cream-style, 4.2%; cottage cheese, dry curd, <1.0%; yogurt is plain, produced from whole milk. See carton for additional information. The analysis for cheeses is not based on low-fat or low-sodium versions currently available. If these versions are used, make the proper adjustments in the profile by using the label information.
- **Cake mixes** which are prepared using package directions include 3 eggs and 1/2 cup vegetable oil.
- **Chicken**, cooked for boning and chopping, has been roasted; this method yields the lowest caloric values.
- **Eggs** are all large. To avoid raw eggs that may carry salmonella as in eggnog or 6-week muffin batter, use an equivalent amount of commercial egg substitute which is pasteurized.
- **Fats**—Oils and shortening used in recipes and profiles are vegetable oils and hydrogenated vegetable shortening made from vegetable oils. Butter and margarine are regular, not whipped or pre-softened products. Whenever large amounts of shortening or oil are used for frying, the profile does not include the shortening or oil since it is impossible to determine the amount that would be absorbed.
- **Flour** is unsifted all-purpose flour unless otherwise specified.
- **Ingredients with alcoholic content** have been analyzed for the basic ingredients, although cooking causes the evaporation of alcohol thus decreasing caloric content.
- **Artificial sweeteners** vary in use and strength so should be used "to taste," using the recipe ingredients as a guideline. Sweeteners using aspartame (NutraSweet and Equal) should not be used as a sweetener in recipes involving prolonged heating which reduces the sweet taste. For further information, refer to package information.

Kathleen S. Aceto
Jeanne C. Addison
Laurel Allen
Miriam April
Shirley Armstead
Ann Armstrong
Helen R. Armstrong
Susan Armstrong
Emily Asplundh
Erich Auerswald
Susan W. Ayres
Lawrence S. Balka
Mark Basnage
Emma Bauer
Susan C. Beebe
Margo Bennett
Grace P. Benson
Camille Beyer
Patty Billings
Ann Bird
Jean Bittenbinder
Caroline Blochberger
Nona Bloom
Lea Bolling

Amy Borer
Blair Both
Hildegarde S. Boylan
June M. Boyle
Leslie L. Branda
Marta Brann
Elizabeth D. Branson
Jean J. Brennan
Toni Brinton
Carole Brodkin
Barbara Brouse
Enid S. Brown
Marie E. Brown
Susan Brown
Margaret A. Browne
Barbara Bruno
Lillian H. Buck
Elizabeth Bullock
Barbara E. Burdick
Ramon Burgos
Eleanore Burns
Beth Butler
Maria Caiola
Peter Callahan

Nancy E. Carlin
Ruth Carver
Toni M. Cavanagh
Walter Chandoha
Dixie Chapman
Cheryl Cheston
Norma Cianfrani
Bernadette Clark
Eleanor Clarke
Ellen Clarke
Herb Clarke
Elly Cleveland
Vera Clift
Barbara Collins
Dottie Conner
P. R. Corso
Elizabeth S. Corson
Florence S. Corson
Carole Cowing
Jeannie Craig
Lonnie Crawford
Elizabeth Crothers
Hutchie Cummin
Charlotte Cunningham

Flo Daday

Dena Dannenberg

Martha B. Darlington

Shirley J. Davies

Aldys C. Davis

Dorothy DeAntonio

Melissa DeAntonio

Elsie L. Denby

Dorothy Denison

Catherine C. DiBona

Edna Dickson

Marlene Diedrich

Carol Dilks

Lynne R. Dillett

Carol A. DiRienzi

Alice M. Doering

Anne R. Donnell

Joyce Douglas

Ronell Young Douglass

Lynn Dowling

Cindy Drager

Christine L. Drake

Beth Dribin

Sonya Driscoll

Samuel S. M. DuBois

Mary Durinzi

Margaret T. Eberz

Beatrice H. Edgar

Elsa R. Efran

Mary L. Emory

Linda Emrich

Jill Evans

Wally Evans

Helen Eveler

Alice Hamilton Farley

Elizabeth B. Farley

Fran Farley

Helen W. Fath

Pat Fox Feehrer

Joyce Fingerut

Donna Fisher

Josephine Fisher

Connie Fleming

Denise Flores

Ruth Flounders

Phyllis Fox

Deborah Frank

Jeanne Franklin

Dorothy A. Freeman

Dorothy C. Freeman

Patricia D. Gaines

Frances C. Gallo

Polly Garnett

Florence Garr

Kitty Genuardi

Lynn Gevjan

Roxie E. Gevjan

Gretchen Gibbons

Delmer Gill

Lee Carter Glancey

Jenifer Post Goetz

Jane Golas

George Graham

Sally Graham

Betsy Gray

Jane C. Greenleaf

Jane Gresh

Dale Gress

Dottie Grosse

June Meinel Gubb

Joan B. Gustafson

Janet Oliver Gyer

John F. Gyer
Deborah Hall
Geraldine M. Hall
Nancy Hammersmith
Barbara Hare
Bobbits Harrington
Ellen Harris
Joan Havens
Laura T. Hawkins
Jeff Hayden
Katherine Z. Heasley
Mary Heckrotte
Nancy B. Heckscher
Nancy H. Heckscher
Sue Hendrixson
Helen Smith Henry
Sue McGovern Herndon
Karla R. Herr
Rebecca Hesse
Eileen S. Hillenmeyer
Nancy Hissey
Nadine Hoffman
Nancy Holst
Bitsy Hood

Sally Humphreys
Martha Hunt
Sondra Hurley
Tunia Hyland
Virginia Ingram
Joanmarie V. Intelisano
Joseph R. Janulewicz
Helena R. Jebb
Beverly Jennings
Betsy Johnson
Joan Brinton Johnson
Ann Kalbach
Bette Kalmbach
Leni Katz
Catherine Makem Kelly
Marilyn Khoury
Barbara B. Kidder
Lorraine Kiefer
Patricia D. Kile
Welthie Kinney
Josephine E. Knapp
Elizabeth Knorr
Frances Kopple
Elsie Kortrey

Margaret Kostow
Dorothy Krape
Sandie Krauss
Sharon Kreitzberg
Emmy Krick
Katharine R. Kriebel
Susan Kriebel
Janie Botto Kwiedis
Mary LaBold
Jocie Lamb
Fannie Lang
Emily Laros
Joan Lenhardt
Kay Leto
Lydia P. Lewis
Betty Leydon
Betty S. Light
Dick and Sally Lighty
Sylvia R. Lin
Christine Gerner Linde
Carol Lindemann
Ed Lindemann
Elizabeth C. Listerman
Rosetta Little

Barbara Allyn Lockwood
Dorothy C. Longaker
Martha B. Loughridge
Rosalinda R. Madara
Deborah L. Majer
Nancy Maliken
Peg Manthorpe
Sandy Manthorpe
Spencer A. Manthorpe
Sadie Marr
Bonny W. Martin
Aline Martinelli
Margarete M. Marvin
Sallie H. Maser
Wilma B. Maslin
Gay Mason
Stella L. Matczak
Cheryl Mattson
William J. Mayer
Evelyn W. McAdam
Veronica C. McAfee
Becky McBrien
Mary Carter McConnell
Esther McCrea

Florence B. McElroy
Gladys H. McGrath
Louise McIlvaine
Judith N. McKee
Helen McKendrick
Judy McKeon
Carol M. McQuade
Sally McQuail
Deb McThenia
Linda Meckley
Mary Ann Meisberger
Anne R. Mendenhall
Judy Meyer
Lynda Meyers
Betty Miller
Diane Miller
Jeffrey Miller
Joanne Miller
Sally Wistar Miller
Sandra Y. Miller
Ruth Molloy
Susan Montgomery
Connie Moore
Jane Z. Moore

Jane Morgan
Melinda C. Moritz
Judy Moroz
Ann and George Morris
Claire Müller
Bernice A. Murphy
Pauline Young Murphy
Jo Muscari
Ruth E. Myers
Dixie Nace
Flossie Narducci
Leigh Narducci
Betty Naylor
Susanne D. Naylor
Dorothy S. Nero
Helen W. Newman
Helen B. Nicholson
Betsy Nutt
Elaine Oeste
Marlene April Ornston
Saralinda Orr
Judith L. Osterman
Joy Ozer
Julia Park

Josephine Parman
Wendy Paul
Elise Payne
Jane G. Pepper
Susan R. Perretta
William D. Perry
Martha Peterson
Isabella W. Pfeil
Audrey Pfeilsticker
Dot Plyler
Daryl Ponder-Rynkiewicz
Kathy Potter
Betty Preston
Frances Prince
Lucile S. Proctor
Kathleen G. Putnam
Joan Putney
Paul Quintavalla
Trish Radey
Ruth J. Rainer
Hannah S. Randolph
Helen A. Reed
Joanna McQuail Reed
Mildred R. Reid

Nancy Resnick
Debra C. Ridgeway
Helen Roback
Betsy Roberts
Celia W. Roberts
Gainor Roberts
Betty Robertshaw
Carmine J. Rodia
Pinkie Roe
Tomasita Romero
Ann Rosenberg
Margot T. Ross
Paula C. Rothermel
Rodman S. Rothermel
Shirley Rubinstein
Joan Sage
Betty Trotta Sandel
Pat Sanders
M. Doris Sandstrom
Nancy Sarcione
Joyce Scheier
Carolyn C. Schelling
Cheryl Schlenker
Joan Schmitt

John Eric Schneider
Nancy H. Schriber
Sue Schubert
Frances M. Schwartz
Kathleen B. Schwartz
Herb Scott
Susanne F. Seltzer
Joan Semple
Martha B. Sharples
Elizabeth H. Shay
Janice Maxine Sherafat
Sybil Siegfried
Florence Slane
Jan and Mike Slater
Elizabeth R. Slattery
Traci M. Slaybaugh
Mary Jane Smedley
Ellen H. Smith
Isabelle B. Smith
Margaret C. Smith
Maria M. Smith
Rosalie Smith
Sharon Smith
Mimi Snyder

Henriette V. Solomon
Laurence Sombke
Marie Stalte
Lucie B. Steele
Florence G. Stephany
Pam Stitley
Molly Stohler
Dorothy Storms
Keith Straw
Joanne Stuart
Patricia A. Taylor
Elizabeth Tetzlaff
Susan Thatcher
Dorothy Thomas
Sara C. W. Thompson
W. S. Thornhill
Ginnie Tietjens
Eleanore G. Tompkins
Sharon E. Turner

Jeannine Vannais
Rosemarie P. Vassalluzzo
Anna Maria Vona
Nancy Wadleigh
Elizabeth Wagoner
Carolyn Waite
Susie Walker
Mark C. Ward
Clare Warfield
Corinne Warner
Mili Dunn Weiss
Polly Weiss
Rosemary Weiss
Diana Wells
Janet M. Welsh
Sue Westrum
Ellen P. Wheeler
Elaine H. White
White Dog Cafe

Alice Whiting
Jane Williams
Phyllis G. Williams
Sybil Williamson
Janet J. Wilson
Nancy Wismer
Patricia Wolanski
Mary Lou Wolfe
Shirley Wolfe
Carol Wolfinger
Hope Middleton Wood
Sally Ann Wood
Barbara Wrightson
Connie Yost
Sally Yow
Marc Zaharchuk
Elizabeth Zanowiak
Theresa Zielinski
L. Wilbur Zimmerman

We also thank Charlotte Archer who did so much for PHS, including providing her famous haute cuisine on a shoestring budget. After her death in 1992, Charlotte's family donated to PHS a copy of her new, privately published cookbook. We include some of her recipes with pride and gratitude.